THE THEATER OF GOD'S GLORY

The CALVIN INSTITUTE OF CHRISTIAN WORSHIP LITURGICAL STUDIES Series, edited by John D. Witvliet, is designed to promote reflection on the history, theology, and practice of Christian worship and to stimulate worship renewal in Christian congregations. Contributions include writings by pastoral worship leaders from a wide range of communities and scholars from a wide range of disciplines. The ultimate goal of these contributions is to nurture worship practices that are spiritually vital and theologically rooted.

RECENTLY PUBLISHED

The Whole Church Sings: Congregational Singing in Luther's Wittenberg
  Robin A. Leaver

Visual Arts in the Worshiping Church
  Lisa J. DeBoer

*Singing God's Psalms: Metrical Psalms and Reflections for Each Sunday
in the Church Year*
  Fred R. Anderson

*Missional Worship, Worshipful Mission:
Gathering as God's People, Going Out in God's Name*
  Ruth A. Meyers

Worship with Gladness: Understanding Worship from the Heart
  Joyce Ann Zimmerman

The Touch of the Sacred: The Practice, Theology, and Tradition of Christian Worship
  F. Gerrit Immink

Evangelical versus Liturgical? Defying a Dichotomy
  Melanie C. Ross

Arts Ministry: Nurturing the Creative Life of God's People
  Michael J. Bauer

From Memory to Imagination: Reforming the Church's Music
  C. Randall Bradley

The Theater of God's Glory

Calvin, Creation, and the Liturgical Arts

W. David O. Taylor

WILLIAM B. EERDMANS PUBLISHING COMPANY
GRAND RAPIDS, MICHIGAN

Wm. B. Eerdmans Publishing Co.
2140 Oak Industrial Drive NE, Grand Rapids, Michigan 49505
www.eerdmans.com

Published 2017
Printed in the United States of America

26 25 24 23 22 21 20 19 18 17   1 2 3 4 5 6 7 8 9 10

ISBN 978-0-8028-7448-1

Library of Congress Cataloging-in-Publication Data

Names: Taylor, W. David O., 1972– author.
Title: The theater of God's glory : Calvin, creation, and the liturgical arts /
    W. David O. Taylor.
Description: Grand Rapids : Eerdmans Publishing Co., 2017. |
    Series: The Calvin Institute of Christian Worship liturgical studies series |
    Includes bibliographical references and index.
Identifiers: LCCN 2017004621 | ISBN 9780802874481 (paperb : alk. paper)
Subjects: LCSH: Worship. | Calvin, Jean, 1509–1564. | Christianity and the arts.
Classification: LCC BV10.3 .T39 2017 | DDC 264—dc23
    LC record available at https://lccn.loc.gov/2017004621

To Phaedra Jean Taylor: *juntos*

Contents

Foreword

Vibrant Christian faith and life today are immeasurably enriched by the work of historians. Praise God for the host of people with gifts in archaeology, paleography, translation, archival organization, and expertise in the history of art, architecture, music, philosophy, theology, scriptural exegesis, political theory, economics, language, and more. Each of these gifts helps us see more deeply into the ways that key figures, communities, and traditions throughout the history of Christianity have worked out their salvation in ordinary life. What a host of analytic and synthetic skills are needed for the large communal enterprise of history to unfold in honest and redemptive ways.

Within this constellation of methods, the volume you are holding offers a unique and essential approach. I would like to dub this approach, appreciatively, the "wrestling Jacob" approach to history—or perhaps, better, the "wrestling Jacob approach to the use of history."

In these pages, David Taylor sets out to wrestle with John Calvin, and ultimately with the triune God, for a blessing on liturgical artists. You can feel this pulse running through these pages: "I will not let you go, unless you bless me!"

In this grappling, Taylor doesn't merely describe or analyze Calvin. He doesn't merely venerate or dismiss Calvin. He wrestles with Calvin's thought—affirming it, challenging it, responding to it. At the end, Taylor is changed. Wise and engaged readers will be, too.

David Taylor's passion is the vital practice of Christian worship today. He has been deeply engaged for years in the work of encouraging, challenging, nurturing, goading congregations to engage worship in graciously intentional and aesthetically thoughtful ways. He is a reformer, an enlivener, a catalyst. He casts a vision for the indispensable ways that the arts can function in prophetic and priestly ways to shape, nurture, and challenge contemporary Christian communities as they seek to faithfully worship the triune God.

Wisely, Taylor has also taken the time to wrestle with history. He rightly intuits that the vast, majestic, and often poetic imagination of John Calvin offers a fascinating site for historical exploration. For there we find both strong prohibitions against perceived misuse of the arts as well as rich veins of exegetical insight, with promise for developing a robust, if chastened, affirmation of artistic engagement.

The genre of this volume, then, is really an example of the use of history. It is an exploration of how historical study can offer us wisdom, poise, inspiration, and correction.

Taylor stands in good company as a passionate liturgical theologian who grounds his vision in historical engagement. John Calvin himself entitled his liturgy *The Form of Prayers and Manner of Ministering the Sacraments According to the Usage of the Ancient Church*. It is a liturgy that, in its own way, is a kind of wrestling match with early church forms—an intense exercise in affirmation and adaptation. In the nineteenth century, American Presbyterian Charles W. Baird's 1857 *Book of Public Prayer* was preceded by a careful historical study of Reformed liturgies, published as *Eutaxia, or the Presbyterian Liturgies: Historical Sketches*; and the Mercersburg theologians pored over patristic sources in search of inspiration and insight. Meanwhile, in the Netherlands, Abraham Kuyper wrote a dynamic series of columns on worship, recently translated as *Our Worship*. Many of his insights were generated in his doctoral research on the history of Polish Reformer Johannes à Lasco's ministry in London. In each case, these historical wrestling matches offer access to historical sources we never would have seen in the same way, even when the resulting work is intentionally as much about the historian's sharpening vision as it is about the subject being studied.

One gift of Taylor's deep attention to Calvin is that this book is so much more than merely (another) defense of the arts in worship. It is, more precisely, an invitation for artists, and then for worshipers, to engage with artworks in the context of worship in certain ways, in ways that align with a profoundly Trinitarian vision and strengthen the community's covenantal engagement with each other and with the triune God. In Taylor's words,

> the arts flourish in a liturgical context *if they are inextricably linked to Word and Spirit, promote order, exhibit beauty, render pious joy,*

and prompt the faithful to "lift their hearts" to God together, rather than
remain entrapped in self-absorbed concerns, and "return" with God to
earth, rather than remain unmoved by the ethical and missional realities
that await them in the world at large.

May every liturgical artist and Christian worshiper be invited into
this dynamic vocation.

Likewise, this book is not merely (another) affirmation of the goodness of materiality, as if a blanket affirmation of the goodness of materiality is a sufficient response to the persistent Gnosticism that creeps back
into our theological imagination, generation after generation. It is an affirmation of materiality inside a Trinitarian theological vision, in which material reality in general, and in artworks specifically, can align with God's
good purposes and express priestly prayer and praise back to God. May
every Christian community embrace this more nuanced affirmation.

With this in mind, I would invite readers to open these pages ready
for their own deep engagement.

Take up this book's invitation not merely to describe but to behold
a compelling Trinitarian vision of liturgical participation—one that embraces rather than avoids the spatial, visual, material, and embodied aspects of public Christian liturgical assemblies.

Take up this book's invitation to imagine the buildings we construct,
the media we curate, the gestures and postures we practice, and the Supper of the Lord we share as profound theological actions.

Take up this book's invitation to study and teach worship by setting
aside simplistic sentimental hagiography of key historic figures and engaging them precisely at the point that their words might offend contemporary sensibilities.

Take up this book's invitation to advocate for the arts in ways that
honor their potential weaknesses and strengths, potential distortions and
contributions.

In his famous sermon on wrestling with Jacob, "Magnificent De-
feat," Frederick Buechner describes the scene in Genesis 32 this way:

> The darkness has faded just enough so that for the first time [Jacob]
> can dimly see his opponent's face. And what he sees is something
> more terrible than the face of death—the face of love. It is vast and
> strong, half ruined with suffering and fierce with joy, the face a man
> flees down all the darkness of his days until at last he cries out, "I will

not let you go, unless you bless me!" Not a blessing that he can have now by the strength of his cunning or the force of his will, *but a blessing that he can have only as a gift.*

That begins to get at the mission here: to establish the vocation of liturgical arts on the basis of nothing less than divine gift, a gift to be cherished and nurtured by all who seek to follow Jesus.

JOHN D. WITVLIET
Calvin Institute of Christian Worship
Calvin College and Calvin Theological
 Seminary
Grand Rapids, Michigan

Acknowledgments

Stanley Hauerwas once described his work as a theologian in the terms of a bricklayer. One writes, like one lays bricks, by putting one thing on top of another, whether bricks or paragraphs, and it is quite impossible to know whether you have done your work well apart from the many people who have instructed you along the way. Hauerwas's metaphor of bricklaying has returned to me again and again in the writing of this book. At one level, it is really no more exciting than putting one thing on top of another; and without a host of good friends and guides, we only muddle along in the dark, with little hope of doing the work right. If this book has any chance to persuade its readers, it is due in no small part to many fine people.

A first debt of gratitude goes to Jeremy Begbie. It was he who first sparked my interest in both theology and the arts nearly twenty years ago. Jeremy has also served as an inspiring model of a scholar-priest. I am likewise grateful to my dissertation committee at Duke Divinity School, where the majority of this book got its start in 2013: to Sujin Pak, Sam Wells, Lester Ruth, and John Witvliet. To all my teachers over the years, who have inculcated in me a love of learning and a desire for God, along with a vision of theology in service of the church, I am immensely grateful. I also express my sincere thanks to Eerdmans for the invitation to publish this book—particularly to Michael Thomson for his gentle patience and to James Ernest for believing that this book could be something better than I had originally imagined.

I owe thanks to an uncommonly talented group of Blue Devil friends, including Bo Helmich, Tanner Capps, Brian Curry, Joelle Hathaway, Jacki

Price-Linnartz, Stephanie Gehring, Carole Baker, and Nate Jones; also, of course, Brian Williams. I am grateful for their gracious, constructive comments along the way. I acknowledge a special debt to Dan Train for reading an early version of this manuscript. To Ken Woo, Thomas Kortus, Steve Breedlove, David Hyman, Brad Wright, Kyle Miller, and Geno Hildebrandt: a heartfelt thanks for your pastoral care. A particular thanks goes to the Calvin scholars who generously corresponded with me on this book: David Steinmetz, Randall Zachman, John Thompson, Richard Muller, Julie Canlis, Todd Billings, Bill Dyrness, David Moffitt, and Beth Felker Jones. I am equally grateful for the feedback from Marianne Meye-Thompson, Steve Guthrie, and Steve Young. And to Joel Green: thank you.

I have long felt that, apart from "the prayers of the people," the Christian faith is rather difficult to sustain. In that light, I deeply appreciate the prayers of the communion of saints scattered across North America who have also offered their words of encouragement and, in some cases, financial support during the particularly challenging season of PhD studies. I acknowledge a special gratitude to my family: to Christine and Cliff, Stephanie and Scranton, my nephews and nieces, and most especially my parents, Bill and Yvonne, for their constant care, their wise counsel, and the gift of friendship. Life would not be nearly as much fun, or worth the while, without my daughter, Ruby Blythe Marie. Thank you, baby girl. Finally, I owe an incalculable debt to Phaedra, my wife, for her enduring love and persistent enthusiasm for the calling that has been entrusted to me. To her I dedicate this book.

Abbreviations

AB	Anchor Bible
AGJU	Arbeiten zur Geschichte des antiken Judentums und des Urchristentums
BECNT	Baker Exegetical Commentary on the New Testament
CO	*Ioannis Calvini Opera Quae Supersunt Omnia* (Baum, Cunitz, Reuss)
Comm.	*Commentaries of John Calvin*
CR	*Corpus Reformatorum* (Braunschweig, 1834–)
ETS	Evangelical Theological Society
HTR	*Harvard Theological Review*
ICC	International Critical Commentary
Institutes	1559 *Institutes of the Christian Religion* (McNeill/Battles)
Institutes (1536)	1536 *Institutes of the Christian Religion* (Battles)
IVPNTCS	InterVarsity Press New Testament Commentary Series
JBL	*Journal of Biblical Literature*
JETS	*Journal of the Evangelical Theological Society*
JSNTSup	Journal for the Study of the New Testament, Supplement Series
NICNT	New International Commentary on the New Testament
NIGTC	New International Greek Testament Commentary
SBLDS	Society of Biblical Literature Dissertation Series
SHR	Studies in the History of Religions
SNTSMS	Society for New Testament Studies Monograph Series
Tracts and Treatises	*Tracts and Treatises of John Calvin* (Beveridge)
WBC	Word Bible Commentary

Introduction

[For] Calvin, it is a mark of true religion to have little need for things of a physical or material nature.

Larry Harwood, *Denuded Devotion to Christ*

[Calvin] confronted the whole colorful world of phenomena with such remarkable and painfully serious restraint. . . . In him we find as little of the supposedly French joy in the concrete and real as we do of the French esprit.

Karl Barth, *The Theology of John Calvin*

This we must do, not only to declare, by tongue and bodily gesture, and by every outward indication, that we have no other God; but also with our mind, our whole heart, and all our zeal, to show ourselves as such.

Calvin, *Institutes* (1536)

In a paper delivered at Wheaton College in 2011 titled "The Future of Theology amid the Arts: Some Reformed Reflections," Jeremy Begbie observed that "as the theology and arts conversation continues to unfold apace, resources from the Reformed world—so often buried beneath an understandable but exaggerated shame—have considerably more to offer than is often supposed, especially if we are seeking to delve more deeply into the plotlines and harmonies of a scripturally rooted and vibrant trinitarian faith."[1]

The question is: Which Reformed resources are those? And might those same resources be helpful to theological reflection on the *liturgical arts*? The wager of this book is that John Calvin, standing at the headwaters of the Reformed tradition, represents such a resource, even if not in the ways one might initially suppose.[2] For both supporters and critics of the Frenchman, such a conclusion will likely be regarded with a measure of skepticism. Voltaire, not surprisingly, held Calvin responsible for the dour artistic life of Geneva, while Orentin Douen believed that Calvin was the "enemy of all pleasure and distraction, as well as of the arts and music."[3] Philip Benedict blames Calvin's heirs for a kind of "visual anorexia,"[4] even as Peter Auksi argues that "Calvin's systematic removal of the regenerate Christian away from . . . over-sensuous involvement in the earthly arts receives its seminal inspiration from a reading and interpretation of several key scriptural models."[5]

To these observations we must add that Calvin's ambivalence toward the liturgical arts is undergirded by a persistently negative view of materiality and that the fate of the former hinges, as it were, on the fate of the latter.[6] Dorothy Sayers, in fact, regards "hatred of the flesh" as one of

1. Jeremy Begbie, "The Future of Theology amid the Arts: Some Reformed Reflections," in *Christ across the Disciplines: Past, Present, Future*, ed. Roger Lundin (Grand Rapids: Eerdmans, 2013), 182.

2. Interest has never been lacking in Calvin's influence on the arts. See, for example, Léon Wencelius, *L'esthétique de Calvin* (Geneva: Slatkine, 1979); Jérôme Cottin, *Le regard et la parole: Une théologie protestante de l'image* (Geneva: Labor et Fides, 1994); Paul Corby Finney, ed., *Seeing beyond the Word: Visual Arts and the Calvinist Tradition* (Grand Rapids: Eerdmans, 1999); Christopher R. Joby, *Calvinism and the Arts: A Reassessment* (Leeuven: Peeters, 2007); William A. Dyrness, *Reformed Theology and Visual Culture: The Protestant Imagination from Calvin to Edwards* (Cambridge: Cambridge University Press, 2004).

3. Both cited in William Edgar, "The Arts and the Reformed Tradition," in *Calvin and Culture: Exploring a Worldview*, ed. David W. Hall and Marvin Padgett (Phillipsburg, NJ: P&R Publishing, 2010), 41; translation mine.

4. Philip Benedict, "Calvinism as a Culture? Preliminary Remarks on Calvinism and the Visual Arts," in *Seeing beyond the Word*, ed. Finney, 31.

5. Peter Auksi, *Christian Plain Style: The Evolution of a Spiritual Ideal* (Montreal and Kingston: McGill-Queen's University Press, 1995), 224. According to Daniel K. L. Chua, *Absolute Music and the Construction of Meaning* (Cambridge: Cambridge University Press, 1999), 33, Calvin believed that the function of music was "to channel human verbiage from the mind to the heart to align concept with passion."

6. For similar critiques of Calvin, see Oliver Millet, "Art and Literature," in *The Cal-*

the "four certain marks" of Calvin's legacy.[7] In *Calvin against Himself*, Suzanne Selinger contends that "abstraction in Calvin the introverted intellectual was above all a dephysicalizing."[8] Such a conclusion is comparable to the one that Carlos Eire draws in his seminal work *War against the Idols*. Eire writes, "Calvin forcefully asserted God's transcendence through the principle *finitum non est capax infiniti* [the finite is incapable of containing the infinite] and His omnipotence through *soli Deo gloria*."[9] Calvin, it needs to be conceded, supplies plenty of evidence in his own writings to corroborate the above judgments.

Calvin's Self-Implication?

In his commentary on the Psalms, Calvin maintains that not only do musical instruments prompt the faithful to cling to "earthly" things, but they also contravene God's requirement for a simple, spiritual, and articulate worship. Now that Christ has appeared, he writes, for the church to persist in the use of musical instruments is "to bury the light of the Gospel" and to "introduce the shadows of a departed dispensation."[10] With respect to the visual shape of worship, Calvin believes that "it would be a too ridiculous and inept imitation of papistry to decorate the churches and to believe oneself to be offering God a more noble service in using organs and the many other amusements of that kind."[11] Calvin insists that

---

vin Handbook, ed. Herman J. Selderhuis (Grand Rapids: Eerdmans, 2009), 424; Auksi, *Christian Plain Style*, 216; William Bouwsma, *John Calvin: A Sixteenth-Century Portrait* (Oxford: Oxford University Press, 1989), 80.

7. Dorothy Sayers, *Further Papers on Dante*, vol. 2: *His Heirs and His Ancestors* (Eugene, OR: Wipf & Stock, 2006), 167. Calvin is not, of course, to be regarded as interchangeable with Calvinism.

8. Suzanne Selinger, *Calvin against Himself: An Inquiry in Intellectual History* (Hamden, CT: Archon Books, 1984), 80. Similarly, Margaret Aston, *England's Iconoclasts* (Oxford: Clarendon, 1988), 10: "Physical erasure was part of the vitalizing ferment of the new age."

9. Carlos Eire, *War against the Idols: The Reformation of Worship from Erasmus to Calvin* (New York: Cambridge University Press, 1986), 316, emphasis original; see also 197–98.

10. *Comm.* Ps. 92:3.

11. From Calvin's sermon on 1 Sam. 18, cited in Percy A. Scholes, *The Puritans and Music in England and New England: A Contribution to the Cultural History of Two Nations* (London: Milford, 1934), 336.

to include images in public worship, as Rome does, arises out of avarice (*cupiditas*), which is a far cry from the pleasure (*oblectatio*) that God allows in the enjoyment of paintings of things imagined.[12] More bluntly, he dismisses the whole affair with icons as "sheer madness."[13] He states his theological conviction clearly: "God's majesty is sullied by an unfitting and absurd fiction, when the incorporeal is made to resemble corporeal matter, the invisible a visible likeness, the spirit an inanimate object, the immeasurable a puny bit of wood, stone, or gold."[14]

In comments such as these we begin to perceive the close link between Calvin's worry over the liturgical arts and his worry over the material realm. While Calvin concedes that certain embodied "exercises of godliness" are needed in public worship, they are offered, to his mind, as accommodations to human weakness.[15] As he remarks in book 4 of the 1559 *Institutes*, since "in our ignorance and sloth (to which I add fickleness of disposition) we need outward helps to beget and increase faith within us, and advance it to its goal, God has also added these aids that he may provide for our weakness."[16] Calvin consistently considers it a regrettable thing that Scripture and preaching are not enough for the faithful.[17] If Christians were "wholly spiritual," like angels, they would not need material symbols of worship.[18] And when he exclaims, "How great is the distance between the spiritual glory of the Word of God and the stinking filth of our flesh!"[19] it is not difficult to imagine why both friend and foe have deemed Calvin to be an enemy of the physical body, a pessimist toward creation, and a negative influence on the liturgical arts.[20]

---

12. 1.11.12. Calvin adds: "Even if the use of images contained nothing evil, it still has no value for teaching."

13. "An Admonition, Showing the Advantages Which Christendom Might Derive from an Inventory of Relics," in *Tracts and Treatises*, 2:297.

14. 1.11.2.

15. *Comm.* John 4:23.

16. 4.1.1.

17. "Confession of Faith, in the Name of the Reformed Churches of France," in *Tracts and Treatises*, 2:152, 159 (hereafter, "Confession of Faith").

18. "Catechism of the Church of Geneva (1545)," in *Tracts and Treatises*, 2:84, 91. Cf. 3.20.30; 4.5.18.

19. *Comm.* John 1:14.

20. Thomas J. Davis, "Not 'Hidden and Far Off': The Bodily Aspect of Salvation and Its Implications for Understanding the Body in Calvin's Theology," *Calvin Theological Journal* 29 (1994): 406-18. Karl Barth states, with a touch of hyperbole, "We have to search his works with a magnifying glass to find any traces that he could laugh" (*The Theology of*

To imagine this, however, is to imagine only half the story, through a glass darkly. For even if Calvin is hardly the first place we go to discover a vision for the flourishing of the liturgical arts, the above comments do not tell the whole story. As I propose in this book, that story is both far more complicated and far more interesting than commentators have often allowed.

The Argument of This Book

In this book I examine Calvin's Trinitarian theology as it intersects his theology of materiality in order to argue for a positive theological account of the liturgical arts. I do so, believing that Calvin's theology of materiality offers itself—perhaps surprisingly—as a rich resource for the practice of Christian worship and opens up a Trinitarian grammar by which we might understand the theological purposes of the arts in public worship.

Using Calvin's commentary on musical instruments as a case study, generally representative of his thinking on all the arts in corporate worship, I identify four emphases that mark his thinking: that the church's worship should be (1) devoid of the "figures and shadows" that marked Israel's praise and should emphasize instead a (2) "spiritual," (3) "simple," and (4) "articulate" worship, suitable to a new-covenantal era. A common feature of these emphases, I suggest, is an anxiety over the capacity of physical things to mislead the worship of the faithful in idolatrous or superstitious ways. As it concerns public worship, Calvin's account of materiality is, quite frankly, largely pessimistic. Here the material creation is seen as an especial temptation to distort the true worship of God and as a lesser vehicle by which the faithful offer their praises to God.

Calvin's account of materiality outside of the liturgical context, however, is distinctly optimistic. A close reading of his views on creation, the resurrected body of Christ, the material symbols of worship, and the material elements of the Lord's Supper points to a more integral role for materiality in the economy of God. And while a nearly exclusive appeal to God's "essential" nature may dominate Calvin's thinking on the physical

---

John Calvin, trans. Geoffrey W. Bromiley [Grand Rapids: Eerdmans, 1995], 126). Sergiusz Michalski, *The Reformation and the Visual Arts: The Protestant Image Question in Western and Eastern Europe* (London: Routledge, 1993), chap. 2; David Morgan, *Icons of American Protestantism: The Art of Warner Salman* (New Haven: Yale University Press, 1996), 6.

shape of public worship, his arguments in these particular doctrinal loci are marked by a distinctly Trinitarian frame of mind. Here the material creation is seen not as especially problematic or "merely there"; instead it is *for* something, *headed* somewhere, caught up in the activities of the Two Hands of God, to use Irenaeus's language.[21]

While setting aside his concern for "articulate" worship as an issue more directly related to the question of metaphor rather than of materiality, I focus this study on the first three emphases: "shadows" (chapters 2–5), "spiritual" (chapters 6–7), and "simple" (chapters 8–9). In a careful investigation of each of these domains of thought in Calvin, I discover a Trinitarian reading of the material creation that, in turn, opens up the possibility of a Trinitarian reading of materiality in public worship. Though I follow the logic of Calvin's theology to conclusions that he himself did not imagine, I believe that they remain sympathetic to his best instincts and that a robust theological account of the liturgical arts is hereby brought to light.

Even, then, as Calvin perceives that God appropriates material things, such as the eucharistic bread or the "affluence, sweetness, variety and beauty" of creation,[22] to form and feed the church, so I argue—sometimes with and beyond Calvin, sometimes against Calvin—that God takes the liturgical arts as intensively material artifacts to form and also feed the church.

With this end in mind, one of the chief aims of this book is to let Calvin speak for himself as often as possible.[23] As such, I attend not only to Calvin's 1559 *Institutes* (as has been done frequently enough) but also to the biblical commentaries, sermons, catechisms, treatises, and worship orders that he authored. Without a proper consideration of these other sources, Calvin's liturgical theology risks certain distortion. On this account, John Witvliet and Nathan Bierma are right to stress that "understanding liturgical partic-

---

21. The "Two Hands" language is peculiar to Irenaeus (e.g., see *Against Heresies* 4.20.1) and is developed at length, along parallel lines, in Julie Canlis, *Calvin's Ladder: A Spiritual Theology of Ascent and Ascension* (Grand Rapids: Eerdmans, 2010), e.g., 20, 187–95, 234–35.

22. *Comm.* Gen. 2:8–9.

23. Calvin, not the "Reformed" tradition or "Calvinism," remains the focus of this book. "A clever theologian can accommodate Calvin to nearly any agenda; a faithful theologian—and a good historian—will seek to listen to Calvin, not to use him" (Richard A. Muller, *The Unaccommodated Calvin: Studies in the Foundation of a Theological Tradition* [Oxford: Oxford University Press, 2000], 188). Whether it is a matter of *how* one uses Calvin, the aim here is to give Calvin himself a careful, charitable hearing.

ipation in Calvin's Geneva requires attention not just to formal liturgical texts, but also to architecture, music, preaching, church order documents, town regulations, and sacramental theology. It requires complementary methods of intellectual, material, and social history, along with attention to scattered liturgical references in the complete corpus of Calvin's writings, including his letters, treatises, sermons, and commentaries."[24] One might of course argue that the *Institutes* functions as a definitive distillation of Calvin's theology, or that his Geneva liturgy represents a final form of his ideal public worship, and that nothing more is needed to discern Calvin's mind. But to do so is to assume, wrongly, that Calvin's theology is simple rather than complex and that his ideas about worship are straightforward rather than complicated—and richly promising, too.

That being said, it is important to state that this book is not a historical study.[25] To borrow Oliver Crisp's language, this book is engaged in a retrieval of Calvin's ideas for the purpose of constructive theology.[26] Where it seems necessary, I note relevant historical data. But while some may wish to argue that Calvin's social location generated the plausible conditions for his intense allergic reaction to "popish" excesses and his rejection of the plastic and performing arts in public worship, I suggest that no necessary causal relation needs to be inferred between historical circumstances, theological ideas, and actual liturgical reforms. And while the historical data rightly temper the judgments of a systematic theologian, those data do not necessarily preclude the possibility of collegial disagreement on theological and liturgical questions. In fact, while I remain sympathetic to Calvin at many points, I part ways with him at times where I think he has gotten it wrong and at other times where I think he has not carried far enough the logic of his own Trinitarian theology. In a sense, this book argues Calvin against himself, but it does so in a chari-

---

24. Witvliet and Bierma, "Liturgy," in *The Calvin Handbook,* ed. Herman J. Selderhuis (Grand Rapids: Eerdmans, 2009), 408. On this account, see also Edgar, "The Arts and the Reformed Tradition," 40-68.

25. The work of historical theologians is of course helpful to this book, for example, David Steinmetz, *Calvin in Context* (Oxford: Oxford University Press, 2010); Carl Trueman, "Calvin and the Calvinists," in *The Calvin Handbook,* ed. Selderhuis, 472-79; as also Muller, Pitkin, Hesselink, and Old. On the use of musical instruments in the sixteenth-century Catholic Mass as a historical backdrop to Calvin's liturgical reforms, see Leslie Korrick, "Instrumental Music in the Early Sixteenth-Century Mass: New Evidence," *Early Music* 18.3 (1990): 359-65, 367-70.

26. Oliver D. Crisp, *Retrieving Doctrine: Essays in Reformed Theology* (Downers Grove, IL: IVP Academic, 2010), viii.

table spirit, trusting that Calvin's theology of the physical creation has something invaluable to offer academy and church alike.

To the extent that Calvin's theological ideas rest on the exegesis of Scripture, as he himself regarded his primary task, I engage Calvin on his own preferred terms. I venture the study of key biblical texts upon which, to his mind, the role of materiality in worship hinges. Three exegetical issues are especially important:

- the relation in Scripture between temple, creation, and worship
- the relation of the physical body to the *imago Dei*
- the relation of John 4:23–24 to the physical shape of worship

Each of these exegetical exercises occupies a substantial place in the book. Inasmuch as Calvin regards himself as a biblical theologian and views his liturgical proposals as the result of a faithful interpretation of Scripture, I provide an extensive reading of the relevant biblical data, at times concurring with his judgments, at other times disagreeing with the exegesis or with the conclusions that he draws from it. Why he parts ways, for example, with Luther, Bucer, or Zwingli on the substance or details of public worship cannot be accounted for on strictly exegetical terms. A careful examination of his theological ideas is thus required in order to illumine the larger landscape of his views of public worship.

The Hope for This Book

The hope for this book is that it might make a modest contribution to Calvin studies and liturgical studies, and perhaps a more significant contribution to the church's thought on and practice of the arts in corporate worship.

For Calvin studies, the hope is that this book offers a correction to erroneous judgments of Calvin's theology of materiality that occur, as often as not, in precipitate fashion. In positive terms, I seek specifically to build on the work of both Julie Canlis and Randall Zachman. With Canlis, I believe that Calvin fails to consistently relate the work of Christ as mediator of the material creation to the work of the Spirit as the one who enables the physical world to be "in Christ."[27] While sympathetic to many of Canlis's conclusions, I nonetheless offer a more intensive treatment

27. See, in particular, chap. 6 in Canlis, *Calvin's Ladder*.

of Calvin's understanding of materiality in a liturgical context. Where Zachman argues against the view that he terms the "old thesis"—wherein Calvin is seen to give exclusive privilege to the knowledge of God that is "heard," rather than "seen"—I, like Zachman, draw attention to the aesthetic features of Calvin's theology of materiality.[28] With Zachman, as with other Calvin scholars, I believe that there is a more integral role for sensory data in Calvin's liturgical theology than the "old thesis" suggests and that Calvin's views of the material creation are more positive than is commonly granted.[29] In a sense, I argue the reverse of Eire's dictum. *Finitum* est *capax infiniti*, I propose, but only because *God* enables creation to become a vehicle of divine glory.

In this vein, my hope is that liturgical studies will yet again discover Calvin as an important resource for theologies and practices of public worship. Hughes Oliphant Old is correct to say that the perception of Calvin as a theologian uninterested in worship "is seriously misleading."[30] Similarly, Witvliet notes that if Calvin is given two paragraphs in liturgical histories, "there may be mention of his un-Zwinglian sacramental theology and his promotion of vernacular metrical psalmody, but no more."[31] In this book I contend that there is indeed far more to be discovered— not least on behalf of the arts in public worship. Building on the work of Reformed theologians, then, this project draws attention to Calvin's Trinitarian thought pattern and suggests that, while Calvin himself did not pursue far enough the implications of his Trinitarian theology for his

28. Randall Zachman, *Image and Word in the Theology of John Calvin* (Notre Dame, IN: University of Notre Dame Press, 2007). Zachman includes Ed Dowey, David Willis, T. F. Torrance, Lucien Richard, Alexandre Ganoczy, Carlos Eire, William Bouwsma, Brian Gerrish, Dawn de Vries, and Bernard Cottret as representative of what he terms the "old thesis."

29. Especially helpful on this account are Mary Potter Engel, *John Calvin's Perspectival Anthropology* (Eugene, OR: Wipf & Stock, 1988); Susan E. Schreiner, *The Theater of His Glory: Nature and the Natural Order in the Thought of John Calvin* (Durham, NC: Labyrinth Press, 1991); Barbara Pitkin, *What Pure Eyes Can See: Calvin's Doctrine of Faith in Its Exegetical Context* (New York: Oxford University Press, 1999).

30. Old, "John Calvin and the Prophetic Critique of Worship," in *Calvin Studies III*, ed. John H. Leith (Davidson, NC: Colloquium on Calvin Studies, 1986), 79. The *Cambridge Companion to John Calvin*, ed. Donald K. McKim (Cambridge: Cambridge University Press, 2004), fails to include any significant treatment of Calvin and worship.

31. Witvliet, "Images and Themes in John Calvin's Theology of Liturgy," in *Worship Seeking Understanding: Windows into Christian Practice* (Grand Rapids: Baker Academic, 2003), 127, and esp. 128.

liturgical proposals, it nonetheless offers itself as a significant resource for theologians, pastors, and worship leaders today.[32]

With a view to the arts, I contend that they should serve the church's worship in their own ways (with their own logics and powers), though not on their own terms. The arts in worship would perform this service for the sake of a deeper fellowship with God and a robust Christian witness in the world. They would do so for good *theological* reasons. For liturgical arts studies, interest in biblical or missional or traditional reasons for any given art form in public worship is plentiful.[33] Often missing, however, is expressly theological argument—even less so, Trinitarian accounts of the arts in worship. At first glance, Calvin's views on the liturgical arts hardly promise such an account. As Calvin sees it, the liturgical arts risk occluding the clear light of the gospel while also endangering the clarion voice of Christ, and they suffer guilt by association with Rome's intemperate liturgies. To borrow from Alan Jacobs's work in *The Book of Common Prayer: A Biography*, Calvin worries that a glut of liturgical arts will allow "the specific language of the prayers to disappear into a sensuous impressionism constructed primarily through architecture, incense, vestments, and melody."[34]

Yet while Calvin may fret that the liturgical arts immerse the faithful in an excess of materiality, he also argues that the physical creation is a "theater" fit for God's glory. I seek then to capitalize upon Calvin's Trinitarian sensibility toward the material realm, but I wish to press it in new directions, specifically on behalf of the material aspects of corporate worship. Calvin's Trinitarian theology includes rich veins in some cases,

---

32. Alasdair Heron, *Table and Tradition* (Edinburgh: Handel Press, 1983), 154, makes this point with respect to the role of the Holy Spirit in Calvin's eucharistic theology. Much the same, Sue A. Rozeboom, "The Provenance of John Calvin's Emphasis on the Role of the Holy Spirit regarding the Sacrament of the Lord's Supper" (PhD diss., University of Notre Dame, 2010), 6, draws attention to Calvin's failure to bring to bear his pneumatologically rich treatment of the Lord's Supper in his *Institutes* into his proposed orders of worship.

33. For example, Eddie Gibbs and Ryan K. Bolger, *Emerging Churches: Creating Christian Community in Postmodern Cultures* (Grand Rapids: Baker Academic, 2005).

34. Jacobs, *The Book of Common Prayer: A Biography* (Princeton: Princeton University Press, 2013), 147. Jacobs in this instance describes the Anglo-Catholic Ritualist Movement of the nineteenth century, associated chiefly with John Mason Neale and John Henry Newman, both of whom sought to restore a love for liturgical ceremony. The Ritualists, Jacobs writes, "transformed [Thomas] Cranmer's powerful words into a kind of ambient music, often heard without acknowledgment, received aesthetically but not necessarily with the ear of understanding."

slight traces in others, which I believe yield a more positive outcome for materiality in worship and, quite possibly, also for the proper flourishing of the liturgical arts. In charting this course, then, I hope that common tensions regarding the arts in worship might be fruitfully addressed, including, for instance, the ways in which order and nonorder are rendered or how the introduction of new art media might form, reform, or malform a given congregation.

The Shape of the Argument

This book begins by arguing that, contrary to what scholars have often held, the language of "shadows" alone cannot account for the logic of Calvin's thought on musical instruments. Nor does it explain the tangle of theological and biblical ideas or historical circumstances that inform his argument, even if we might discover in them a clear enough cast of mind. To the language of "shadows" must be added three distinctive emphases in Calvin's thinking: "spiritual," "simple," and "articulate." Together, as I suggest in chapter 1, these four emphases establish the complex shape of his argument against musical instruments in public worship, while a common thread in each of these emphases is a view of materiality as problematic. While Calvin argues his case against instruments by appealing to the "essence" of God, I suggest that a Trinitarian line of thought opens up the possibility of a more positive regard for the material and aesthetic shape of the church's worship.

Calvin's ideas about the physical creation, the subject of chapter 2, function as the starting point for this possibility. Calvin's commentary here involves a keen regard for the "theater" of God's glory. As the "hands and feet" of God in Christ, upheld by the Spirit, the physical creation is a place for something: for goodness, pleasure, beauty, and praise. And though sin vitiates humanity's capacity to enjoy God in and through creation, sin does not rob creation of its capacity to stage a spectacle of God's powers. Whereas Calvin avoids using the language of symbol to describe the material creation, he uses it frequently to refer to the God-ordained media that serve to disclose specific knowledge of God. This is the concern of chapter 3. For Calvin, the material symbols of God's presence, in both the Old and New Testament, raise the faithful up to God for the sake of a gracious encounter with God. As the case may be, these symbols also are provided on account of human ignorance or "childishness."

While the physical world is capable of bearing witness to God, as a "mirror" or "insignia" of God, which Israel's worship, with its physically dense symbolism, exemplified, Calvin's comments on the symbols of worship in the New Testament reflect a consistent anxiety that their *physicality* is somehow hazardous to the church. Something about the coming of Christ has generated in Calvin's thinking a theological disjunction between the work that the physical creation performed in Israel's worship and the work that the physical creation performs in the setting of the new covenant. In chapter 4 I propose that Calvin's ideas about the physical aspect of worship are haunted by a metaphysical dualism, which, in turn, makes him suspicious of the capacity of the material realm to mediate the presence of God to the church. While exceptions exist, it is generally true that, for Calvin, material symbols of worship are, at best, an unfortunate necessity and, at worst, inert powers whose chief function is to activate the faculties of the soul.

With chapter 5 I turn to more constructive work. I suggest here that the material creation does not cease to be significant for public worship with the advent of Christ. Rather, it receives a new orientation under the constitutive work of the Spirit and is caught up in a double movement: the movement of creation's praise at large and the movement of the Two Hands of God to enable creation to become the theater of God's glory. Likewise, I contend that the language of "weakness," which Calvin uses to describe the material symbols of worship, is not the preferred language of the New Testament. In its stead, and working with elements of Calvin's Trinitarian theology, I suggest that a "temple theology" provides a more compelling way to read the worship-creation relationship. To use Calvin's own language, the church at worship exists in the "school of the beasts," learning to see and to love God *in* and *through* the physical stuff of creation.

As I seek to show in chapter 6, Calvin is at his most persuasive when he interprets the meaning of the human body in light of Christ's resurrected body. He also persuades when he traces out the logical implications of the body as a "temple of the Spirit." And when faced with what he regarded as the hypocritical conduct of the so-called Nicodemite believers, Calvin brings body and soul into a mutually determinative relation. Where Calvin is less persuasive is in a rhetorical habit that fails to do justice to the more positive role of the body that Holy Scripture presents to us and in his insistent stress for "spiritual" worship, which prioritizes the interior activities of the soul in relation to the theological priority of God's nonmaterial essence. In chapter 7 I argue that Jesus's Spirit-constituted

Introduction

body shows us what bodies are for, while it is the Spirit who enables the faithful to partake now of the sort of physical life that the ascended Christ enjoys, thereby enabling all other human bodies to discover their proper end. With a view to public worship, human bodies, as bearers of a distinct glory, are to be seen not as sources of exceptional provocation to sin, nor as lesser servants of the soul, but rather as domains of the Spirit's habitation, reordered to Christ's bodily order, through which the faithful in the context of worship engage in re-formative corporeal activities, not only internal and invisible ones.

Similar to Calvin's ideas about "shadowy" and "spiritual" worship, a close examination of Calvin's notion of "simple" points not to a single meaning but rather to a complex of meanings. In chapter 8 I concentrate on the link between "simple" and the language of John 4:23–24, "in spirit and truth." I do so because of the central role that this Johannine passage plays in Calvin's liturgical theology. While Calvin's understanding of "simple" worship involves two distinct, but interrelated, concerns—that is, the need for a minimal number of ceremonies and a minimal role for materiality in worship—the primary focus of my examination remains on the relation between "simple" and materiality. In contrast to previous investigations, here I find myself parting ways with Calvin to a greater degree. Over against Calvin, I argue in chapter 9 that the narrative of John's Gospel follows a Trinitarian rather than a narrowly "essentialist" line of thought, that John 4:23–24 is concerned with a christological and pneumatological orientation to worship rather than an anthropological one, and that a positive regard for materiality is discernable throughout the Johannine narrative rather than a negative one. With and beyond Calvin, I suggest that matter *matters* in John precisely for the kind of worship that the Father seeks in this "new hour."

As I propose in the conclusion to this book, Calvin's "creaturely pessimism" is unwarranted on his own terms. What the Spirit accomplishes in Christ's whole humanity, to which the faithful are made partakers by that same Spirit, augurs a much more positive role for human bodies in public worship. Likewise, the material condition of public worship is not to "get out of the way" but rather to be caught up in the work of the triune God. A more integral role for the physical creation, and therefore also for the arts, is possible on Calvinian terms. Even, then, as Calvin perceives that God appropriates material things, such as the sweetness of creation or the eucharistic bread, to form and feed the church, so I argue that God may take the liturgical arts to form and also feed the church.

13

CHAPTER 1

Musical Instruments in Calvin

[Calvin's] exemplary liturgy will be simplex, pura and spiritualis, "plain," "unadorned" and "spiritual."

Peter Auksi, "Simplicity and Silence"

I have no doubt that playing upon cymbals, touching the harp and the viol, and all that kind of music, which is so frequently mentioned in the Psalms, was a part of the education; that is to say, the puerile instruction of the law.

Calvin, *Comm.* Psalms

Calvin's appreciation for both music and the psalms is well known by those who count themselves his liturgical heirs. In his *Epistle to the Reader*, his foreword to the very popular Genevan Psalter, he writes: "Now among the other things which are appropriate for recreating people and giving them pleasure, music is either the first or one of the principal, and we must value it as a gift of God deputed to that use."[1]

The singing of psalms, Calvin remarks in 1537, "can incite us to lift up our hearts to God and move us to an ardor in invoking and exalting with praises the glory of his Name."[2] It is estimated that, on average, Genevan

---

1. John Calvin, "Foreword to the Genevan Psalter," in *John Calvin: Writings on Pastoral Piety*, ed. Elsie A. McKee (New York: Paulist Press, 2001), 95 (hereafter *Pastoral Piety*).
2. John Calvin, "Articles concerning the Organization of the Church and of Worship

Christians would have sung at any given service between sixteen and thirty psalm stanzas, which, according to Paul Jones, amounts to "the equivalent of five hymns of up to 6 stanzas each."[3] In the tradition that followed Calvin, the singing of metrical psalms would become one of the singular distinguishing features of Calvinists of the sixteenth and seventeenth centuries.[4] How Calvin viewed musical instruments, however, is a mixed bag. While he envisions a legitimate place for their use "at home" and "in the fields," he does not regard them as appropriate to corporate worship. Typical of his thinking is this observation: "For even now, if believers choose to cheer themselves with musical instruments, they should, I think, make it their object not to dissever their cheerfulness from the praises of God. But when they frequent their sacred assemblies, musical instruments in celebrating the praises of God would be no more suitable than the burning of incense, the lighting up of lamps, and the restoration of the other shadows of the law."[5]

If scholars take notice of Calvin's ideas about instruments, it will be to observe that he locates them under the era of "figures and shadows." More often, the matter is left altogether untreated. In the case of Charles Garside's seminal essay "The Origins of Calvin's Theology of Music: 1536–1543," for example, the focus remains exclusively on music as a general topic.[6] H. P. Clive's treatment does more than most, for he rightly situates Calvin's concerns about instruments within a wider historical context and thus brings to light the kind of historical "pressures" that may account for the Reformer's conclusions in a way that exegetical or theological scrutiny alone cannot.[7] The aim of this chapter is to press the topic in a more thoroughgoing manner and to suggest that Calvin's thinking on musical instruments in public worship is far more complicated and interesting than commentators have often allowed.

---

at Geneva Proposed by the Ministers at the Council, January 16, 1537," in *The Library of Christian Classics*, vol. 22: *Calvin: Theological Treatises*, trans. J. K. S. Reid (Philadelphia: Westminster, 1954), 53 (hereafter "Articles").

3. Paul S. Jones, "Calvin and Music," in *Calvin and Culture: Exploring a Worldview*, ed. David W. Hall and Marvin Padgett (Phillipsburg, NJ: P&R Publishing, 2010), 235.

4. Horton Davies, *Worship and Theology in England*, vol. 1: *From Andrewes to Baxter and Fox, 1603–1690* (Princeton: Princeton University Press, 1975), 270–72; see also James H. Nichols, *Corporate Worship in the Reformed Tradition* (Philadelphia: Westminster, 1968), 38–40.

5. *Comm.* Ps. 33:2.

6. Garside, "The Origins of Calvin's Theology of Music: 1536–1543," *Transactions of the American Philosophical Society* 4 (1969): 1–36.

7. H. P. Clive, "The Calvinist Attitude to Music, and Its Literary Aspects and Sources," *Bibliothèque d'Humanisme et Renaissance* 19.1 (1957): 80–102.

Song and Instruments

Calvin and Congregational Song

In order to put Calvin's ideas about musical instruments in context, it will be helpful to summarize his view of congregational song:

1. Singing obtains not only a possible place in the liturgy but a positive place, for it intensifies our capacity to worship God.
2. Not just any singing will do. We must sing rightly, which involves a consideration for both the mind and the heart, for both understanding and affection.
3. The kind of singing that pleases God most is the kind that is done commonly (i.e., in unison), as if with "the same mouth."
4. Because our worship must accord with God's holy Word, God has provided us with good, fitting words—namely, the psalms of David; when these are sung well, they lead to maximal edification and to right moral formation.
5. Because not any melody will do for corporate worship but only that which befits congregational song, God has provided us with skilled musicians to compose melodies suitable to corporate worship.

Whereas the 1559 *Institutes*, the "Articles" (1537), and the *Epistle to the Reader* omit mention of musical instruments, Calvin directly addresses their use in his commentaries on the Psalms. The context he presumes in these commentaries is public worship, while the aim is, as always, "pure worship." Calvin makes two kinds of statements about musical instruments: positive and negative. I take each in turn.

Positive Comments on Musical Instruments

Positively, musical instruments perform a double benefit for Israel's worship. On the one hand, they incite the heart to exuberant praise: they *express* ardent affection for God,[8] they *stimulate* increased devotion to God, stirring the worshiper "up more actively to the celebra-

---

8. *Comm.* Pss. 33:2; 57:8.

tion of the praise of God with the heart,"[9] and they *indicate* that even the "most ardent attempts" to celebrate God's mighty deeds will fall "short of the riches of the grace of God."[10] In his comments on Psalm 150, Calvin regards the enumeration of instruments as a kind of metaphor for corporate singing. Even as the sound of one instrument piles on top of that of another, producing an exuberant sound, so our individual praise piled on top of the praises of others, producing a kind of exuberant praise, cannot capture the full measure of adoration that God deserves. For the Jews, however, instruments attained that kind of vibrant adoration.

On the other hand, musical instruments serve as deterrents to an "unruly flesh" and therefore performed a crucial moral function in Jewish life. They protect the worshiper not only from a "cold faith" but also from the possibility of sliding into error.[11] God commands a multiplicity of songs, Calvin explains in his commentary on Psalm 150:3, in order that "he might lead men away from those vain and corrupt pleasures to which they are excessively addicted, to a holy and profitable joy. Our corrupt nature indulges in extraordinary liberties, many devising methods of gratification which are preposterous, while their highest satisfaction lies in suppressing all thoughts of God. This perverse disposition could only be corrected in the way of God's retaining a weak and ignorant people under many restraints, and constant exercises."[12]

Negative Comments on Musical Instruments

On the negative side, Calvin's argument against instruments in a new-covenantal liturgy involves four contentions. First, he stresses that instruments belong to *the era of figures and shadows.* For Calvin, instruments represent the "infancy of the Church,"[13] forming a "part of the training

9. *Comm.* Ps. 92:3.

10. *Comm.* Ps. 98:5–6.

11. See his comments in *Sermons on 2 Samuel: Chapters 1–13*, trans. Douglas Kelly (Carlisle, PN: Banner of Truth Trust, 1992), 409.

12. *Comm.* Ps. 150:3.

13. *Comm.* Ps. 149:3. Calvin makes a similar argument with respect to Miriam and the women of Exodus 15:20 and to David's dancing in 2 Samuel 6:14. See Jon Balserak, *Divinity Compromised: A Study of Divine Accommodation in the Thought of John Calvin* (Dordrecht: Springer, 2006), 78–79.

of the Law"[14] "under the legal economy,"[15] and correspond to the "dispensation of shadows and figures," which characterized Jewish believers. When the Israelites used harp and lyre, it was done because of the "generally prevailing custom of that time."[16] Christians are not to insist on their continuation, for to do so is to perpetuate "the ceremonies of the law."[17] God commanded timbrels and trumpets to "train his people, while they were as yet tender and like children, by such rudiments, until the coming of Christ";[18] the Jews, "who were yet under age," required the use of "such childish elements." In one sense, Calvin says, instruments were not in themselves necessary; they were only "useful" as elementary aids to the people of God. Now that the church has "reached full age," instruments can be set aside.[19]

Second, Calvin insists that the reintroduction of instruments into public worship leads people to cling to "earthly" things when God has expressly commanded that they worship him in *spiritual* fashion.[20] He comments: "We are to remember that the worship of God was never understood to consist in such outward services, which were only necessary to help forward a people, as yet weak and rude in knowledge, in the spiritual worship of God."[21] He elaborates on this point in a sermon on 2 Samuel, arguing that to reinsert such external elements "would be nothing but a silly performance now, which would obscure the spiritual worship spoken of in the fourth chapter of St. John. For there our Lord Jesus Christ declares to us how we must no longer govern ourselves by the Law."[22]

In this light, musical instruments risk contaminating the true praise of God. As Selderhuis observes, Calvin "fears that, by using musical instruments, the correct balance would be disturbed between the joy caused by music and the joy due to the praise of God."[23] Calvin asks: "Does anyone object, that music is very useful for awakening the minds

---

14. *Comm.* Ps. 71:22.
15. *Comm.* Ps. 150:3–5.
16. *Comm.* Ps. 71:22.
17. *Comm.* Ps. 98:5.
18. *Comm.* Ps. 81:2–3.
19. *Comm.* Ps. 92:3.
20. *Sermons on 2 Samuel*, 234–39. Cf. *Comm.* Col. 3:16.
21. *Comm.* Ps. 92:3.
22. *Sermons on 2 Samuel*, 412; see also 236, 310.
23. Herman J. Selderhuis, *Calvin's Theology of the Psalms* (Grand Rapids: Baker Academic, 2007), 209. Echoes of Augustine can be heard here.

of men and moving their hearts? I own it; but we should always take care that no corruption creep in, which might both defile the pure worship of God and involve men in superstition."[24] The use of instruments in public prayers, in short, defiles such worship.

Third, Calvin insists that God is more pleased with *simple* worship. This idea functions as a kind of corollary to the first, where the opposite of "shadowy" worship is "simple" worship. Likewise, the opposite of a ceremonially and materially extravagant worship is a ceremonially and materially simple worship. Papists "ape" Israel in their employment of instruments. They do so, Calvin maintains, in "a senseless and absurd manner," "exhibiting a silly delight in that worship of the Old Testament which was figurative, and terminated with the Gospel."[25] Fond of "outward pomp," Rome persists in a "wicked and perverse obstinacy," causing Christians to stumble into superstitious activities.[26] In contrast, simple worship occurs under "the clear light of the gospel,"[27] which has dissipated the shadows of the law. To the extent that musical instruments represented a form of "outward service," they were necessary for a people who are weak, ignorant, and frail.[28] Because Christ has now appeared, however, for the church to persist in the use of musical instruments is "to bury the light of the Gospel" and to "introduce the shadows of a departed dispensation."[29]

Finally, instruments fail St. Paul's requirement that praise be offered in an *articulate* voice. This contention appears as a new line of argument. While "simple" worship operates as an obverse to an externally "thick" worship, the idea of "articulate" worship functions as an ancillary argument to the above contentions, while also remaining central to Calvin's presuppositions about public worship. As Calvin forthrightly states: "The name of God, no doubt, can, properly speaking, be celebrated only by the articulate voice."[30] More strongly even, Calvin argues that instruments

24. *Comm.* Ps. 33:2. In *Comm.* Ps. 93:2 Calvin adds that, unlike humans, God does not take delight "in mere melody of sounds." Cf. Jeremy Begbie, "Music, Word, and Theology Today: Learning from John Calvin," in *Theology in Dialogue: The Impact of the Arts, Humanities, and Science on Contemporary Religious Thought; Essays in Honor of John W. de Gruchy*, ed. Lyn Holness and Ralf Wustenberg (Grand Rapids: Eerdmans, 2002), 24–27.

25. *Comm.* Ps. 92:3.

26. *Comm.* Ps. 33:2.

27. *Comm.* Ps. 81:2.

28. See Calvin's thoughts in *Comm.* 1 Sam. 18; *Comm.* 2 Cor. 4:16; *Comm.* 1 Tim. 4; and "Confession of Faith," 152, 159.

29. *Comm.* Ps. 92:3.

30. *Comm.* Ps. 33:2.

"are banished out of the churches by the plain command of the Holy Spirit."[31] For this judgment Calvin appeals to 1 Corinthians 14:13–16. From this New Testament passage, Calvin infers that instruments can generate only an inarticulate voice and ipso facto cannot meet the standards of right worship. Curiously, Calvin excludes chanting on similar grounds because it "fills the ears with nothing but an empty sound."[32]

Questions

A few questions arise at this point. How exactly did instruments "train" the Israelites? If they intensified the affections and enlarged the praise of God,[33] do Christians no longer require such training? Did Calvin place musical instruments under the era of "figures and shadows" because of their ceremonial function or because of their status as physical media?[34] Calvin argues that instruments, by virtue of their resemblance to an "inarticulate" voice, cannot properly praise God. If that is the case, what do we make of the worship that Israel offered God with pipes and cymbals? Is St. Paul's command in 1 Corinthians 14 an arbitrary command—that while God was once pleased to command and receive both articulate (vocal) and inarticulate (instrumental) worship, God no longer deems such worship pleasing? If answers are to be found to these questions, they will be discovered, first, by following Calvin into his reading of John 4 and 1 Corinthians 14.

Instruments and the New Testament

John 4

Calvin summarizes the exchange between Jesus and the Samaritan woman in John 4:23–24 by noting that their conversation concerns the nature of "the pure worship of God."[35] Pertinent to our concerns, Calvin notes that, with the coming of Christ, the era of ceremonies has come to an end. Now,

31. *Comm.* Ps. 71:22.

32. *Comm.* Ps. 33:2.

33. On this point, see Jeffrey T. VanderWilt, "John Calvin's Theology of Liturgical Song," *Christian Scholar's Review* 25.1 (1995): 63–82.

34. *Comm.* Col. 2:17.

35. *Comm.* John 4:23. Cf. Eire, *War against the Idols*, 197–212.

nothing "is hidden or obscure."[36] The substance of the gospel brings to light what Jews, with their use of incense, candles, holy garments, altar, and vessels, could know only in "shadow" form. Rome's burden is precisely the "foolish affectation of copying Jewish ceremonies."[37] Such practices obscure Christ again. What does it mean, then, to worship "in the spirit"? It means, in this context, to worship spiritually, which is another way of saying that God must be worshiped inwardly. "The worship of God is said to consist in the spirit, because it is nothing else than that inward faith of the heart which produces prayer, and, next, purity of conscience and self-denial, that we may be dedicated to obedience to God as holy sacrifices."[38]

To stress the chiefly inward character of pure worship, Calvin describes it as "faith, prayer, thanksgiving, purity of heart, and innocence of life"; and to reinforce the point, he adds that "at no time did [God] delight in any other sacrifices." Conversely, nonspiritual worship corresponds to outward or external worship, which is the kind of worship that the Jewish people had grown accustomed to but that Christ had now abolished. Does this mean that Jewish worship was devoid of spiritual content? No, to the contrary, says Calvin. Such worship as God had commanded the Jewish people was in fact spiritual, only it was concealed under figures and shadows—"it was enveloped in so many outward ceremonies that it resembled something carnal and earthly."[39] Calvin cites Paul's statement in Galatians 4:9 as warrant for this conclusion. There Paul describes ceremonial practices, such as the observance of "days and seasons," as "weak and worthless elemental things."[40]

Is there a place, then, for "outward exercises of godliness"? Calvin concedes that Christians will indeed need these, but he insists that they be few, moderate, and sober and that they not "obscure the plain truth of Christ." With such "plain and simple worship" God is well pleased. The "simple" truth of Christ, then, must express itself in a "simple" liturgy. Anything more, Calvin insists, will "deprive the Church of the presence of Christ." While the "spirit" was indeed concealed by the shadows of the law, the masks of popery "disfigure" it altogether. "Therefore we must on no account connive at such horrible and unworthy corruptions." Why do we need such outward exercises? Calvin answers: "our weakness renders"

36. *Comm.* John 4:23.
37. *Comm.* John 4:20.
38. *Comm.* John 4:23.
39. *Comm.* John 4:23.
40. *Comm.* Gal. 4:9.

them necessary. What constitutes worship "in spirit and truth"? Answer: "It is to remove the coverings of the ancient ceremonies and retain simply what is spiritual in the worship of God. For the truth of the worship of God rests in the spirit, and ceremonies are so to say adventitious."[41]

For Calvin, the phrase "spirit and truth" functions as a hendiadys. Rather than referring to two distinct realities, they describe a common one, namely, that worship with the coming of Christ designates chiefly an inward reality.[42] While "spirit" can be seen to describe for Calvin the interior domain of worship, whether as faith or prayer, "truth" seems to refer to their "substance." "Truth" is not contrasted with falsehood but rather with "the outward addition of the figures of the Law." To restate his point, Calvin notes that the kind of worship that the Father seeks "is the pure and simple substance of spiritual worship."[43] Finally, what does Jesus mean when he says that "God is Spirit"? Calvin answers that this sentence describes the essential nature of God. Against certain patristic theologians, who employed this text to defend the full deity of the Spirit, Calvin believes that Jesus simply wished to underscore the "spiritual" nature of his Father. Calvin stresses this idea with strong, perhaps exaggerated, language: "God is so far from being like us, that those things which please us most are the objects of his loathing and abhorrence."[44]

First Corinthians 14

In order to get a sense of Calvin's reading of 1 Corinthians 14, it might be helpful to summarize Paul's train of thought in 14:6–19.[45] Revolving around a discussion of the relative place of tongues and prophecy in public worship, Paul uses musical instruments as a metaphor to explain human speech. If a flute or bugle is blown indiscriminately, he reasons, only a jumble of sounds will result (vv. 7–8). Conversely, if a person were to blow distinct sounds through a bugle, then one might prepare oneself for battle. All human languages, Paul argues analogously, retain a meaning,

41. *Comm.* John 4:23.
42. Calvin elaborates on his meaning of "outward man" in his commentary on 2 Cor. 4:16–18.
43. *Comm.* John 4:23.
44. *Comm.* John 4:24.
45. Cf. Gordon Fee, *God's Empowering Presence: The Holy Spirit in the Letters of Paul* (Peabody, MA: Hendrickson, 1994), 221–35.

but only for the one who recognizes the intent of the language. Otherwise, it will be like speaking to a foreigner or "barbarian" (v. 11). In the context of corporate worship the aim should be to "abound for the edification of the church," which can occur only if the speech is "intelligible" (v. 12; cf. vv. 3–4, 6).[46] Tongues benefit the "spirit" (*pneuma*) but not the "mind" (*nous*, v. 14; cf. vv. 2, 4). "Therefore," Paul writes, "let one who speaks in a tongue pray that he may interpret" (v. 13) so that edification may ensue for the church.[47] Paul's resolution is noteworthy: "I will pray with the spirit and I will pray with the mind also; I will sing [*psalō*] with the spirit and I will sing [*psalō*] with the mind also" (v. 15; cf. vv. 27–33, 39!). If, Paul adds, prayer occurs only with the spirit (i.e., in tongues), others will neither understand what is being prayed nor be edified (vv. 16–17); and then he ends his admonition with a hyperbolic declaration: "In the church I desire to speak five words with my mind so that I may instruct others also, rather than ten thousand words in a tongue" (v. 19).[48]

Whereas Paul employs musical instruments as a metaphor, Calvin interprets Paul to mean them literally. And whereas Paul enjoins both prophecy and tongues (appropriately exercised), Calvin concludes that only prophecy, as a work of the mind, will result in an edifying experience for the assembly.[49] "How foolish then it is and preposterous in a man, to utter in an assembly a voice of which the hearer understands nothing."[50] And again, paraphrasing, "What can be plainer than this prohibition—'let not prayers or thanksgivings be offered up in public, except in the vernacular tongue'?"[51] As Calvin sees it, Paul argues that all public prayer must involve the mind: "Let us take notice, that Paul reckons it a great fault if the mind is not occupied in prayer."[52] With regard to 14:15, Calvin notes that Paul teaches that "it is lawful, indeed, to pray with the spirit, pro-

---

46. Verse 26 reiterates this point, but in a way that might in fact undermine Calvin's conclusion.

47. Fee, in *God's Empowering Presence*, 228, notes that the presumed conclusion to Paul's point here would be that prophecy should prevail over tongues in worship, but, he writes, "prophecy is not Paul's first concern, intelligibility is."

48. Fee, *God's Empowering Presence*, 261.

49. In *Comm.* 1 Cor. 14:14, Calvin stresses the inwardness of such worship: "As prayer is the spiritual worship of God, what is more at variance with the nature of it, than that it should proceed merely from the lips, and not from the inmost soul?"

50. *Comm.* 1 Cor. 14:11. In Calvin's mind the "papists" fail repeatedly on this account.

51. *Comm.* 1 Cor. 14:16.

52. *Comm.* 1 Cor. 14:14.

vided the mind be at the same time employed";[53] or put negatively, "the prayers of every one of us will be vain and unfruitful, if the understanding does not go along with the voice."[54] He grants that "spirit" prayer has a place in the assembly, so long as the mind is also at work, but he appears here to conflate in a single experience what Paul envisions as separate experiences for the believer.

A Cast of Mind

As a way toward clarity, I propose that it might be useful to speak in terms of a cast of mind. Whereas any given line of argument in Calvin's writings lands us in disparate hermeneutical and dogmatic territory, certain patterns of reasoning remain consistent. I suggest at least three distinctive casts of mind: biblical, theological, and pastoral.

Biblical Cast of Mind

Calvin's biblical approach is not one we might initially suspect. While he argues repeatedly that the church's worship should accord with God's explicit commands in Scripture, this is not the approach that he adopts toward musical instruments. Calvin *does not* say: God fails to command or commend instruments in the New Testament (as God does with song), therefore we ought to avoid them.[55] Calvin *does* say: instruments belong to the era of figures and shadows, therefore we ought to leave them there. To bring them into public worship is to "ape" Israel's worship, to "bury Christ," and to "pervert" true Christian worship. Where he does appeal to command language in his Psalms commentaries is in reference to two decisive texts: John 4 and 1 Corinthians 14. God commands worship that is "in spirit and truth" and "articulate."

Calvin's biblical logic, then, might be summarized this way: just as we have received the "clear light of the gospel," so we must worship God in substantially inward, formally simple, and rationally intelligible fashion.[56]

53. *Comm.* 1 Cor. 14:15.
54. *Comm.* 1 Cor. 14:16.
55. Cf. Eph. 5:19; Col. 3:16; James 5:13; Heb. 2:12; 1 Cor. 14:15.
56. Acts 2 might also be seen to factor significantly in Calvin's thinking here.

Theological Cast of Mind

Calvin's theological cast of mind involves a conflict of interest: between an enthusiastic doctrine of creation (largely outside of the context of public worship) and a "creaturely pessimism" (largely within the context of public worship).[57] As Begbie points out, Calvin's affirmation of creation as the theater of God's glory might lead us to believe that musical instruments will be given their own distinctive contribution to human flourishing, grounded, that is, in a theology of creation rather than in a theological anthropology.[58] But in Calvin's argument it does not. While, for example, the Lord was "pleased to use such visible figures" (like the embodied practice of baptism),[59] we also find, in Calvin, that God "did not delight in these external things" (like the ornaments of Israel's worship) but rather made them available "because of the infirmity of the times."[60] While Calvin affirms that the glory of God rightly shines "in the several parts of our bodies," he concedes that material ceremonies are permitted because our "weakness renders these necessary."[61]

In Calvin's theological logic, then, the "spiritual" nature of God, the "gravity" of heavenly worship, and the "crude and weak" capacity of humans, prone to misuse material reality, require an internally oriented, sober public worship. To include musical instruments in worship is "to make a confused mixture which confounds heaven and earth."[62]

Pastoral Cast of Mind

With respect to Calvin's pastoral cast of mind, the following points are key. Calvin accepts the patristic line of thinking almost exclusively, except in his encouragement of instruments "at home" and "in the fields."[63] Following the Antiochene rather than the Alexandrian exegesis of mu-

---

57. Canlis employs this phrase in *Calvin's Ladder*, 243.

58. Jeremy S. Begbie, *Music, Modernity, and God* (Oxford: Oxford University Press, 2013), 34.

59. 4.15.14.

60. *Sermons on 2 Samuel*, 413.

61. 3.20.31.

62. *Sermons on 2 Samuel*, 241.

63. Hughes Oliphant Old, *The Patristic Roots of Reformed Worship* (Zürich: Theologischer Verlag, 1975), 45.

sic, Calvin echoes the patristic concern for "logocentricity," "together-
ness" in worship, the moral power of music, and the close link between
"spiritual" and "internal."[64] With respect to the humanist scholars of the
day, Calvin reiterates their concern for simplicity, decorum, intelligibility, clarity, and a respectful deference to the "ancients."[65] While Erasmus,
for instance, allowed space for musical instrumentation in the Mass, he
strongly warned against semiprofane ceremonies, the indulgent behavior
of choristers, "lascivious" melodies, and song that was disconnected from
the text.[66] As a pastor, Calvin had good reason to worry over the liturgical
conditions for ready abuse (per Rome) and over the human proclivity to
turn material objects to idolatrous and superstitious use (per the Genevan
Christians under his care).[67]

According to Calvin's pastoral logic, then, it is better to remove
the sources of temptation. The human tendency to abuse material aids
to worship is "a contagion disease of sorts,"[68] and only an "economical"
ceremonial apparatus is able to preserve the believer in the right worship
of God.[69]

Critical Questions

What kind of initial critical response might we offer in light of the above?

A Comment on Calvin's Exegesis

With respect to Calvin's exegesis, we might begin by questioning his reading of the principal texts. In Calvin's writings, the notion of "spiritual"

64. Particularly helpful on this account is Everett Ferguson, "Toward a Patristic
Theology of Music," *Studia Patristica* 24 (1993): 266–83.

65. Hyun-Ah Kim, "Erasmus on Sacred Music," *Reformation and Renaissance Review*
8.3 (2006): 277–300. See also Clement A. Miller, "Erasmus on Music," *Musical Quarterly*
52.3 (1966): 332–49; Charles Garside Jr., "Calvin's Preface to the Psalter: A Re-Appraisal,"
Musical Quarterly 37.4 (1951): 566–77.

66. Kim, "Erasmus on Sacred Music," 290–96.

67. See Clive, "The Calvinist Attitude to Music," 94, 98.

68. Eire, *War against the Idols*, 231–32.

69. John H. Leith, *Introduction to the Reformed Tradition: A Way of Being the Christian Community* (Atlanta: John Knox Press, 1977), 167, believes that "economical" is preferable to "austere" in describing Calvin's liturgical sensibility.

is expressed in two ways: on the one hand, to designate the inward encounter with God and, on the other, to indicate a minimal ceremonial apparatus. For Calvin, at issue in John 4 is the invisible essence of God, which confronts the human spirit by way of heart and mind.[70] Might a careful rereading of the Johannine narrative, however, lead us to a different conclusion? If the phrase "God is Spirit" describes not the nature of God but rather the person of the Spirit, and if "Spirit and Truth" identifies something about God instead of humanity, the narrative would press us to read this passage in a rather more Trinitarian light than in an essentialist one. When we consider certain trajectories in John, we might also discover a healthy estimation of the material dimension of creation—from the enfleshed Logos to the new-creation subtext that runs throughout. From these emphases, John's narrative invites us to infer a far more integral relationship between the "spiritual" and the "material" dimensions of corporate worship than perhaps Calvin himself imagined. We take up this matter in chapter 8.

According to Calvin, the so-called simplicity of Christ requires a simple liturgical ceremony.[71] Heirs of the Frenchman have questioned this rationale. Hughes Old, for example, writes, "The Scriptures themselves do not even suggest that [the musical accompaniment in worship] should be restrained, simple or unadorned. If the early Reformed Church was of that opinion, it was probably more because of the warnings of the Church Fathers than because of the directions of either Old or New Testament."[72] Philip Butin argues that an "unnecessarily spare" worship in Reformed churches betrays a defective Trinitarian orientation,[73] while Auksi, more forcefully, contends that Calvin's liturgical aesthetic drives "towards ultimate simplicity in means and ends, towards an intense spiritualism independent of sensory stimulation," and away from "the profound actuality of a tangible communion."[74] Chapter 9 addresses these concerns in detail.

70. In *Sermons on 2 Samuel*, 232, 235, 311, Calvin states that God's essence is "spiritual," "invisible," and "celestial."

71. On this account, Calvin argues for a certain translation of the phrase in 2 Corinthians 11:3 that is not widely followed by New Testament scholars, believing that the phrase modifies Christ rather than the believer.

72. Old, *The Patristic Roots of Reformed Worship*, 268–69, esp. 269n1.

73. Philip Butin, "Constructive Iconoclasm: Trinitarian Concern in Reformed Worship," *Studia Liturgica* 19 (1989): 140.

74. Peter Auksi, "Simplicity and Silence: The Influence of Scripture on the Aesthetic Thought of the Major Reformers," *Journal of Religious History* 10.4 (1979): 361, 363.

With respect to Calvin's reading of 1 Corinthians 14, we point out a possible discrepancy. If Calvin has read Paul rightly, that "spirit" prayer can occur in corporate worship only if the mind is involved, the analogy to musical instruments still breaks down. Calvin affirms that prayer involving the "spirit" (i.e., inarticulate prayer), even in its subordinate status to prayer involving the mind (i.e., articulate prayer), belongs in the church's liturgy.[75] But for reasons that cannot be explained from his Corinthians exegesis alone, his argument in the Psalms commentaries cannot envision a way that musical instruments—as a form of "spirit" and therefore inarticulate prayer—could also be included in corporate worship. On the reasoning of his Corinthian exegesis, one might argue for instruments so long as they were exclusively used as accompaniment and therefore in a subordinate role to congregational song. If St. Paul has not proscribed the use of tongues-speaking in public worship (a big "if," I grant), then surely there is a place for musical instruments as an analogous means of inarticulate though still intelligible worship. What Calvin, unlike Bucer, could not countenance was a place for instrumental music alone, where believers did not lend their voices with "understanding" in the praise of God.[76]

A Comment on Calvin's Theology of Materiality

With Calvin's theological reading of materiality, we encounter a rhetoric that remains consistently wary of the physical media of worship. In his exegesis of Psalm 9:11, Calvin remarks: "The design of God from the commencement in the appointment of the sacraments, and all the outward exercises of religion, was to consult the infirmity and weak capacity of his people. Accordingly, even at the present day, the true and proper use of them is, to assist us in seeking God spiritually in his heavenly glory, and not to occupy our minds with the things of this world, or keep them fixed in the vanities of the flesh."[77]

---

75. Calvin does, in fact, concede Paul's argument (in 14:26–33) that tongues, while not as enthusiastically commended as prophecy, do have a place in the church's worship.

76. R. Gerald Hobbs, "'Quam Apposita Religioni Sit Musica': Martin Bucer and Music in the Liturgy," *Reformation and Renaissance Review* 6.2 (2004): 174. Bucer also conceded the use of Latin in the church's liturgical song.

77. *Comm.* Ps. 9:11. Cf. Eire, *War against the Idols*, 200–202; Canlis, *Calvin's Ladder*, 120–21. See also 4.19.15; 17.5, 10.

As God is "spiritual," Calvin writes in the *Institutes*, so "only spiritual worship delights him."[78] God "descends to us," he adds in his sermons on 2 Samuel, "not to stupefy or bind our senses in these low and feeble things . . . but rather that we should be lifted on high to adore him spiritually, and that we should thereby rise above the world by our faith."[79]

Calvin repeatedly warns against the abuse of external aids to worship, and rightly so.[80] False attachments to them jeopardize faithful worship. Yet one is frequently left with the impression that Calvin, much like Zwingli, remains suspicious of external aids *as such*. His ambiguous use of "ascent" language to describe the purpose of material aids often gives the impression that they are unfortunate requirements.[81] The "prison house of our flesh" leads us to crave external aids, while "the idle splendor of the flesh" accounts for Rome's attraction to a "mass of ceremonies."[82] When combined with a sharp turn toward "interiority," a curious fascination with the incorporeal nature of angels, and the frequent emphasis on the "crude," "feeble," "cold," "lazy," "vain," and "rude" nature of humanity, one wonders whether the "weakness" that concerns Calvin pertains to *sinful* physical reality or to *creaturely* physical reality.[83] One wonders why the work of the Spirit to make us partakers of Christ's "flesh" carries so little theological weight in Calvin's formulation of public worship. We address these issues in chapters 2–7.

A Comment on Calvin's Historical Context

With respect to Calvin's historical context, it is important that we not presume simple lines of causality. The liturgical practices of a Catholic Geneva, a generation prior to Calvin's arrival, cannot be said to have *caused* Calvin to act one way or another. Calvin is his own man, just as he is a man

---

78. 2.7.1; cf. 1.13.1.

79. *Sermons on 2 Samuel*, 235–36. See also *Comm.* Exod. 25:8; Canlis, *Calvin's Ladder*, 169.

80. See esp. 2.10.8, 23 and 3.20.30.

81. On this account, see Witvliet's excellent exposition in *Worship Seeking Understanding*, 133–40.

82. See his comments on Psalms 24:7 and 28:2 and on John 4:23.

83. In *Comm.* Jer. 31:4, Calvin interprets mention of tambourines and dances as a reference to "holy joy" rather than actual musical instruments. Cf. Garside, "Origins," 9; Elsie McKee, "Context, Contours, Contents," *Princeton Theological Seminary Bulletin* 16 (1995): 167–68.

of his own times. This is perhaps to state the obvious, but it still bears mentioning. Why he parts ways with Luther, Bucer, or Zwingli in his vision of liturgical music, then, cannot be accounted for on exegetical terms alone. Where Luther extolled the psychological tonic of music, Calvin, like Augustine, influenced by Plato, fretted over its ability to distort the heart, despite his belief that Israel had benefited from music's affective powers. Where Luther praised both the music of nature (*musica naturalis*) and instrumental music (*musica artificialis*), Calvin could make room only for the human voice (*musica humana*) in public worship. Where, in this vein, Luther engages the medieval cosmological outlook on music, Calvin remains silent on it.[84] With Zwingli, Calvin stressed the importance of rational understanding in the people's praise. Unlike the Zurich pastor, however, who insisted that St. Paul's meaning in Colossians argued for a voiceless singing of the heart, Calvin believed that the mind, heart, and voice *could* sing to God in one accord.[85]

Whereas Bucer's typological reading of Israel's worship made room for instruments in Christian worship, Calvin's reading excluded them altogether.[86] Where Bucer, appealing to the principle of simplicity, saw how they might provoke the believer to a "more fulsome praise of God," Calvin, likewise appealing to the need for simplicity, saw them as real distractions.[87] His commendation of "restrained" singing appears to be at odds, we might add, to the kind of singing that the Psalter itself commends—with its exhortations to shout, burst, revel, clap, and cry unto the Lord. And the fact that angels in heaven repeatedly blow trumpets fails to factor in Calvin's understanding of the eschatological dimension of worship.[88] This view is in contrast, on the one hand, to Bucer, who believed that instrumental praise anticipated "the blessed festivities of the life to come,"[89] and, on the other,

84. Cf. Begbie, *Music, Modernity, and God*, 27ff. Luther also grounds his musical propositions in a doctrine of creation, which is something Calvin fails to do. See *Luther's Works*, vol. 53: *Liturgy and Hymns* (Philadelphia: Fortress, 1965), 321–24.

85. Charles Garside Jr., *Zwingli and the Arts* (New Haven: Yale University Press, 1966), 37, 45, 53.

86. Hobbs, "Quam Apposita Religioni Sit Musica," 165, 169, 175–76. Key textual loci for Bucer include Col. 3, Eph. 5, Deut. 6, and the narratives of King David and the prophet Elisha. Bucer also made space for hymns, not just psalms, so long as they were "in conformity with Scripture."

87. Hobbs, "Quam Apposita Religioni Sit Musica," 170, 176–77.

88. Cf. *Pastoral Piety*, 94–97. See also *Comm.* 1 Cor. 15:52; *Comm.* 1 Thess. 4:16; *Comm.* Matt. 24:31.

89. Hobbs, "Quam Apposita Religioni Sit Musica," 170.

to Luther, who believed that the music of heaven directly influenced the music of the church.[90] Finally, while experience compels him to include song as a stimulant to praise and a medicine for cold affections, it is curious that Calvin also appeals to experience to exclude musical instruments in the public assembly.[91]

Calvin's concerns for right worship are shared not only by fellow Reformers but also, in various ways, by Catholic Europe.[92] From Erasmus of Rotterdam to Martin Navarrus, a Spanish professor of canon law, a pattern of worries emerges—over melodies that drew attention away from the Mass and over musical practices that caused the assembly to engage in activities such as talking, joking, laughing, and carrying on business in neglect of faithful worship. The changes decreed by the Council of Trent represent an attempt, in its own way, to address what were perceived as problematic practices in liturgical music. From a committee of deputies who met on September 10, 1562, a series of changes were recommended:

> The whole plan of singing in musical modes should be constituted not to give empty pleasure to the ear, but in such a way that the words may be clearly understood by all, and thus the hearts of listeners be drawn to the desire of heavenly harmonies, in the contemplation of the joys of the blessed. . . . They shall also banish from church all music that contains, whether in the singing or in the organ playing, things that are lascivious or impure; as also all secular actions; vain and therefore profane conversations, all walking about, noise, and clamour, that so the house of God may be seen to be, and may be called, truly a house of prayer.[93]

90. Andreas Loewe, "'Musica est Optimum': Martin Luther's Theory of Music," http://mcd.academia.edu/loewe/Papers/1074845/Musica_est_optimum_Martin_Lu thers_Theory_of_Music, 33–38.

91. See 3.20.31; *Sermons on Job* 21:2, trans. Rob McGregor (Edinburgh: Banner of Truth Trust, 1993), vol. 1.

92. For an introduction to liturgical music in Catholic churches of sixteenth-century Europe, see Gustave Reese, *Music in the Renaissance* (New York: Norton, 1959), 358–62, 448; Christopher Boyd Brown, *Singing the Gospel: Lutheran Hymns and the Success of the Reformation* (Cambridge, MA: Harvard University Press, 2005); Joseph Herl, *Worship Wars in Early Lutheranism: Choir, Congregation, and Three Centuries of Conflict* (Oxford: Oxford University Press, 2004), 25–26; and Friedrich Blume, *Protestant Church Music: A History* (New York: Norton, 1974), 127–85.

93. As cited in David W. Music, *Instruments in Church: A Collection of Source Documents* (Lanham, MD: Scarecrow Press, 1998), 68–69.

The diversity of liturgical music throughout Catholic Europe notwith-standing,[94] the Mass, prior to Trent, would have been linguistically unin-telligible to the average layperson (because in Latin), vocally expressive (on account of polyphonic and choral practices), extrabiblical (in its use of secular materials), and musically difficult (in view of the use of pro-fessionals, such as court musicians and cathedral choirs).[95] Calvin's so-cial location, under this light, perhaps accounts to some degree for the intensity of his concern for the aesthetic dimension of public worship. A serious pastoral, and even psychological, matter was at stake. Long-standing habits required, one might concede, a forceful word with a res-olute conviction.[96]

Conclusion

While Calvin's contemporaries invariably appealed to common biblical texts in their proposals for the church's worship, the actual musical shape of that worship varied significantly from case to case, hinging, as it did, on a range of theological priorities, exegetical habits, and pastoral cir-cumstances. Disagreements existed among them over what constituted a "childish" practice of Israel's worship and what could be fittingly trans-lated into Christian worship. At stake for many of them was the manner in which materiality could mediate the presence of God and the way in which the arts might serve the purposes of "acceptable" worship. As this chapter has attempted to show, Calvin's argument against musical in-struments cannot be attributed solely to his appeal to the notion of "fig-ures and shadows"; the issues are far more complicated and interesting.

94. On this issue, see Korrick's excellent treatment in "Instrumental Music in the Early Sixteenth-Century Mass: New Evidence," esp. 360–63; Francis Higman, "Music," in *The Reformation World*, ed. Andrew Pettegree (London: Routledge, 2000), 491–504; Rob-ert M. Kingdon, "The Genevan Revolution in Public Worship," *Princeton Seminary Bulletin* 20.3 (1999): 264–80; and Jeffrey Dean, "Listening to Sacred Polyphony, c. 1500," *Early Music* 25.4 (1997): 611–36.

95. Especially helpful on these points is Lewis Lockwood, "Music and Religion in the High Renaissance and the Reformation," in *The Pursuit of Holiness in Late Medieval and Renaissance Religion*, ed. Charles Trinkaus, with Heiko A. Oberman (Leiden: Brill, 1974), 500–502.

96. Elsie Anne McKee, "Reformed Worship in the Sixteenth Century," in *Christian Worship in Reformed Churches Past and Present*, ed. Lukas Vischer (Grand Rapids: Eerd-mans, 2003), offers a valuable pastoral perspective on Calvin's context in Geneva.

Equally important, as he understood it, was the need for the church's worship to be "spiritual," "simple," and "articulate." A common feature in all these emphases was a sense that the *material* aspect of musical instruments was somehow hazardous to the church's worship.

CHAPTER 2

The Work of the Material Creation

All creatures are aflame with the present glory of the Lord.

Jürgen Moltmann, *The Source of Life*

We see, indeed, the world with our eyes, we tread the earth with our feet, we touch innumerable kinds of God's works with our hands, we inhale a sweet and pleasant fragrance from herbs and flowers, we enjoy boundless benefits; but in those very things of which we attain some knowledge, there dwells such an immensity of divine power, goodness, and wisdom, as absorbs all our senses.

Calvin, *Comm.* Genesis

As we saw in chapter 1, one key element of Calvin's argument against musical instruments is that they belong to the "shadowy" dispensation of the church. It is for this reason that they must not be brought forward into the "clear light" of New Testament worship. While God was pleased to use such material aids under the old covenant, Calvin believes that they were made available to the church because "the dullness of men is so great, that they do not perceive the presence of God unless they are put in mind by external signs."[1] To inquire into the nature of "shadowy" worship, then, is to inquire, among other things, after the question of continuity: between old- and new-covenantal worship.

---

1. *Comm.* Ps. 99:7. Cf. *Comm.* John 4:23; 4.15.14; *Sermons on 2 Samuel*, 413.

For the biblical writers, the advent of Christ and of the Spirit undoubtedly necessitated liturgical changes. Certain practices would need to be discontinued, while other practices would certainly be continued but perhaps in a different manner. What required careful discernment was the role that physical helps might play in a new-covenantal worship. In chapters 2 and 3, I examine Calvin's thinking on the physical creation itself and on the physical creation within the context of Israel and the church's worship. I do so in order to discover lines of continuity and discontinuity in Calvin's understanding of the "work" of the physical creation in general and the "work" of the physical creation in a liturgical context.

At stake here, I suggest, is the telos of materiality in the doxological purposes of God for the church.

The Witness of the Material Creation

"If ever there was a theologian who saw the universe sacramentally it was Calvin. For him, reality was drenched with sacrality. . . . Calvin's reforms meant a radical turn towards the world. But for him . . . the world to which one turns is a sacrament of God."[2] Nicholas Wolterstorff's observation here surprises, perhaps even strains credulity, but a close look at Calvin's commentary on creation appears at some level to bear out his observation. In "The Argument" of his Genesis commentary, Calvin writes that God "gives signs of his presence" everywhere in creation. For those who rightly wish to know God, he argues, "let the world become our school." In fact, to ignore the witness of God in creation is to be "deaf and insensible to testimonies so illustrious." Even without a human tongue, the created realm functions as an eloquent herald of the glory of God.[3] The glory of God, then, not only shines in heaven and on earth, bearing witness to our eyes; it also "resounds" in them, testifying thereby to the ears. For Calvin, creation fulfills this doxological role by operating according to the good purposes of God, and it is in this sense, we might say, that the creation is *for* something, caught up in the work of the triune God *in* the world and *on behalf of* the world and the church.

Working with metaphors adapted from Diana Butler, I argue that,

---

2. Nicholas Wolterstorff, *Until Justice and Peace Embrace: The Kuyper Lectures for 1981, Delivered at the Free University of Amsterdam* (Grand Rapids: Eerdmans, 1983), 160.

3. *Comm.* Gen., "The Argument."

for Calvin, creation performs five roles: epiphanic (revealing the invisible God), pedagogical ("schooling" the church), aesthetic (awakening delight through beauty), admonitory (rebuking ingratitude and pride), and doxological (enacting and summoning the praise of God).[4] I take each in turn, with the hope that the reader will be able to discern a kind of grammar in Calvin's theology: the work creation performs, the manner in which creation performs it, and the ends to which creation exists in relation to animate and inanimate creatures, on the one hand, and, on the other, to God. This review will constitute a first step in our investigation of Calvin's doctrine of creation, followed by a second step in our examination of the role that Calvin believes the material creation performs in the external symbols that accompany the church's public worship.

An Epiphanic Role: Making the Invisible God Visible by His Work

In a preface to his Genesis commentary, Calvin writes, "We know God, who is himself invisible, only through his works. . . . This is the reason why the Lord, that he may invite us to the knowledge of himself, places the fabric of heaven and earth before our eyes, rendering himself, in a certain manner, manifest in them." Because God's eternal and infinite existence is inaccessible to human beings, and because to seek to penetrate the essence of God would plunge the mind into a labyrinth from which it could not hope to escape, Calvin encourages the reader to accept the more modest task of learning about God through "the guidance and instruction of his own works."[5] God "clothes himself" with the image of the world. Before the fall, Calvin writes, "the state of the world was a most fair and delightful mirror of the divine favor and paternal indulgence towards man."[6] On Hebrews 11:3, he states: "Correctly then is this world called the mirror of divinity; not that there is sufficient clearness for man to gain a full knowledge of God, by looking at the world, but . . . the faithful, to whom he has given eyes, see sparks of his glory, as it were, glittering in every created thing. The world was no doubt made, that it might be the theater of divine glory."[7]

Not only is the universe a mirror of God's powers, then, it is also

---

4. Cf. Diana Butler, "God's Visible Glory: The Beauty of Nature in the Thought of John Calvin and Jonathan Edwards," *Westminster Theological Journal* 52 (1990): 13–26.

5. *Comm. Gen.*, "The Argument."

6. *Comm. Gen.* 3:17.

7. *Comm. Heb.* 11:3.

a "theater" or "spectacle" of God's glory.[8] This theater serves as a "bare and simple testimony" to God, so that wherever the faithful cast their eyes, "all things they meet are works of God."[9] On Psalm 104:31 Calvin observes, "It is no small honor that God for our sake has so magnificently adorned the world, in order that we may not only be spectators of this beauteous theater, but also enjoy the multiplied abundance and variety of good things which are presented to us in it."[10] Added to the imagery of mirror and theater language is the language of painting. Calvin writes in the *Institutes*: "We must therefore admit in God's individual works—but especially in them as a whole—that God's powers are actually represented as in a painting. Thereby the whole of mankind is invited and attracted to recognition of him, and from this to true and complete happiness. Now those powers appear most clearly in his works."[11]

What divine "powers" exactly are humans able to discover in creation?[12] Calvin consistently returns to five: wisdom, justice, majesty, order, and goodness. In the heavens, Calvin writes, are displayed the "wisdom and power" of God.[13] As architect of the world, God "shows how admirable is His power, His wisdom, His goodness, and especially His tender solicitude for the human race."[14] Susan Schreiner, in *The Theater of His Glory*, notes that the importance of "order" in the works of God appears as a constant concern in Calvin's writings.[15] Calvin stresses, for example, that God the Artificer has "stationed, arranged, and fitted together the starry host of heaven in such wonderful order that nothing more beautiful in appearance can be imagined."[16]

Perhaps more than order, however, the idea of God's goodness governs Calvin's thinking on creation.[17] In the provision of a garden to Adam and Eve, God can be seen as "the bountiful Father of a family, who

8. 1.5.5.

9. 1.5.15; 1.14.20.

10. *Comm.* Ps. 104:31.

11. 1.5.10.

12. Cf. 1.14.20. So also *Comm.* Ps. 148:7, "Wherever we turn our eyes we meet with evidences of the power of God."

13. *Comm.* Ps. 19:1; 8:1.

14. *Comm.* Gen., "The Argument." See also 1.14.22; *Comm.* Ps. 8:1; *Comm.* Ps. 148:7; *Comm.* Isa. 40:12.

15. Schreiner, *The Theater of His Glory*, 22.

16. 1.14.22; 1.5.2.

17. In *Comm.* Ps. 104:10, Calvin remarks that God's provisions for the wilderness and for the arable fields "furnish manifest tokens of the Divine goodness."

has omitted nothing essential to the perfection of his edifice."[18] About Genesis 3:17, Calvin writes, "Only, lest sadness and horror should overwhelm us, the Lord sprinkles everywhere the tokens of his goodness."[19] Calvin employs especially intimate language, noting that God shows himself to be a "nurse and a father" in his care for the animal kingdom, "the brute creation."[20] In short: God "has so wonderfully adorned heaven and earth with as unlimited abundance, variety, and beauty of all things as could possibly be, quite like a spacious and splendid house, provided and filled with the most exquisite and at the same time most abundant furnishings."[21]

In sum, although God is invisible, for Calvin, God's glory is "conspicuous enough" to the human creature. The invisibility of God, we might say, is not strictly a problem for Calvin, either ontologically or epistemologically. The God of Abraham, Isaac, and Jacob, the God who exists above the highest heavens, Calvin consistently seems to argue, can still be known through sensory means. The so-called transcendent otherness of God does not imply unknowability.[22] Though the essence of God remains impenetrable to contingent creatures, and while salvific knowledge of God comes only by way of the spectacles of Scripture (the other "Book," besides the book of nature) and the inner testimony of the Holy Spirit, which together show us Christ, the perfect image of the Father,[23] Calvin maintains that "this does not prevent us from applying our senses to the consideration of heaven and earth, that we may thence seek confirmation in the true knowledge of God."[24] As he explains,

> In respect of his essence, God undoubtedly dwells in light that is inaccessible; but as he irradiates the whole world by his splendor, this is the garment in which He, who is hidden in himself, appears in a manner visible to us. . . . That we may enjoy the sight of him, he must come forth to view with his clothing; that is to say, we must cast our eyes upon the very beautiful fabric of the world in which he wishes to

18. *Comm.* Gen. 2:2. The language of mirror appears again in 1.5.1.
19. *Comm.* Gen. 3:17.
20. *Comm.* Ps. 147:9. See also *Comm.* Gen. 3:14, 19.
21. 1.14.20.
22. Contra Eire, *War against the Idols.*
23. *Comm.* Ps. 19:7.
24. *Comm.* Gen., "The Argument."

be seen by us, and not be too curious and rash in searching into his secret essence.[25]

The proper aim of humans, then, is not to seek God "above the clouds" but "in the clouds," not beyond creation but through creation. To seek God in this way yields a knowledge of God that is mediated *by* creation, not despite creation, and it is to be regarded not simply as a knowledge about God but also as a communication of God himself to human creatures. As Calvin reasons in book 1 of the *Institutes*, the right way to seek God "is not for us to attempt with bold curiosity to penetrate to the investigation of his essence, which we ought more to adore than meticulously to search out, but for us to contemplate him in his works whereby he renders himself near and familiar to us, and in some manner communicates himself."[26]

Anticipating my argument below, we could say that, for Calvin, such an experience cannot be grounded in the human creature itself, but rather in Christ. "For Christ is that image," Calvin writes in the prologue to his Genesis commentary, "in which God presents to our view, not only his heart, but also his hands and his feet. I give the name of his heart to that secret love with which he embraces us in Christ: by his hands and feet I understand those works of his which are displayed before our eyes."[27] Such an experience is possible for human creatures only because of the Holy Spirit, who enables them to see and to love the work of God in creation.[28]

An Aesthetic Role: Awakening Delight through Beauty

Calvin repeatedly argues that human beings are not only to see the glory of God in creation but also to enjoy the creation. As he puts it, God would not have us be "mere witnesses" of creation but "to enjoy all the riches" that are there exhibited.[29] Or, as elsewhere, "It is no small honor that God for our sake has so magnificently adorned the world, in order that we may not only be spectators of this beauteous theater, but also enjoy the multiplied abundance and variety of good things which are presented

25. *Comm.* Ps. 104:1.
26. 1.5.9.
27. *Comm.* Gen., "The Argument."
28. Cf. 1.5.13; 1.7.4.
29. *Comm.* Gen., "The Argument."

THE THEATER OF GOD'S GLORY

to us in it."[30] We take joy in creation, Calvin significantly insists, because God himself takes joy in creation. In a comment on Genesis 1:4, Calvin writes, "Here God is introduced by Moses as surveying his work, that he might take pleasure in it."[31] Because our pleasure in creation is grounded in God's own pleasure, it is not a passive but an active engagement of the sensory riches of creation. Calvin writes: "We have never been forbidden to laugh, or to be filled, or to join new possessions to old or ancestral ones, or to delight in musical harmony, or to drink wine."[32] Wine exists on earth precisely because of "God's superabundant liberality." Even more positively, "It is lawful to use wine not only in cases of necessity, but also thereby to make us merry."

It is clear, then, that for Calvin this experience of creation is an intensively sensory one. The faithful ought never to run over the good things in creation "with a fleeting glance; but we should ponder them at length, turn them over in our minds seriously and faithfully, and recollect them repeatedly."[33] What results from such reflection? A recognition that, when properly considered under the governorship of the Creator, creation is offered to humanity both for sociobiological needs *and* for aesthetic needs. Calvin summarizes as follows a rightly ordered life in 3.9.2 of the *Institutes*:

> Has the Lord clothed the flowers with the great beauty that greets our eyes, the sweetness of smell that is wafted upon our nostrils, and yet will it be unlawful for our eyes to be affected by that beauty, or our sense of smell by the sweetness of that odor? What? Did he not so distinguish colors as to make some more lovely than others? What? Did he not endow gold and silver, ivory and marble, with a loveliness that renders them more precious than other metals or stones? Did he not, in short, render many things attractive to us, apart from their necessary use?

It is important here to stress that Calvin does in fact believe that it is possible to be rightly related to the material creation—both to enjoy it as such ("in the raw," as it were) and to enjoy what humans make of it

30. *Comm.* Ps. 104:31.
31. *Comm.* Gen. 1:4.
32. 3.19.9.
33. 1.14.21.

(e.g., bread, wine, oil, music). While he acknowledges the possibility for human perversion of creation, this concession does not diminish his consistent enthusiasm for the material-aesthetic delights with which God has endowed humanity. Calvin also believes that a delight in earthly things may lead to a delight in heavenly things. "For in this world God blesses us in such a way as to give us a mere foretaste of his kindness, and by that taste to entice us to desire heavenly blessings with which we may be satisfied."[34]

What seems to hold all these ideas together in Calvin is a certain notion of beauty, two characteristics of which recur in Calvin's application of the term. One characteristic points to a sensuous and desirable quality in creation. In his comment on Genesis 2:8, he writes, "God, then, had planted Paradise in a place which he had especially embellished with every variety of delights, with abounding fruits, and with all other most excellent gifts. For this reason it is called a garden, on account of the elegance of its situation, and the beauty of its form."[35] Additionally, "not only was there an abundant supply of food, but with it was added sweetness for the gratification of the palate, and beauty to feast the eyes." A more habitual use of the term is intended to draw attention to the harmonious arrangement of creation. When God pronounces his final benediction on the original creation, he does so "that we may know that there is in the symmetry of God's works the highest perfection, to which nothing can be added."[36] A "beautiful arrangement and wonderful variety" characterize both the heavenly bodies and the things of earth. Everything fits; everything has its place, and all things are rightly related to each other.[37]

While the physical creation makes possible, in some fashion, the knowledge of God, creation also entails the worship of God when it fulfills the purpose for which it has been made. "For does not the sun by his

desirable + harmonious [margin note]

---

34. *Comm.* 1 Tim. 4:8.
35. *Comm.* Gen. 2:8.
36. *Comm.* Gen. 1:31. Cf. *Comm.* Ps. 19:1.

is this true worship? [handwritten note]

37. *Comm.* Isa. 40:2: "All who shall observe, that amidst the vast number and variety of the stars, so regular an order and course is so well maintained, will be constrained to make this acknowledgment. For it is not by chance that each of the stars has had its place assigned to it, nor is it at random that they advance uniformly with so great rapidity, and amidst numerous windings move straight forwards, so that they do not deviate a hairbreadth from the path which God has marked out for them. Thus does their wonderful arrangement show that God is the Author and worker, so that men cannot open their eyes without being constrained to behold the majesty of God in his works."

light, and heat, and other marvelous effects, praise his Maker?" Calvin asks, "The stars when they run their course, and at once adorn the heavens and give light to the earth, do they not sound the praises of God?" They do. And in doing so, the "affluence, sweetness, variety and beauty" of creation can train men and women to choose the good and to reject the evil.[38]

A Pedagogical Role: Schooling the Church

"The contemplation of heaven and earth," Calvin writes, "is the very school of God's children."[39] And again: "Let the world become our school if we desire rightly to know God."[40] The heavens are "preaching the glory of God like a teacher in a seminary of learning."[41] The science of astronomy is like an "alphabet of theology," inasmuch as the stars "contribute much towards exciting in the hearts of men a high reverence for God."[42] "Even irrational creatures," Calvin comments on Isaiah 1:3, "give instruction." "Under their tuition," the heavens teach all people without distinction, and all receive profit "at the mouth of the same teacher."[43] All people may "read" about the glory of God in the heavens—"with the greatest ease," even![44] Yet, while an immediate goal of creation's instruction is to show how God has provided all things that they may be "useful and salutary" to humanity, the larger goal is to foster the twin virtues of obedience and love in the human creature.[45]

Explaining the purpose of Genesis, Calvin says that "all things were ordained for the use of man, that he, being under deeper obligation, might devote and dedicate himself entirely to obedience towards God."[46] God places the sun and the moon in their respective places "to teach us that all creatures are subject to his will, and execute what he enjoins upon them."[47]

---

38. *Comm.* Ps. 148:3.
39. 1.14.20; cf. 1.5.1–12; *Sermons on Job* 9:7–15.
40. *Comm.* Gen., "The Argument."
41. *Comm.* Ps. 19:4.
42. *Comm.* Ps. 148:3.
43. *Comm.* Ps. 19:3.
44. *Comm.* Ps. 19:4.
45. 1.14.22.
46. *Comm.* Gen., "The Argument."
47. *Comm.* Gen. 1:14. The "lucid bodies," Calvin writes, obey the command of God.

[handwritten note: what does creation tell us about God?]

But more than simple obedience, the invitation of the Creator to the creature is heartfelt trust in a benevolent Father. Calvin remarks, "Invited by the great sweetness of his beneficence and goodness, let us study to love and serve him with all our heart."[48] Such a love inspires not just our present life but our future one too. "Knowledge of this sort, then, ought not only to arouse us to the worship of God but also to awaken and encourage us to the hope of the future life."[49]

An Admonitory Role: Chiding Ingratitude and Pride

A fourth role that creation performs is admonitory. As such, creation exposes our ingratitude to God and unmasks human pride before God.

> How great ingratitude would it be now to doubt whether this most gracious Father has us in his care, who we see was concerned for us even before we were born! How impious would it be to tremble for fear that his kindness might at any time fail us in our need, when we see that it was shown, with the greatest abundance of every good things, when we were yet unborn! Besides, from Moses we hear that, through His liberality, all things on earth are subject to us. It is certain that He did not do this to mock us with the empty title to a gift. Therefore nothing that is needful for our welfare will ever be lacking to us.[50]

In a comment on Genesis 2:9, Calvin writes, "And certainly it was shameful ingratitude, that he [Adam] could not rest in a state so happy and desirable."[51] With regard to humanity's prideful proclivities, Calvin argues that human beings repeatedly substitute nature for God (1.5.4), defraud God of his rightful praise (1.5.5), succumb to the "evil imaginings of our flesh" (1.5.11), and fall into a mental labyrinth wherein all sorts of ignorant, foolish, and idolatrous fictions are spawned (1.5.12),[52] whereas a proper consideration of heaven and earth should have the very opposite effect. To behold the works of God in creation ought to inflame us "with love to God,

---

48. 1.14.22.

49. 1.5.10.

50. 1.14.22. See also Calvin's comments in *Comm.* Ps. 19:1; *Comm.* Ps. 95:1; *Comm.* Ps. 100:3–5; *Comm.* Ps. 104; *Comm.* Gen. 1:28; 2:9; *Comm.* 1 Cor. 15:36; *Comm.* Rom. 8:22.

51. *Comm.* Gen. 2:9.

52. See also 1.6.1, 3; 1.13.21; 3.2.2–3; 3.6.2; 3.8.1; 3.19.7; 3.21.1; 3.25.11; 4.7.22.

Is general revelation only found in creation?

that we may be stirred up to the practice of godliness, and that we may not suffer ourselves to become slothful and remiss in celebrating his praises."[53]

A Doxological Role: Enacting and Summoning Praise of God

While creation performs an admonitory function over against human beings who really should know better, for Calvin the more forceful role of creation is to arouse us to worship the Lord of heaven and earth. For Calvin, creation serves as a context for praise, creation enacts praise, creation summons praise, and creation subsists to the extent that right praise is lifted up to the Creator. About Genesis, Calvin writes, "For this is the argument of the Book: After the world had been created, man was placed in it as in a theater, that he, beholding above him and beneath the wonderful works of God, might reverently adore their Author."[54] Not only does creation at large and in the temporal framework of the Sabbath day serve as a context for the "pure and lawful worship of God," creation also enacts its own peculiar praise. In a preface for the 1534 French translation of the New Testament by his cousin, Pierre Robert Olivetan, Calvin famously writes: "It is evident that all creatures, from those in the heavens to those under the earth, are able to act as witnesses and messengers of God's glory. . . . For the little birds that sing, sing of God; the beasts clamor for him; the elements dread him, the mountains echo him, the fountains and flowing waters cast their glances at him, and the grass and flowers laugh before him."[55]

In a note on the phrase "the beasts of the field shall honor me," in Isaiah 43:20, Calvin writes, "The meaning is, that the power of God will be so visible and manifest [when God does a 'new thing'], that the very beasts, impressed with the feeling of it, shall acknowledge and worship God. . . . [And] they will stand still, as if in astonishment, when they see the miracles."[56] "Irrational" creatures of all sorts, in fact, praise God day and night: trees, seas, stars, fishes, beasts of the field, planets, each in its own way proclaiming "loudly and distinctly enough" the glory of God. While creation resounds with the praise of God, it also invites humanity to join in that praise.[57] On Psalm 139:13, Calvin says, "The true and proper

---

53. *Comm.* Ps. 8:7–9.
54. *Comm.* Gen., "The Argument."
55. In *Calvin: Commentaries* (Philadelphia: Westminster, 1958), 60.
56. *Comm.* Isa. 43:20.
57. *Comm.* Ps. 95:3.

view to take of the works of God . . . is that which ends in wonder."[58] If humans were not at present sinful creatures, Calvin argues, creation would in fact suffice to excite the pure worship of God.[59] Yet "we are stone-blind, not because the manifestation is furnished obscurely, but because we are alienated in mind . . . we lack not merely inclination, but ability."[60] So God chooses to "daunt us and tame us" in order to enable us to see this theater properly.[61]

Creation's praise is not, however, a whip upon the human conscience. Nor does the Creator harangue the human creature to fulfill its doxological calling. God wishes to ravish humanity by his creation and so summon love and a willing obedience from the human heart. "If one feather of a peacock is able to ravish us," Calvin preaches in a sermon on Job 39:8–40:6, "if wild beasts are able to stop men's minds . . . what will God's infinite majesty do?"[62] If a hawk can ravish and amaze us, "what ought all his works do when we come to the full numbering of them?"[63] Indeed, the glory of the Creator "is surpassingly great as to ravish us with the highest admiration."[64] So intimately does Calvin link the work of creation with the work of worship that the welfare of both is at stake if either is lost or neglected. "The stability of the world depends on the rejoicing of God in his works."[65] On Psalm 115:17, Calvin writes, "If on earth such praise of God does not come to pass, if God does not preserve His church to this end, then the whole order of nature will be thrown into confusion and creation will be annihilated when there is no people to call upon God."[66]

Conclusion

As we anticipate part 2 of our exposition of Calvin, it might be helpful to make note of a few things. The first is that, whatever else we find in Calvin's thinking, we do not find a meager regard for the cosmos. Here we

58. *Comm.* Ps. 139:13.
59. *Comm.* Ps. 19:7.
60. *Comm.* 1 Cor. 1:21; cf. 1.5.15.
61. Cf. *Sermons on Job* 4:20ff.
62. *Sermons on Job* 39:8–40:6.
63. *Sermons on Job* 39:22–35.
64. *Comm.* Ps. 8:3–4.
65. *Comm.* Ps. 104:31.
66. *Comm.* Ps. 115:17; cf. 3.20.43.

have nothing less than a grand theater where humanity is invited to delight in the workmanship of the universe. As the "hands and feet" of God in Christ, upheld by the Spirit of God, creation is a place *for* something: for goodness, pleasure, beauty, vitality and fruitfulness, action, the worship of God, and the mediation of God's presence to humanity. Though sin vitiates humanity's capacity to enjoy God in and through creation, it does not rob creation of its capacity to stage a spectacle of God's powers. And while it is only with the help of the law, of faith in Christ through the preaching of the gospel, and of the internal witness of the Holy Spirit—each serving as spectacles to rectify a poor vision—that the faithful are able to see and to enjoy creation fully, for Calvin, the human eye is in its own way capable of discerning the glory of God in creation.

A second observation is that Calvin's argument follows what he believes to be a faithful reading of the Apostles' Creed. In Calvin's theology of the physical world there is very little christological or pneumatological reasoning. Calvin also avoids the language of symbol to describe the material creation. While he employs the vocabulary of image, mirror, painting, school, fabric, and preacher to describe creation's functional relationship to the Creator, the language of symbol appears only in his discussion of particular material phenomena, like the ark of the covenant, which God commands and which allow the invisible God to become visible in order that God may be known. How, then, do the media of the tabernacle and temple, with their respective aesthetic and ceremonial paraphernalia, function as symbols of God's presence in the world? How does Calvin understand the purpose of the material creation in these prescribed aids to worship? What continuities and discontinuities do we discover in relation to the grammar of creation that we have just examined? It is to these questions that we now turn.

CHAPTER 3

The Work of the Material Symbols of Worship

Calvin links the Word to the symbol not primarily to authorize the creation of the symbol, but because it is the Word in particular that gives to the symbol its upward dynamic, leading the godly from the contemplation of the symbol to God in heaven.

Randall Zachman, *Image and Word*

Paul likens the Jews to children, Christians to young men [Gal. 4:1–7]. What was irregular about the fact that God confined them to rudimentary teaching commensurate with their age, but has trained us through a firmer and, so to speak, more manly discipline? Thus, God's constancy shines forth in the fact that he taught the same doctrine to all ages, and has continued to require the same worship of his name that he enjoined from the beginning. In the fact that he has changed the outward form and manner, he does not show himself subject to change. Rather, he has accommodated himself to men's capacity, which is varied and changeable.

Calvin, *Institutes*

Three comments, pulled together here, offer a kind of précis for Calvin's understanding of material symbols in God's economy. In the 1539 *Institutes* (3.25), he observes: "God, indeed, from time to time showed the presence of his divine majesty by definite signs, so that he might be said

47

to be looked upon face to face. But all the signs that he ever gave forth clearly told men of his incomprehensible essence. For clouds and smoke and flame [Deut. 4:11] restrained the minds of all, like a bridle placed on them, from attempting to penetrate too deeply."[1]

In a remark on the tree of life in Genesis 2:9, Calvin adds, "For we know it to be by no means unusual that God should give us the attestation of his grace by external symbols."[2] By them, in fact, God "stretches out his hand to us, because, without assistance, we cannot ascend to him." And third, in a note on the cherubim of Genesis 3:23, he writes, "I call them vehicles and ladders, because symbols of this kind were by no means ordained that the faithful might shut up God in a tabernacle as in a prison, or might attach him to earthly elements; but that, being assisted by congruous and apt means, they might themselves rise towards heaven."[3]

In each of these statements we perceive a pattern that will be repeated in Calvin's writing. Positively, a material symbol raises us up *to* God for the sake of a gracious encounter *with* God. It is also an aid given *by* God, both because of our inability to ascend through our own powers and because of the inadvisability of penetrating the essence of God.[4] Such creaturely symbols are fitting ("congruous and apt") for the human creature. Negatively, a material symbol fails its divinely intended purpose if it imprisons God on earth or if it binds humanity to earth, preventing an ascent to heaven. It likewise fails if it is detached from the promise of God.

As the case may be, material symbols are provided on account of human ignorance,[5] weakness,[6] infirmity,[7] sloth,[8] and childishness.[9] Consistently, then, there are things that are to be affirmed, things that are to be warned against, and a persistent anxiety over the domain of physicality. In what follows, I consider, first, what Calvin says about the material

---

1. The language of "face" is pervasive in Calvin's thought, anchoring both his protology and his eschatology. To look on God's face, he writes in 1.1.2, is the beginning of true self-knowledge. In a comment on 2 Cor. 3:18, Calvin defends Paul's use of the term "unveiled face" as a way to describe our present experience of God. See Pitkin, *What Pure Eyes Can See*, 7.

2. *Comm.* Gen. 2:9.

3. *Comm.* Gen. 3:23.

4. *Comm.* Gen. 3:23.

5. *Comm.* Acts 7:40.

6. *Comm.* Acts 17:25.

7. *Comm.* Ps. 42:2.

8. 4.1.1.

9. *Comm.* John 4:23.

symbols of the tabernacle and temple, and, second, more briefly, what Calvin says about particular symbols of God's presence in New Testament worship.

Material Symbols of God's Presence in Tabernacle and Temple

Echoing language he employs in his discourse on creation, Calvin argues in a comment on John 5:3 that the Jerusalem temple was "a most noble theater" of the goodness of God.[10] A splendid structure marked by astonishing beauty, the temple was "an image of spiritual things."[11] About Isaiah 66:1, he writes, "The Temple is called God's rest, because he gave the sign of his presence in the temple; for he had chosen it as the place where men should call on him, and from which he would give a display of his strength and power."[12] While the faithful should always guard against the temptation to become "wholly engrossed by the outward forms of worship," the psalmist "does not in the least degree detract from the holiness of the temple, which alone of all places of the earth God had chosen as the place where he was to be worshipped."[13] Even more strongly, the temple "was a sign and symbol of religion, where the face of God shown forth."[14]

Extending this visual idiom further, Calvin argues that it is possible to speak of the ark of the covenant as a symbol that "everywhere denominated" God's face.[15] Indeed, "it is called the Ark of his strength, not a mere idle shadow to look upon, but what certainly declared God's nearness to his Church."[16] Of the priestly garments, mentioned in Exodus 28:2, Calvin comments: "But God would show by this symbol the more than angelic brightness of all the virtues which was to be exhibited in Christ."[17] On the bells and pomegranates: "In this allegory there is nothing too subtle or far-fetched: for the similitude of the smell and the sound naturally leads us to the honoring of grace, and to the preaching of the

---

10. *Comm.* John 5:3.
11. *Comm.* Ps. 27:4.
12. *Comm.* Isa. 66:1.
13. *Comm.* Ps. 99:5.
14. *Comm.* Amos 4:2. Cf. 4.1.5.
15. *Comm.* Ps. 27:8.
16. *Comm.* Ps. 132:8.
17. *Comm.* Exod. 28:2.

gospel."[18] The elaborate garments mentioned in Exodus 39:1, moreover, serve a specific typological purpose: "Since Christ was vividly represented in the person of the high priest, this was a most important part of the legal service . . . [for the] purpose of placing before men's eyes all that faith ought to consider in Jesus Christ."[19] Indeed, as Calvin remarks in a note on Acts 6:14, "The great value of the temple and the usefulness of the ceremonies consists rather in their being ascribed to Christ as to their original pattern."[20]

By maintaining this christological emphasis, Calvin is able to clarify the nature of continuity in the work of God through both old and new covenants and to define the fundamental purpose of material symbols, which is to pull the faithful up into a lively participation in the life of Christ.[21] When, for instance, God promises Israel in Jeremiah 31:12 that they will once again enjoy wine, oil, and wheat, Calvin explains that "something better and more excellent than food and sufficiency is promised; and that what is spiritual is conveyed under these figures, that the people might, by degrees, ascend to the spiritual kingdom of Christ, which was yet involved in shadows and obscurity."[22] When it is said in Psalm 84:2 that David longs for the courts of the Lord, Calvin believes that David "knew that the visible sanctuary served the purpose of a ladder, because, by it the minds of the godly were directed and conducted to the heavenly model."[23] Conscripting language typical of the prophets, Calvin remarks on Psalm 132:7, "While God dwells in heaven, and is above all heavens, we must avail ourselves of helps in rising to the knowledge of him; and in giving us symbols of his presence, he sets, as it were, his feet upon the earth, and suffers us to touch them."[24]

While affirming the ostensible purposes of the material media in Israel's public worship, Calvin warns against specific dangers. God descends to his people "not to occupy their minds with a gross superstition, but to raise them up by degrees to spiritual worship."[25] When it is said that

18. *Comm.* Exod. 28:31
19. *Comm.* Exod. 39:1. The sacrificial animals mentioned in Ps. 56:12, Calvin comments, are "outward symbols of thanksgiving."
20. *Comm.* Acts 6:14.
21. Cf. Canlis, *Calvin's Ladder*, 238–42.
22. *Comm.* Jer. 31:12.
23. *Comm.* Ps. 84:2.
24. *Comm.* Ps. 132:7.
25. *Comm.* Exod. 16:32.

God dwells "in the midst of his people" in Acts 7:49, "he is neither fixed to the earth, nor contained in any place, seeing that they seek him spiritually in heaven."[26] Not only do the people of God indulge the habit of dragging "God off his heavenly throne" and thereby making him "part and parcel with the elements of the world," Calvin worries that they themselves will cling to earth, refusing to ascend to God in heaven.[27] In commenting on Deuteronomy 4:12, Calvin notes that the visions of the patriarchs were testimonies of God's glory intended "rather to elevate men's minds to things above than to keep them entangled amongst earthly elements."[28] And finally, on Psalm 42:2, "it behooved the faithful in seeking to approach God, to begin by those things. Not that they should continue attached to them, but that they should, by the help of these signs and outward means, seek to behold the glory of God, which of itself is hidden from sight."[29]

In sum, for Calvin the function of external symbols in the Old Testament was to present a sensory attestation of God's grace to his people. They made visible through material media what remained invisible to the unaided eye, namely, the spiritual blessings that inhere to the promises of God. These symbols could not enclose God, nor could they circumscribe his infinite essence or drag God down from "heaven." Nor could they remain effective if humans clung exclusively to the symbol's external signification. They remained effective only if humans submitted to the divinely established dynamic, which was to raise the faithful to heaven through earthly means.

Preliminary Assessment

What exactly is the sensory realm capable of, and for what purpose does God reveal his powers and promises through creaturely media? While more will be said below, here we consider two lines of argument that predominate in Calvin's thinking. On the one side, Calvin seeks to remain faithful to the *temporal* logic of salvation history, which he discerns in the typological language exhibited throughout Holy Scripture. On the other side, Calvin attempts to make sense of the *spatial* logic of salvation his-

26. *Comm.* Acts 7:49.
27. *Comm.* Acts 17:24.
28. *Comm.* Deut. 4:12.
29. *Comm.* Ps. 42:2.

tory, especially as it unfolds in the New Testament. To put it simply, with the one, it is a question of *then vs. now*; with the other, it is a question of *above vs. below*.

Paradigmatic of the first line of argument is Calvin's statement on Hebrews 7:12: "Moses kept the people under a veil: that since the reality was not yet shown forth he represented a foretaste of Christ in types and shadows: that he adapted himself to convince the ignorant people and did not rise above the childish elements."[30] When it is said in Psalm 3:4 that David directs his prayers to the tabernacle, Calvin surmises: "By these words he intimates that he kept a middle way, inasmuch as he neither despised the visible sign, which the Lord had appointed on account of the rudeness of the times, nor by attaching a superstitious importance to a particular place, entertained carnal conceptions of the glory of God."[31] Of Exodus 30:23, Calvin writes, "For we have already often seen that there had been set before this rude people a splendor in sacred symbols, which might affect their external senses, so as to uplift them as it were by steps to the knowledge of spiritual things."[32] To Calvin's thinking, the movement from a dense display of material symbols in an old-covenantal liturgy to a more spare display in a new-covenantal liturgy parallels a movement of maturation for the church: metaphorically, from infancy to adulthood.

While it is obvious that the ceremonial shape of public worship has fundamentally changed with the coming of Christ, it is less obvious how the material symbols of such worship ought to be regarded "in the clear light of day." Are they symbols fit only for "slow men," as Calvin seems to suggest in a comment on Acts 17:24?[33] Are they helps that our "frail" earthly life uniquely requires?[34] In what manner do the prophets "figure spiritual things too high for human sense by corporeal and visible symbols"?[35] Are they too high for the human intellect also or too high only for the human senses? Has the cognitive domain replaced the physical domain as the preferred locus for the mediation of knowledge and love of God? Calvin believes that the fathers and prophets "painted a portrait

30. *Comm.* Heb. 7:12.

31. *Comm.* Ps. 3:4.

32. *Comm.* Exod. 30:23.

33. *Comm.* Acts 17:24: God uses symbols "as intermediaries with which to introduce himself in a familiar way to slow men, until, step by step, they ascend to heaven."

34. Cf. Calvin's comment on Jer. 11:5. See also Canlis, *Calvin's Ladder*, 62–65.

35. Cf. Calvin's comment on the Spirit as a wind in Ezekiel in his *Psychopannychia*, in *Tracts and Treatises*, 3:422–25.

such as to lift up the minds of the people above the earth, above the elements of this world and the perishing age, and that would of necessity arouse them to ponder the happiness of the spiritual life to come."[36] Was this portrait not also painted positively *in* and *through* the elements of the world?[37] In a comment on Hebrews 12:18, Calvin contrasts Mount Sinai, which "can be touched with hands," with Mount Zion, which "can only be known by the spirit."[38] Does an encounter of Mount Zion not also involve tangible media? These are the sorts of questions that Calvin's exposition prompts, inviting further investigation as we turn to his commentary on New Testament worship.

Material Symbols of God's Presence in New Testament Worship

While it is tempting to suppose that Calvin presumptively dismisses the importance of material symbols in a new-covenantal liturgy, Randall Zachman argues that such a judgment would be hasty. As Zachman summarizes: "According to Calvin, the gestures, rites, and ceremonies of the godly serve two necessary purposes: they are exercises of piety, and they are also expressions of the worship of God in body as well as in soul," for "it is right, that not the mind only, but the body also, should be employed in the service of God."[39] Bracketing off, for now, the practice of the Lord's Supper, Calvin makes a number of significant remarks about the church's external aids to worship. In a note on Psalm 95:6, for example, Calvin emphatically argues that the worship of God demands "our whole strength. . . . Mention is made not only of inward gratitude, but the necessity of an outward profession of godliness . . . to discharge their duty properly, the Lord's people must present themselves a sacrifice to him publicly, with kneeling, and other marks of devotion."[40] While the church should not rest in outward ceremonies, it should nonetheless imitate David, who took advantage of ceremonies "as a ladder by which he might ascend to God, finding he had not wings with which to fly thither."[41]

---

36. *Institutes* (1536), 7.20.
37. *Comm.* Heb. 9:1.
38. *Comm.* Heb. 12:18.
39. Zachman, *Image and Word*, 359. Cf. *Comm.* Exod. 4:31.
40. *Comm.* Ps. 95:6.
41. Cf. *Comm.* Ps. 42:2.

The Benefits of Kneeling and Hand-Raising

In addition to enabling one's whole person to rise to God in rightful praise, ceremonies "train" the church. As Calvin remarks in a note on Psalm 52:10, "By these, and our common sacraments, the Lord, who is one God, and who designed that we should be one in him, is training us up together in the hope of eternal life, and in the united celebration of his holy name."[42] The body, perhaps surprisingly, is a key to right praise for Calvin: "As for the bodily gestures customarily observed in praying, such as kneeling and uncovering the head, they are exercises whereby we try to rise to a greater reverence for God."[43] Kneeling as such expresses a "serious" disposition of the heart. Like musical instruments for Israel, kneeling stimulates the soul, since "the outward exercise of the body helps the weakness of the mind."[44] Kneeling, in this way, both symbolizes and activates the interior domain. As Calvin says, "It reminds us of our inability to stand before God, unless with humility and reverence; then, our minds are better prepared for serious entreaty, and this symbol of worship is pleasing to God."[45]

While kneeling signifies a condition of humility, the raising of hands signifies the church's "confidence and longing" for God.[46] In a remark on Lamentations 2:19, Calvin writes, "Except this ceremony were to raise up our minds (as we are inclined by nature to superstition), every one would seek God either at his feet or by his side."[47] Raised hands, in fact, strengthens an ecstatic movement: "to go forth, as it were, out of ourselves whenever we call on God."[48] When the "inward feeling corresponds with the external gesture," we arrive at "the right way of praying."[49] About Psalm 47:1, the psalmist enjoins the nations, in light of their joy in God, "to clap their hands, or rather exhorts them to a more than ordinary joy, the vehemence of which breaks forth and manifests itself by external expressions."[50] Although Israel suffered the fall of David's kingdom, all sorts of

---

42. *Comm.* Ps. 52:10.
43. *Institutes* (1536), 9.27.
44. *Comm.* Acts 9:40.
45. *Comm.* Dan. 6:10.
46. *Comm.* Acts 20:36.
47. *Comm.* Lam. 2:19.
48. *Comm.* Lam. 2:19.
49. *Comm.* Lam. 3:41.
50. *Comm.* Ps. 47:1. Cf. *Comm.* Ps. 26:8.

calamities, the captivity, and a dispersion, Calvin notes that Israel as "the faithful" is still summoned by the Holy Spirit "to continue clapping their hands for joy, until the advent of the promised Redeemer."[51]

The Particular Dangers of External Aids to Worship

As with Israel, the New Testament church should likewise avoid certain dangers. One danger is the unnecessary multiplication of ceremonies. "Accordingly, to keep that means [of pure worship], it is necessary to keep fewness in number, ease in observance, dignity in representation, which also includes clarity." And again: "God has given us a few ceremonies, not at all irksome, to show Christ present."[52] A second danger is hypocrisy. "If we do not begin with [worship in the heart], all that men profess by outward gestures and attitudes will be empty display."[53] Idolatry is a third danger: "For if any man shows any appearance or indication of idolatry at all or takes part in wicked and superstitious rites, even if in his soul he is perfectly upright—which is impossible—he will still be guilty of having defiled his body."[54] Superstitious attachments to these material symbols is, for Calvin, a constant vocational hazard.

A crucial danger is the rupture of Word from symbol. "Since the promise is the very soul of the sign, whenever it is torn away from the sign, nothing remains but a lifeless and vain phantom."[55] Bringing into intimate relationship the functions of eye and ear, Calvin comments on Numbers 9:18, "I do not doubt that the name of word was given to the sign, inasmuch as God speaks as much to the eye by outward signs as he does to the ears by his voice. Still, from this mode of expression we may gather that the use of signs is perverted and nullified, unless they are taken to be visible doctrine, as Augustine writes."[56] Added to the language of word,

---

51. *Comm.* Ps. 47:1.

52. *Institutes* 4.10.14. Against Romish practices, Calvin writes in *Institutes* 4.10.29, "We see such an example in the theatrical props that the papists use in their sacred rites, where nothing appears but the mask of useless elegance and fruitless extravagance."

53. Cf. *Comm.* Isa. 29:13.

54. Cf. *Comm.* 1 Cor. 7:1. Echoes of the Nicodemite controversy can be heard here.

55. *Comm.* Gen. 17:9.

56. *Comm.* Num. 9:18. In *Comm.* Gen. 17:9, Calvin states that circumcision is the "visible word, or sculpture and image," of the covenant with Abraham, "which the word more fully illustrates." Cf. Zachman, *Image and Word*, 163. On the visual register of Calvin's

promise, and doctrine, which Calvin uses synonymously in this context, is specifically christological language. Calvin affirms, "There are no true religious symbols except those which conform to Christ."[57] Not only must Word be joined to symbol, Word must also be joined to the ceremonies that compose a new-covenantal liturgy. "For God's promise and Word is like the soul which gives life to ceremonies. Take away the Word, and all rites which men observe, although apparently belonging to the worship of the godly, are nothing but decaying or silly superstition."[58]

For Calvin, to dislodge the material symbols from the Word is to rob them of their upward, or Godward, inertia. Zachman helpfully summarizes this point:

> Calvin links the Word to the symbol not primarily to authorize the creation of the symbol, but because it is the Word in particular that gives to the symbol its upward dynamic, leading the godly from the contemplation of the symbol to God in heaven. . . . If maintaining the proper distinction between God and creation keeps us from affixing or confining God to the symbol of God's presence, then the Word of God conjoined to the symbol guides us step by step from the visible symbol to the invisible God in heaven, so that the symbol serves its proper purpose.[59]

Finally, in a manner similar to his commentary on the symbols that accompanied Israel's worship, Calvin exhibits a proclivity to regard the materiality of liturgical symbols as *in itself* somehow troubling. In the opening salvo of book 4 of the 1559 *Institutes*, Calvin explains the reason for God's providing the faithful with external means by which they might partake of Christ. Since "in our ignorance and sloth (to which I add fickleness of disposition) we need outward helps to beget and increase faith within us, and advance it to its goal, God has also added these aids that he may provide for our weakness [*infirmitati*]."[60] To Calvin's mind, there exists a kind of unhealthy dynamic between earthlings and earthly media. He remarks that "men are indolent and slow by nature and tend down-

language for creation, see Jerome Cottin, "'Ce beau chef d'œuvre du monde': L'esthétique théologique de Calvin," *Revue d'histoire et de philosophie religieuses* 89 (2009): 489–510.

57. *Comm.* Heb. 8:5.
58. *Comm.* John 19:40.
59. Zachman, *Image and Word*, 227.
60. 4.1.1.

wards by their earthly spirit and need such arousing or rather vehicles to raise them to God."[61] Because the redeemed have not yet "scaled the heights" of angels, they need "inferior aids" to nurture their relationship with God in Christ.[62] Calvin insists that there "are indeed among us today certain outward exercises of godliness which our childishness needs. But they are moderate and sober enough not to obscure the naked truth of Christ."[63]

To summarize: for Calvin, material symbols are divinely ordained media, inextricably joined to the Word, which both disclose the character of God and raise us to heavenly life. In their own way they communicate grace, thereby feeding and forming the faithful. The abiding worry with material symbols is their capacity to keep God or the human creature caged to earth. More precisely, it is the tendency of humans to pervert a material symbol that worries Calvin, though there is always a lingering sense that there might be something intrinsically problematic with the symbol's materiality.

Preliminary Assessment

While Zachman rightly highlights the positive role that creation plays in Calvin's theology of worship, there is tension in Calvin that Zachman fails to emphasize enough, which, in turn, problematizes Zachman's enthusiastic apology for the Frenchman's "living images." This tension also highlights our two-part concern over continuity: on the one hand, continuity between old- and new-covenantal worship, particularly in its aesthetic dimension, and, on the other, continuity between the material creation at large and the material creation as it occurs in public worship. Zachman writes, "One of the essential purposes of the public worship of the Church is that the worshiping community might give voice to the praises of God that silently sound forth from all creatures. Since the godly have been given the ability to see, feel, and enjoy the powers of God set forth in God's works as in a painting, they ought to testify to these powers in their language of worship."[64] While Calvin's theology of creation does seem

---

61. *Comm.* John 17:1.
62. See *Comm.* 1 Cor. 13:12.
63. *Comm.* John 4:23.
64. Zachman, *Image and Word*, 355, with respect to a comment on Ps. 145:10.

to bear out this synopsis, his liturgical theology does not. The following statement from Calvin's 1539 *Institutes* is characteristic of a persistent cast of mind: "[To nourish the Old Testament saints better in the hope of eternal life, God] displayed it for them to see and, so to speak, taste, under earthly benefits. But now that the gospel has more plainly and clearly revealed the grace of the future life, *the Lord leads our minds to meditate upon it directly*, laying aside the lower mode of training that he used with the Israelites."[65]

Something about the coming of Christ has generated in Calvin's thinking a theological disjunction between the work that the physical creation performs in Israel's worship and the work that the physical creation performs in a new-covenantal setting—oriented around different teloi, in fact. And while in Calvin's commentary on the universe, creation is *somehow* capable of bearing witness to God, which Israel affirms in its cultic practices, Calvin's commentary on the symbols of public worship in the New Testament leads one to believe that this positive function no longer obtains—that discontinuity is the chief hallmark between creation's praise and the church's praise. Moreover, while there is plenty of data to corroborate the principle *finitum* est *capax infiniti* in the former,[66] it seems that the opposite principle, *finitum* non est *capax infiniti*, governs the thinking on the latter.[67]

While in the former Calvin affirms creation as the mirror of God, replete with "insignia" that sketch out a living likeness of God in the world, in the latter Calvin worries that the material creation will distort the knowledge of God.[68] While Calvin is bold enough to say that, in gazing upon the physical works of God, we are "restored by his goodness," in Calvin's discussion of the church's worship he repeatedly warns against the temptation to become overly distracted by material media.[69]

---

65. 7.25, emphasis added.

66. Cf. *Comm.* Dan. 3:6–7.

67. It is significant whether we translate *capax* as "fit for" or "contain." On the troubled history of this phrase and of its polemical appropriation by both Lutheran and Reformed theologians, see Heiko A. Oberman, "The 'Extra' Dimension in the Theology of Calvin," *Journal of Ecclesiastical History* 21.1 (1970), esp. 61–62. It is crucial to note that this phrase does not appear anywhere in Calvin. As Oberman explains, the phrase is taken up by subsequent Reformed historians and accorded a principled status in a genuinely Calvinistic theology.

68. Cf. 1.5.1, 6.

69. 1.5.9. In 1.5.5 Calvin even goes so far as to say, with the appropriate qualifications, that "nature is God."

And whereas creation at large becomes an arena to display the variety and abundance of God's "workmanship," the material quality of liturgical symbols appears to be an unfortunate necessity.[70] An occasion for "cataphatic" feasting, that is, albeit a temperate one, stands over against an insistence on "apophatic" restraint. Although creation may function as a context and stimulus for human praise, existing side by side with the praise of irrational creatures, such a function remains muted or missing altogether from public worship.

Conclusion

Several questions arise at this point, all of them revolving around the pressing issue of continuity. How do we account for such different linguistic and theological patterns in Calvin's writings on the physical creation? What relationship exists between "shadowy" worship and the material shape of that worship? What fate does the material creation suffer in the move from so-called childhood to adulthood in Calvin's eschatology? What precisely constitutes the human "weakness" that necessitates material symbols of worship? How does Calvin's language cohere with the actual language of Holy Scripture? And what role might Calvin's Christology and pneumatology play in the outcome of these questions? It is my aim in the following two chapters to address these questions.

70. 1.5.4.

CHAPTER 4

The Twin Problem of Materiality and Mediation

Some people read books in order to find God. But the very appearance of God's creation is a great book. Look above you! Look below you! Take note! Read!

Augustine, cited in Karlfried Froehlich, "Take Up and Read"

It is a truth, which may serve as a most powerful stimulant, and may lead us most fervently to praise God, when we hear that Christ leads our songs, and is the chief composer of our hymns.

Calvin, *Comm.* Hebrews

In the present chapter I argue that Calvin's ideas about worship and the material creation are haunted by a metaphysical dualism. There is no doubt that Calvin regards the capacity of the material realm to mediate the presence of God to the church with considerable suspicion. Discontinuity, rather than continuity, is the primary way that Calvin perceives the relationship between the material creation as such and the material creation in the context of public worship.

Two Nonoverlapping Trajectories for the Physical Creation

As a way to address the overarching question of continuity, I propose that Calvin's thinking involves two nonoverlapping trajectories for the mate-

60

rial creation. One on side stands the trajectory of creation at large, which ends in its restoration. Here the material dimension of creation remains good from beginning to end. On the other side stands the trajectory of the external aids to worship, which ends in their abolition at the eschaton. Here the material dimension of liturgical symbols remains ambiguous or negative, depending on the context of Calvin's writing. While a material optimism consistently marks the former,[1] a material pessimism tends to mark the latter; and whereas the New Testament operates with an eschatological dualism vis-à-vis creation, Calvin's rhetoric about the material shape of public worship is colored by a metaphysical dualism that is resisted only by a dogged commitment in Calvin to biblical language about the final destiny of the "new earth."

Calvin's Theological Methodology

As a first critical observation, I note that the conflicting rhetorical patterns that we detect in Calvin's discussion of creation may be provisionally accounted for by his theological methodology.[2] As arranged in the 1559 *Institutes*, the bulk of Calvin's exposition on creation occurs under the heading "The Knowledge of God the Creator," mirroring, as the case may be, the outline of the Apostles' Creed or Paul's book of Romans.[3] Here the material creation is discussed in relation both to the "natural man" and to the faithful. Here we find creation described as a work of God, yielding a limited knowledge of God and affording the faithful enjoyment of both creation and the Creator, hedged only and always by the possibility of sin. The majority of Calvin's discussion of material symbols of worship, in contrast, falls under books 2–4 of the *Institutes*, where knowledge of

1. Cf. Cornelis van der Kooi, *As in a Mirror: John Calvin and Karl Barth on Knowing God; A Diptych*, trans. Donald Mader (Leiden: Brill, 2005), 75–84. "All our pores are open" to God, Van der Kooi summarizes, though not apart from the mediation of the Son and the Spirit (76).
2. While the individual passages of Calvin's commentaries may mitigate this point, the fact that Calvin regarded the *Institutes* as an interpretive guide ("the sum of all religion") to his biblical commentary leads us to believe that the methodology observed in the *Institutes* is representative of his thought generally.
3. On this point, see Charles Partee, *The Theology of John Calvin* (Louisville: Westminster John Knox, 2008), 35–36, 121. In the preface to his commentary on Romans, Calvin writes, "If we have gained a true understanding of this Epistle, we have an open door to all the most profound treasures of Scripture."

3

God the Redeemer, the ways in which we are made partakers of the divine life, and the external means by which we are sustained in that life predominate. Here the material creation is discussed chiefly in relation to the redeemed. Here we find material symbols described as a command of God, yielding discrete knowledge of the Savior by the Spirit and affording the faithful ascent into fellowship with God and thereby also with one another. Here the material aspect of symbols is not to be enjoyed in itself but is regarded only as an instrument that delivers the church on to so-called heavenly life.

Calvin says as much in his résumé of public worship: "Believers have no greater help than public worship, for by it God raises his own folk upward step by step. . . . As if it were not in God's power somehow to come down to us, in order to be near us, yet without changing place or confining us to earthly means; but rather by these to bear us up as if in chariots to his heavenly glory, a glory that fills all things with its immeasurableness and even surpasses the heavens in height!"[4]

What precisely Calvin means by his use of "heaven" language will be addressed below. For now, if we are right in saying that the *Institutes* follows the logic of the Creed or of St. Paul's epistle, then his theological method will bring with it similar strengths and weaknesses: for example, understandably beginning with the work of God the Father, Maker of heaven and earth, but separating it too sharply from the work of Son and Spirit, who are equally though distinctly at play in the creation of the world and who together, in loving fellowship with the Father, constitute the telos of creation and therefore define the sorts of things we may, and indeed *must*, say about creation in any given context, liturgical or otherwise.[5]

The New Testament's Silence on Musical Instruments

A second, and perhaps obvious but still necessary, observation is that the New Testament itself remains silent on the use of musical instruments

---

4. 4.1.5.

5. "Although [Calvin] affirms the doctrine of creation out of nothing in his commentary on Genesis, there is surprisingly little interest in it in the *Institutes*. . . . In some contrast to the rest of his theology, there is in Calvin's account of the relation of God and the world little substantive part played by Christ and the Holy Spirit" (Colin Gunton, *The Triune Creator: A Historical and Systematic Study* [Grand Rapids: Eerdmans, 1998], 150, 152).

in corporate worship.[6] While this silence may imply their definitive pro-scription, as some liturgical biblicists would argue,[7] Calvin feels it neces-sary to offer an explication in order to infer the "mind" of the early church and to justify Genevan practices over against "Romish" ones. For this rea-son, as we have already seen, he appeals to the category of shadows.

"Shadowy" as Childishness and Weakness

Third, Calvin's appeal to the language of Colossians (2:17) and Hebrews (8:5; 10:1) involves for him two distinct lines of thought: shadowy as "childishness" (so Gal. 4:3) and shadowy as "weakness" (so Gal. 4:9).[8] The first term is a biblical shorthand to describe the changes that the church's worship incurs with the revelation of Christ and the descent of the Spirit.[9] At an obvious level for Calvin, this change includes no Jerusa-lem temple, no purity laws, no Aaronic priesthood, no animal sacrifices, no circumcision, and no corresponding calendar of annual festivals. More specifically, Calvin argues that, while the symbols of Israel's worship con-tain the same "spiritual" meaning as New Testament worship,[10] there is something qualitatively greater that marks the latter, which, among other

6. Calvin regards the mention of trumpets in 1 Cor. 15:52 and 1 Thess. 4:16 as met-aphorical. No comment is made on the trumpets that appear in the book of Revelation. T. H. L. Parker, *Calvin's New Testament Commentaries* (Edinburgh: T&T Clark, 1993), 119, hazards a guess as to why Calvin refused to write a commentary on the book of Revelation: "Apocalyptic, involving the use of allegory, was part of the Old Testament method of teach-ing; and he treated, even though more from a sense of duty than with pleasure, the apoca-lyptic parts of Ezekiel and Daniel, as witness his lectures on those books. But he may have considered that apocalyptic is foreign to the New Testament as if it involved a re-veiling of the clear and unambiguous Gospel."

7. See, for example, R. Scott Clark, *Recovering the Reformed Confession: Our Theol-ogy, Piety, and Practice* (Phillipsburg, NJ: P&R Publishing, 2008), and Michael Bushell, *The Songs of Zion* (Pittsburgh: Crown & Covenant Publications, 1980).

8. It is important to point out that Paul uses the term "weak" (*asthenē*, Gal. 4:9) to describe the "elemental things," that is, practices of the old covenant, to which the Galatian Christians wrongly returned, such as the celebration of days, months, seasons, and years, rather than remaining "true sons" of God (Gal. 4:1–10). Cf. *Comm.* Gal. 4:9: in the economy of God, "weak" is synonymous with "childishness."

9. Cf. Calvin's comments on John 4:23; Heb. 7:12; Gal. 4:1; Col. 2: 8–23; 2.11.13.

10. See, for example, *Comm.* Heb. 8:5; *Comm.* Exod. 15:20; *Comm.* 2 Sam. 6:14; *Comm.* Ps. 150:3; *Institutes* (1536), 4.8; 7.20; *Comm.* 1 Cor. 10:3; *Comm.* Heb. 10:1; *Comm.* Col. 2:17.

things, is the fact that, fourth, material media are less needed or desirable. His comment on Hebrews 12:18 is representative:

> Mount Sinai can be touched with hands, but Mount Zion can only be known by the spirit. The things which we read about in the nineteenth chapter of Exodus were visible figures; but what we have in the kingdom of Christ is hidden from fleshly experience. If anyone objects that there was a spiritual meaning in all the former things, and that today there are external exercises of holiness by which we are carried up to heaven, I reply that the apostle is speaking comparatively about the greater and the lesser. There is no doubt that when the Law and the Gospel are contrasted, what is *spiritual* predominates in the latter while *earthly* symbols are more prominent in the former.[11]

As the faithful move from childhood to adolescence, then, they require not only fewer ceremonies but also fewer material helps in their worship of God. On what grounds? Calvin appears to argue both a biblical and a theological line of thought, though it may be more accurate to say that he argues according to the economy of salvation—that is, what the Scriptures require of the church during the present age (its adolescence) and what eschatology imagines for the church in the age to come (its adulthood). Biblically, the New Testament commands few external aids, which, for Calvin, implies a negative regard for materiality. Theologically, the end of this age envisions a "face to face" encounter with God, devoid of material symbols, which, for Calvin again, implies a negative judgment on their present use.

Calvin repeatedly describes the movement from childhood to adulthood in terms of an ascent, where the faithful by degrees rise "to the spiritual kingdom of Christ."[12] Or as he writes on John 8:54, "Faith has its degrees of seeing Christ."[13] The apogee of this ascent is an immediate experience of God, face to face. While it is clear that glorification, or the movement to "adulthood," involves the cessation of liturgical ceremonies, it is less clear whether this experience of immediacy is, for Calvin, best

11. *Comm.* Heb. 12:18. See also *Comm.* 2 Cor. 3:7. Cf. David C. Steinmetz, "The Reformation and the Ten Commandments," *Interpretation* 43 (1989): 263.
12. *Comm.* Jer. 31:12. Cf. *Comm.* Gen. 32:29, "The Lord manifested himself to [the OT prophets] by degrees."
13. *Comm.* John 8:54.

captured in terms of intimacy or, said indirectly, in terms of the most minimal material mediation possible. A case can be made that Calvin favors the former. "But now that we rely on Christ the Mediator," he remarks on Hebrews 7:25, "we enter by faith right into heaven, because there is no longer any veil to obstruct us. God appears to us openly, and invites us lovingly to meet him face to face."[14] Still, there remains a lingering sense that the "weakness" that characterizes the church's "shadowy" worship points not just to a reduction of material symbols or a shift in the economy of God's dealings with the church but to a problem intrinsic to materiality itself—that is, the desideratum in the immediate experience of God may in fact be the absence of material mediation and, more crucially, that the absence of physical media in glory implies an antipathetic view of the present use of such media.

On Angels, Human Bodies, Heaven, and the Heavens

As enthusiastic as Julie Canlis is that Calvin's doctrine of ascension, governed by the idea of *koinōnia*, denotes a positive outcome for creation, where creation "is the ground and grammar of an ascent that is not away from materiality but a deepened experience of communion within it," she still admits that Calvin's rhetoric "can leave a lingering taste of Platonism in the mouth."[15] She writes, "Perhaps Calvin's primary weakness is that his language of earth and heaven is usually cast in terms of mutual exclusivity, giving a sense that the 'upward call' is not so much that their 'eyes are turned to the power of the resurrection' in the here and now (III.9.6), but rather the abandonment of the here and now."[16] Canlis wonders whether in Calvin the "carnal" is to be left behind eschatologically.[17] There is sufficient evidence, I suggest, to believe that the latter may in fact be true. This position is initially detectable in his comments on angels, human bodies, the humanity of Christ, and astronomical-heaven-over-against-earth, all of which, fifth, draw sharp attention to the mediating purposes of the material realm.

14. *Comm.* Heb. 7:25.
15. Canlis, *Calvin's Ladder*, 54, 120.
16. Canlis, *Calvin's Ladder*, 120. See also Lucien Richard, *The Spirituality of John Calvin* (Atlanta: John Knox, 1974).
17. Canlis, *Calvin's Ladder*, 120. See also Todd Billings, *Union with Christ: Reframing Theology and Ministry for the Church* (Grand Rapids: Baker Academic, 2011), 80.

In book 2 of the *Institutes*, arguing against Osiander's doctrine of the *imago Dei*, Calvin notes that angels enjoy "the direct vision of God." He adds, "If we believe in Christ, we shall take on the form of angels [Matt. 22:30] when we are received into heaven, and this will be our final happiness."[18] What exactly will constitute the human resemblance to angels?[19] Calvin answers variously. For one, we gain angel-like existence when we achieve an unaided vision of God, a point he stresses in his comment on 1 Corinthians 13:12. We cite it at length because of the connections to themes investigated in the previous chapters:

> The mode of knowledge which we now have is appropriate to our imperfect state, and what you might call our childhood; because we do not yet have a clear insight into the mysteries of the Kingdom of heaven, and we do not yet enjoy *the unclouded vision.* . . . For God, who is otherwise invisible, has appointed these [i.e., the ministry of the Word] as means for revealing Himself to us. Of course this can also be made to embrace the whole structure of the universe, in which the glory of God shines out for us to see, as we find expressed in Rom. 1:20 and Heb. 11:3. The apostle describes the created things as mirrors in which God's invisible majesty is to be seen, but since Paul is dealing particularly here with spiritual gifts, which are of assistance to the ministry exercised by the Church, and go along with it, we shall not digress further. I say that the ministry of the word is like a mirror. *For the angels do not need preaching, or other inferior aids, or sacraments.* They have the advantage of another way of seeing God, for God does not show them His face merely in a mirror [*in speculo*], but He presents Himself openly before them. But we, who have not yet scaled such heights, look upon the likeness of God [*imaginem Dei speculamur*] in the Word, in the sacraments, and, in short, in the whole ministry of the Church.[20]

In some manner, which only the angels now know, our vision of God in the eschaton ("at close quarters") will involve an immediate sight of God, seeing him as he sees us. While this statement appears to contra-

19. On Calvin's view of the nature and function of angels, and of the particular danger devotion to angels posed to Christians, see Schreiner, *The Theater of His Glory*, 39–53.

20. *Comm.* 1 Cor. 13:12, emphasis added. Cf. Van der Kooi, *As in a Mirror*, 57–63.

dict Calvin's comment in book 1 of the *Institutes* that angels are famous for their reluctance to gaze directly at God,[21] the redeemed will experience "a mutual seeing" with God, akin to the angelic experience.[22] Arguing with this end in mind, Calvin asks what purpose is to be served "by a restoration of the world, since the children of God will not be in need of any of this great and incomparable plenty but will be like the angels [Matt. 22:30], whose abstinence from food is *the symbol of eternal blessedness*. But I reply that in the very sight of it there will be such pleasantness, such sweetness in the knowledge of it alone, without the use of it, that this happiness will far surpass all the amenities that we now enjoy."[23]

Like angels, humans will have no need of physical food. To require it, conversely, is a kind of weakness. He makes a similar point in his remark on 1 Corinthians 15:44: "To make it quite clear, let the present quality of the body be called 'animation'; and its future quality, 'inspiration.' For as far as the soul's giving of life to the body now is concerned, that involves the intervention of many aids; for we need drink, food, clothing, sleep and other things like them. That proves to us beyond the shadow of a doubt how *frail* a thing 'animation' is. But the power of the Spirit for giving life will be much fuller, and for that reason independent of necessities of that sort."[24]

This angelic quality not only rests on the power of the Holy Spirit but also is exhibited prototypically in the resurrected Christ. Christ indulges the weakness of the disciples, Calvin argues, by eating fish, though not because he had need of it. "As He had won newness of life in heaven, He had no more need than the angels of food and drink, but He freely condescends to join in mortals' common usage."[25] Furthermore, it seems that humans might be better off if, like angels, they possessed no bod-

---

21. In 1.11.3 Calvin states that it is absurd to drag the cherubim from a "childish age" to our present day.

22. *CO* 26:156. Curiously, Calvin feels that human eyes should take their cue, to some degree, from cherubim and seraphim. "Through this covering of the Ark they stopped the human eye from contemplating God. . . . If the Papists say that there were images of cherubs in the Ark, this really refers to . . . the necessity of closing our eyes when the need comes to have recourse to God and of not approaching him except through the mediation of his voice."

23. 3.25.11, emphasis added.

24. *Comm.* 1 Cor. 15:44, emphasis added.

25. *Comm.* Luke 24:42. Over against this interpretation, see Joel B. Green, *Body, Soul, and Human Life: The Nature of Humanity in the Bible* (Grand Rapids: Baker Academic, 2008), 167-68.

ies, as Calvin wonders out loud in his explication of our need of sacraments. "For if we were incorporeal (as Chrysostom says), he would give us these very things naked and incorporeal. Now, because we have souls engrafted in bodies, he imparts spiritual things under visible ones."[26] The good news, Calvin believes, is that at death our souls "will then be set free from our bodies, and will have no further need of either the external ministry or other inferior aids."[27] Calvin affirms that the faithful will resemble angels, though not in all respects: "only so far as they shall be rid of every *weakness* of this present life, no longer liable to the necessities of an existence of *infirmity* and *corruption*."[28] And like angels, humans will be immortal, freed from "the prison of the body."

The Problem of Materiality

While we could make the case that Calvin's primary concern is the sinless, incorruptible life that the faithful will share with the "elect angels," there is still a sense that human embodied life, which while blessed "in the beginning," is now something that must be patiently endured until we reach the age to come. Food, drink, clothing, sleep, and procreation (all original "goods"), along with liturgical media (all biblical "goods"), are here classified as weaknesses, alongside the infirmities and corruptions that accompany the fallen condition of humans. And while I will treat at length in chapter 6 Calvin's language of "prison" to describe the physical body,[29] it is noteworthy that he also uses it to describe Christ's own body. He writes that "when Christ commended his spirit to the Father and Stephen his to Christ they meant only that when the soul is freed from the prison house of the body, God is its perpetual guardian."[30] More worryingly, at first glance at least, are Calvin's comments on 1 Corinthians 15:27. When Christ returns the kingdom back to the Father, Calvin writes:

[This] does not mean that He will abdicate from the Kingdom in this way, but will transfer it in some way or other from His humanity to His glorious divinity, because then there will open up for us a way of

26. 4.14.3.
27. *Comm.* 1 Cor. 13:12.
28. *Comm.* Matt. 22:30, emphasis added.
29. Cf. 3.25.1; 3.6.5n9; 3.9.4; 3.25.3.
30. 1.15.2.

approach, from which we are now kept back by our weakness. In this way, therefore, Christ will be subjected to the Father, because, when the veil has been removed, we will see God plainly, reigning in His majesty, and the humanity of Christ will no longer be in between us to hold us back from a nearer vision of God.[31]

What sort of "immediate" encounter should the faithful yearn for in their encounter with the Father? Should they desire to "leave the earth" in their prayers as Christ did in his intercourse with the Father?[32] What does Calvin mean that, following Christ's resurrection, "everything carnal which belonged to Christ should be consigned to oblivion and discarded, in order that we may make it our whole study and endeavor to seek and possess him in spirit"?[33] Do the "organs of the body" play no positive role in the external means that sustain Christian faith, yielding instead to the ostensibly superior operations of the so-called organs of the soul (mind, heart, will, spirit)? The sense that the physical creation plays a largely peripheral role in Calvin's liturgical thinking is reinforced, incidentally but still significantly, by the apparently worthier nature of the *astronomical* heavens over against the earth.

Calvin writes that "the nearer we approach to God, the more conspicuous becomes his image. For truly God there exercises his own power and wisdom much more clearly than on earth."[34] The contemplation of the physical heavens, in fact, constitutes "the last step of our ascent to God."[35] Calvin's comment on Jeremiah 51:15–16, echoing Plato in the *Timaeus*, is equally representative: "The wisdom of God is visible throughout the whole world, but especially in the heavens."[36] And again, "As a

---

31. *Comm.* 1 Cor. 15:27. Richard A. Muller addresses the charge of Nestorianism against Calvin's Christology in "Christ in the Eschaton: Calvin and Moltmann on the Duration of the Munus Regium," *HTR* 74.1 (1981): 31–59. Cf. Todd Billings, "Encountering a Mystery in Union with Christ: On Communion with the Incomprehensible God," in *Union with Christ*, chap. 3. For a summary discussion, see Charles A. M. Hall, *With the Spirit's Sword: The Drama of Spiritual Warfare in the Theology of John Calvin* (Zurich: EVZ Verlag; Richmond, VA: John Knox Press, 1968), 86–90, 207–29. See also Colin Gunton, "Aspects of Salvation: Some Unscholastic Themes from Calvin's *Institutes*," *International Journal of Systematic Theology* 1.3 (1999): 253–65.

32. *Comm.* John 17:1.

33. In "An Inventory of Relics," in *Tracts and Treatises*, 1:290.

34. *Comm.* Ezek. 1:22.

35. Zachman, *Image and Word*, 43.

36. *Comm.* Jer. 51:15–16.

more distinct image of [God] is engraven on the heavens, David has particularly selected them for contemplation, that their splendor might lead us to contemplate all parts of the world."[37]

While the ladder of ascent, we might say, involves a profitable lookabout of the earth below, the evidence suggests that what we may have, in Calvin, is an escalator of ascent, moving one way, upward. The purpose of physical symbols of God's presence involves the near-exclusive purpose of inducing the faithful to raise their souls "higher and rise to heaven."[38] The fear that humans will get stuck on earth, on the one hand, and that God will be "shut up within bars of wood or iron,"[39] on the other, is so strong for Calvin that he interprets these symbols in rhetorically uniform fashion: as aids to raise the mind "up to heaven" and the eyes "above this world," without any sense that the material realm is left with theologically positive work to do, *for the sake of a physical, earthy good,* not just a so-called spiritual, heavenly good.[40] Finally, while the explicit focus for many of the passages cited above is anthropological, Calvin's eschatological commentary informs what he regards as the appropriate present liturgical practices of the church.

The Problem of Mediation

One may certainly argue, as Canlis does, that Calvin rightly understood "heaven" as the fulfillment of communion with God.[41] As she summarizes Calvin: "Heaven represents God's freedom *from* human manipulation and *for* communion," and thus by implication "heaven" involves good news for both "the heavens and the earth."[42] One may also argue that Calvin operates with an eschatological rather than a metaphysical dualism in light of his principled christological vision for the created realm.[43] One may further argue that the church's material symbols are justifiably in-

37. *Comm.* Ps. 19:1.
38. *Comm.* Isa. 66:1.
39. *Comm.* Ps. 78:41.
40. *Comm.* Isa. 40.
41. Canlis, *Calvin's Ladder*, 118–21. Cf. Calvin's "Catechism of the Church of Geneva," 76, where he describes heaven as synonymous with "exalted, might, incomprehensible."
42. Canlis, *Calvin's Ladder*, 119, emphasis original.
43. Cf. Schreiner's observation, *The Theater of His Glory*, 22–30, that creation, in Calvin's view, existed in a constant state of instability.

ferior, functionally rather than ontologically, compared to a face-to-face knowledge of God. With Richard Muller, one may argue that, when the saints are fully united to the person of Christ and "cleave completely to God,"[44] they will attain an immediate vision of God, not because Christ's humanity has receded but because theirs has "advanced according to the economy of salvation."[45]

And with Todd Billings, one may finally assert that the beatific vision in Calvin is simply ambiguous,[46] where certain affirmations of the eternal mediation of the incarnate Christ must be kept in tension with the sense "that the incarnate Christ's 'standing in the middle' is only a temporary phenomenon."[47] Yet at a certain point Calvin's rhetorical patterns acquire a position that signifies a state of mind regarding the material conditions of worship. Calvin fails to see how throughout Scripture creation provides the mediating context for all enactments of public worship, now and in the age to come. He likewise fails to press to its logical conclusion the mediating work of Christ and the Spirit in all activities proper to the human creature.

If we wish to speak of an immediate (i.e., face-to-face) encounter with God by the glorified elect, this can be done only in a carefully qualified sense—qualified in two ways, specifically. If the faithful are promised a face-to-face encounter with God, it will be a hypostatic one, where the person of the Spirit mediates the creature's encounter with the person of the Father through the person of the Son,[48] rather than a mingling of essences or, as it were, a direct "plug-in" of humanity to the divine essence.[49] And if the blessed saints can look forward to an immediate vision of God, in an optical sense, it will not be a straightforwardly empirical one, where

44. *Comm.* 1 Cor. 15:27. Cf. Oberman, "The 'Extra' Dimension in the Theology of Calvin," 43–64.

45. Muller, "Christ in the Eschaton," 44, 48.

46. See, for example, Calvin's comments on 1 Pet. 1:21, John 1:18, and 2 Pet. 1:4.

47. Billings, *Union with Christ*, 83. He adds, "Absent from Calvin's account of this final vision of God is the normal vocabulary of accommodation, of God's condescension in Christ to limited human capacity in order to make knowledge of God possible" (83–84).

48. On this point, Calvin notes, in *Comm.* Heb. 1:3, "God is revealed to us in no other way than in Christ. The radiance in the substance of God is so mighty that it hurts our eyes, until it shines on us in Christ. It follows from this that we are blind to the light of God unless it illumines us in Christ . . . while God is incomprehensible to us in Himself, yet His form appears to us in the Son."

49. On this point, see Thomas G. Weinandy's excellent treatment in *The Father's Spirit of Sonship: Reconceiving the Trinity* (Edinburgh: T&T Clark, 1995).

the simple act of opening glorified eyeballs will yield the "unclouded vision" of God. Nor will it be a "spiritual" one, by virtue of something that inheres in the human spirit. Instead, it will be a *Spirit*-mediated sight of God, as it always has been, except now undistorted by a sinful state.[50]

The blessed will behold the face of God in Christ precisely because of the Spirit's work to enable the redeemed to see God in a manner commensurate to the way in which God sees them. To see God, for glorified humanity, will be to enjoy the intimate presence of God, which the Spirit shall make possible.[51] Not only, then, is it appropriate to speak of the Spirit's eternal mediation of our knowledge of God in Christ as such; it is also necessary to speak of the mediation that will occur *in and through the resurrected body*,[52] of the continual mediation that will take place through the *new creation*, and of the *material symbols of worship* that the blessed saints employ in glory (trumpets, songs, and God only knows what else), all of which will be accounted to the work of Christ and the Spirit.[53] It is ever and always a Two Hands work, which occurs through, and not despite, creaturely realities.

Conclusion

One of the distinctive characteristics of Calvin's language about the material form of public worship is the way in which it is marked by a vertical

50. *Comm.* John 6:46, "For these two things must be joined: there can be no knowledge of Christ until the Father enlightens by His Spirit those who are blind by nature; and yet it is useless to seek God unless Christ leads the way, for the majesty of God is higher than men's senses can reach."

51. Calvin makes this point in his *Sermons on Job* 21:13: "Forasmuch then as God is present with us by means of the word . . . we must desire always to be in His presence. . . . Not only therefore should we have God before our eyes but we should desire Him to look upon us and guide us." He adds on Job 14:13 that, though the present disfigured *imago* creates a blindness in the human creature, "God enlightens us by His Spirit and in such a way that we are able to behold Him, as far as we need for the transforming of us into His glory and for the reforming of us by His Holy Spirit."

52. David M. Moffitt, in "Unveiling Jesus' Flesh: A Fresh Assessment of the Relationship between the Veil and Jesus' Flesh in Hebrews 10:20," *Perspectives in Religious Studies* 37 (2010): 71–84, stresses the importance of Jesus's corporeal life in his mediatorial work in heaven.

53. Suzanne McDonald, "Beholding the Glory of God in the Face of Jesus Christ: John Owen and the 'Reforming' of the Beatific Vision," in *The Ashgate Research Companion to John Owen*, ed. Mark Jones and Kelly Kapci (Aldershot, UK: Ashgate, 2012), 141–58, advances a similar argument on behalf of John Owen.

(upward-to-heaven) and unidirectional (earth-to-heaven) orientation. Calvin repeatedly stresses the need for the faithful to ground their worship in both a heavenly originating and a heavenly ending point. Earth, conversely, plays a largely negative role, serving chiefly as a one-way launching point—*away* from earth, *up* to heaven. For Calvin, God descends through the material symbols of worship so that the human creature might in turn ascend to him, but without any notion of creation's ongoing *material* participation in that ascent. Nor is there a sense in which the faithful "return" to created reality with a heavenly "operating system," where the ascent to heaven grounds, orients, and inspires the church's worship on earth, the proper domain of earthlings. Earthy matter in this context is largely left behind.

Concomitantly, creation's fundamental dynamism is transferred to the domain of heaven, where the "real" action is perceived to take place, while the center of liturgical gravity is relocated from the whole of humanity to the internal regions of human life. While individual exceptions exist to the following judgment of Calvin's liturgical theology, it is generally true that in Calvin the material symbols of worship become, at best, an unfortunate necessity and, at worst, inert powers whose chief function is to activate other faculties of the soul. We have also seen how Calvin's thinking is generally marked by a radical discontinuity as it relates to the material character of public worship: (1) discontinuity between old- and new-covenantal liturgy vis-à-vis material symbols, and (2) discontinuity between the material creation at large and the material creation in the church's worship.

Might it be possible to conceive a stronger sense of continuity between these respective spheres? The conviction of the following chapter is, Yes, we can.

CHAPTER 5

The Double Movement of Creation in Worship

Temple and cosmos [in Scripture] are largely synonymous (homological), each representing an image of the other.

John H. Walton, "Creation in Genesis 1:1–2:3"

As soon as we acknowledge God to be the supreme architect, who has erected the beauteous fabric of the universe, our minds must necessarily be ravished with wonder at his infinite goodness, wisdom, and power.

Calvin, *Comm.* Psalms

When the Scriptures are read through what might be called a temple theology, I argue that it is possible to perceive a more richly dynamic relationship between the "heavenly" and the "earthly" orientations of public worship, as well as between the "work" of worship and the "work" of creation. Faithful worship according to the prophets and apostles is oriented simultaneously backward historically, to the original creation, and forward eschatologically, to the new creation, while always linked (figuratively) upward to the kingdom of heaven, the domain of God's perfect rule. From this viewpoint creation can be seen to play an important role in the church's worship, precisely because it is God's unswerving pleasure through his Two Hands to establish worship on earth as it is in heaven.

In light of this framework, I suggest that we may discover a way in which the material condition of public worship is caught up in a double movement: in the movement of creation's praise at large and in the movement of Christ and the Spirit to enable creation to become a dynamic theater of God's glory. I propose, accordingly, that Calvin's original instincts about creation were the right ones, even if he failed to carry them far enough. I also offer the beginning of a christological and pneumatological line of argument for the physical and aesthetic character of the church's liturgical life.

[handwritten: Calvin didn't take it far enough.]

The Temple Theology of Scripture

In his work *The Ideology of Ritual*, F. H. Gorman writes that, for Israel, "cosmos provides the necessary context for correct enactment of ritual; ritual only has meaning with a specific cosmos."[1] Three lines of imagery— cosmological, horticultural, and architectural—are repeatedly brought together by the biblical authors in theologically constitutive ways to describe the locus of the temple, the place that betokens both the presence and the order of God in fullness, "on earth as it is in heaven."[2] And while it can be said that *temple imagery* permeates the New Testament writings, I propose that a *temple theology* frames the mind of the apostolic church and as such reinforces the intimate relation between creation and worship.

The Garden

[handwritten: It starts in the garden.]

We begin with the garden. Gordon Wenham represents the general consensus in biblical scholarship when he writes: "The garden of Eden is not viewed by the author of Genesis simply as a piece of Mesopotamian farmland, but as an archetypal sanctuary, that is a place where God dwells and where man should worship him."[3] The linguistic parallels between Gen-

---

1. F. H. Gorman Jr., *The Ideology of Ritual: Space, Time, and Status in the Priestly Theology* (Sheffield, UK: JSOT Press, 1990), 47, 39.

2. Cf. Nicholas Perrin, *Jesus the Temple* (Grand Rapids: Baker Academic, 2010), 67.

3. Gordon J. Wenham, "Sanctuary Symbolism in the Garden of Eden Story," in *"I Studied Inscriptions from before the Flood": Ancient Near Eastern, Literary, and Linguistic Approaches to Genesis 1–11*, ed. Richard S. Hess and David T. Tsumura (Winona Lake, IN: Eisenbrauns, 1994), 399. Jon D. Levenson, *Resurrection and the Restoration of Israel: The Ultimate Victory of the God of Life* (New Haven: Yale University Press, 2006), 86–87, adds: "Like temples, [gardens] are walled off from quotidian reality, with all its instability

esis and the ceremonial system of Israel are significant. God's command to Adam "to till and keep" the garden, for example, is the same language used in Exodus 3:12 and Numbers 28:2 to describe sacrificial offerings (cf. Num. 3:7–8 and 8:26). If Eden is functioning as a sanctuary, "then perhaps Adam should be described as an archetypal Levite."[4] The verb *hithallek*, in Genesis 3:8, "to walk to and fro," is the same term used to describe the divine presence in the later tent sanctuaries of Leviticus 26:12, Deuteronomy 23:15, and 2 Samuel 7:6–7.

The cherubim who guard the east entrance to the garden evoke the cherubim of Solomon's temple, who guard the entrance to the inner sanctuary (1 Kings 6:23–28).[5] The tree of life adumbrates the menorah candelabrum, while God clothes Adam and Eve in a manner similar to the way that Moses clothes the priests (Exod. 28:41; 29:8; 40:14; Lev. 8:13).[6] The water in the garden brings to mind the great river that flows out of the New Jerusalem temple to sweeten the Dead Sea, and the seventh day of rest, in an Ancient Near Eastern context, symbolized the day when the gods, by entering the temple place, took control of the cosmos. John Walton explains, "When Genesis indicates that God rested on the seventh day, it tells us that in this account of the functional origins of the cosmos, the cosmos is being portrayed as a temple."[7] The garden, as a microcosm of "the heavens and the earth," represents thus the house of God, a place of ordered flourishing under the personal rule of Yahweh.[8]

---

and irregularity and the threats these pose, and thus they readily convey an intimation of immortality."

4. Wenham, "Sanctuary Symbolism," 401.

5. See also Exod. 25:18–25; 1 Kings 6:29.

6. Peter Enns, *The Evolution of Adam: What the Bible Does and Doesn't Say about Human Origins* (Grand Rapids: Brazos Press, 2012), 73, argues that Israel's temple informs its narrative of the creation story, not the other way around.

7. John H. Walton, "Creation in Genesis 1:1–2:3 and the Ancient Near East: Order out of Disorder after *Chaoskampf*," *Calvin Theological Journal* 43 (2008): 61.

8. While God is the God of the heavens (Dan. 2:18–19), dwelling in the heavens (Ps. 115:3), where his throne is located (Ps. 11:4), with the earth as his footstool (Isa. 66:1–2), nonetheless there is a basic sense that God occupies all space in heaven and on earth (1 Kings 8:27; Ps. 139:7). The parallels between Genesis 1 and Exodus 25–40 are also seen by many scholars to reinforce the intimate relationship between *cosmos* and *cultus*. Work in both domains is *completed*; the *Spirit of* God hovers over both labors; the architects of both projects (God, Moses) *see* the work unfolding and then *bless* the *finished* work. Cf. P. J. Kearney, "Creation and Liturgy: The P Redaction of Ex 25–40," *Zeitschrift für die alttestamentliche Wissenschaft* 89 (1977): 375–78.

The Tabernacle and Temple

With the advent of the tabernacle (along with all the little tabernacles that marked the time of the patriarchs), the presence of God occupies a specific cultic place, rather than the entire universe. "The presence of God is not diminished but concentrated."[9] Whereas the world in its fullness represented the dwelling of God, now, after the distortion of creation, which resulted from sin, a "divine contraction" points to the temple as the "holy space" of God. Yet with both major and minor prophets there is always a persistent hope that the earth would once again "be filled with the knowledge of the glory of God" (Hab. 2:14). The Jerusalem temple as such functions both protologically and eschatologically, looking backward and forward.[10] It serves here "as a survival of the primal paradise lost to the 'profane' world, the world outside the sanctuary (Latin, *fanum*) and as a prototype of the redeemed world envisioned by some [e.g., Isa. 44:28; Jer. 33:10–11; Ezek. 40–48] to lie ahead."[11]

Israel's chief sanctuary, in short, represents a liturgical nexus of the primal and the final, where each of its constituent parts engenders a decisive cosmology. The three spaces (outer courts, inner courts, holy of holies), the "molten sea," the altar of incense, the twelve bronze bulls, the lampstands, the lilies, gourds, palm trees, and pomegranates, also the woodwork decorated with inlaid gold, the ark of the covenant, the priestly garments, the curtains, the precious stones—together all of this symbolized a miniature cosmos ordered according to God's rule and thus also an eschatological hope.[12] As Gregory Beale explains, "The temple was a small-scale model and symbolic reminder to Israel that God's glorious presence would eventually fill the whole cosmos and that the cosmos would be the container for God's glory and not a mere small architectural container."[13]

9. Jon Levenson, "The Temple and the World," *Journal of Religion* 64.3 (1984): 297.

10. Ps. 78:69 (ESV), "He built his sanctuary [the Jerusalem temple] like the high heavens, like the earth, which he has founded forever."

11. Levenson, *Resurrection and the Restoration of Israel*, 90.

12. Cf. Allen P. Ross, *Recalling the Hope of Glory: Biblical Worship from the Garden to the New Creation* (Grand Rapids: Kregel, 2006), parts 2–4; G. K. Beale, "Cosmic Symbolism of Temples in the Old Testament," in *The Temple and the Church's Mission: A Biblical Theology of the Dwelling Place of God* (Downers Grove, IL: IVP, 2004), 29–80; Craig G. Bartholomew, *Where Mortals Dwell: A Christian View of Place for Today* (Grand Rapids: Baker Academic, 2011), chap. 4; T. D. Alexander, *From Paradise to the Promised Land: An Introduction to the Pentateuch* (Grand Rapids: Baker Academic, 2002).

13. Beale, *The Temple and the Church's Mission*, 19.

The Prophetic Vision of a New Temple

With Ezekiel 33–48 we discover a theological *via media* between Israel's temple and the vision of St. John in the Apocalypse. In both narratives we find a visionary transport of the prophet to a high mountain, the sight of a new world with Jerusalem at the center, the dwelling of God in the midst of his people, which produces a state of perfect well-being, the presence of the glory of God in the city, a heavenly interpreter with a measuring rod with which he measures the city, and the presence of the river of life.[14] Looking back to Eden, Susan Niditch discerns the same cosmogonic emphases in Ezekiel that one finds in Genesis 1–11. Looking forward to the New Eden,[15] the prophet's vision anticipates the renewal of both spiritual and physical realms, of both interior and exterior life.[16]

This renewal, in each of these paradigmatic texts, is owed to the Spirit of God. With the outpouring of the Spirit comes the redemption and re-creation of the whole earth, a "holy space," like the space of the temple, saturated with the glory of God.[17] While certain prophecies saw the temple extending over all of Jerusalem (Isa. 4:5–6; Jer. 3:16–17; Zech. 1:16—2:13), other prophecies envisioned the temple spreading over all of the land of Israel (Ezek. 37:26–28), and even over the entire earth (Dan. 2:34–35, 44–45), while the book of Revelation insists that the entire cosmos has become the temple (21:1–22:5).[18] In this sense, the intended design of Israel's temple will have been completed: the divine presence "will again fill the whole earth and heaven and become co-extensive with it. Then the eschatological goal of the temple of the Garden of Eden dominating the entire creation will be finally fulfilled."[19] Richard Bauckham

---

14. Daniel I. Block, *The Book of Ezekiel: Chapters 25–48* (Grand Rapids: Eerdmans, 1998), 502–3. Discrepancies of course exist, but the parallels are sufficiently strong to warrant a legitimate comparison. Cf. Joel 4:17–18; Zech. 14:5b–11; John 7:38; Rev. 22:1–2.

15. Susan Niditch, "Ezekiel 40–48 in a Visionary Context," *Catholic Bible Quarterly* 48.2 (1986): 208–24.

16. Block, *Ezekiel*, 701–2.

17. Robin Routledge, "The Spirit and the Future in the Old Testament: Restoration and Renewal," in *Presence, Power, and Promise: The Role of the Spirit of God in the Old Testament*, ed. David G. Firth and Paul D. Wegner (Downers Grove, IL: IVP Academic, 2011), 362–66.

18. G. K. Beale, "Eden, the Temple, and the Church's Mission in the New Creation," *JETS* 48.1 (2005): 28.

19. Beale, "Eden, the Temple, and the Church's Mission in the New Creation," 25. Cf. Bartholomew, *Where Mortals Dwell*, 111, 161–63. William J. Dumbrell, *The End of the Beginning: Revelation 21–22 and the Old Testament* (Grand Rapids: Baker Books, 1985), 38.

summarizes: "Like his presence in the temple (e.g. Ezek. 43), this eschatological presence of God entails holiness and glory. As his eschatological
presence, it is also the source of the new life of the new creation. . . . God's
presence . . . means life in the fullest sense: life beyond the reach of all
that now threatens and contradicts life, life which is eternal because it is
immediately joined to its eternal source in God."[20]

The Enfleshed New Temple

With the New Testament, the idea of the temple is substantially reconfigured.[21] In John's Gospel, Jesus is presented as the new temple, the one
who personifies the presence of God par excellence (John 2:19, 21). Evok-
ing a memory of the Genesis account (Gen. 3:8), God in Christ becomes
ambulatory again, tabernacling "among us" (John 1:14). More simply perhaps, holy space has now been "Christified."[22] Jesus is the singular and supreme "place" of God on earth, which redefines all other places.[23] Along
with this connotation of temple, Nicholas Perrin points to the second
shift in meaning that the temple undergoes in the New Testament:

> The body of the crucified and risen Lord was the portal through which
> true worshippers gained access to the heavenly temple (of which Is-
> rael's temples heretofore were only a copy); Christ's body, soon iden-
> tified with the Church itself, was also the ingress through which the
> heavenly temple would take shape in creation. God's breaking into
> earthly reality, which amounted to God's establishing the heavenly
> temple on earth, was signaled by the Spirit's presence. By virtue of

20. R. J. Bauckham, *The Theology of the Book of Revelation* (Cambridge: Cambridge
University Press, 2003), 140-41.

21. Joel B. Green, *The Gospel of Luke*, NICNT (Grand Rapids: Eerdmans, 1997), 131,
puts the point incisively: "Given the respect assigned earlier to the Jerusalem temple and
particularly to its sanctuary as the *axis mundi*—the meeting place between the heavenly
and the earthly, the divine and the human—this appearance of divine glory is remarkable.
God's glory, normally associated with the temple, is now manifest on a farm! At the birth
of his son, God has compromised (in a proleptic way) the socio-religious importance of the
temple as the culture center of the world of Israel."

22. W. D. Davies, *Gospel and the Land: Early Christianity and Jewish Territorial Doctrine* (Berkeley: University of California Press, 1974), 368.

23. Enns, *The Evolution of Adam*, 75, offers that we might also say that holy time has
been Christified, inasmuch as a new creation bursts forth under a new age.

their possession of the Spirit, believers deemed themselves to be the true temple of God, but only in an anticipatory sense.[24]

While Jesus is recognized as the true temple only as the risen, ascended Lord, it is with the descent of the Spirit at Pentecost that the church discovers *itself* as the temple (1 Cor. 3:16–17; Eph. 2:21; Rev. 3:12; cf. 1 Pet. 2:9).[25] And though the temple's center of gravity, as it were, remains in the "heavenly realm," where Christ is seated at the right hand of the Father, temple life irrupts on earth through the Spirit-possessed church.[26] As Beale writes, "This is why the book of Revelation usually portrays the 'temple' (*naos*) in heaven (11 of 15 times), though related to believers on earth (e.g. 1:13; 11:1–4) through their identification with the Spirit existentially (cf. Rev. 1:4 and 4:5 with 1:13; 2:2; 11:4) and with Christ (cf. 3:12 with 21:22) and their representative angels positionally (cf. 1:13 and 1:16; 2:1)."[27] As with Jesus, so with the church: "Sacred space is wherever Jesus is present with his followers."[28] It might be more accurate, however, to say that Jesus's followers exhibit "templeness" *only because the Spirit inhabits them.*[29]

Rather wondrously, finally, the faithful discover that their individual bodies are also a kind of temple. In a comment on 1 Corinthians 6:19–20, N. T. Wright remarks, "It is, for Paul, a matter of transferring the holy worship of Israel from the Jerusalem Temple to the bodies of individual members of the church, even in Corinth—especially in Corinth! Once more, the Spirit has taken the place of the Shekinah."[30] Where the glory of the Lord is, the dynamic presence of the Holy Spirit becomes concrete,[31] and because the promise remains certain, the whole earth shall

24. Perrin, *Jesus the Temple*, 49.

25. On the intertextual as well as the socioreligious tension that opens up between the Jerusalem temple and the new *naos* oriented around Jesus as it is played out in the book of Acts, see Perrin, *Jesus the Temple*, 64–65.

26. See G. K. Beale, "The Descent of the Eschatological Temple in the Form of the Spirit at Pentecost," *Tyndale Bulletin* 56 (2005): 73–102.

27. Beale, *The Temple and the Church's Mission*, 388–89.

28. J. K. Riches, *Conflicting Mythologies: Identity Formation in the Gospels of Mark and Matthew* (Edinburgh: T&T Clark, 2000), 293.

29. N. T. Wright, "Worship and the Spirit in the New Testament," in *The Spirit in Worship—Worship in the Spirit*, ed. Teresa Berger and Bryan D. Spinks (Collegeville, MN: Liturgical Press, 2009), 11.

30. Wright, "Worship and the Spirit in the New Testament," 13–14.

31. Beale, *The Temple and the Church's Mission*, 258.

be filled with the glory of God (Num. 14:21; Ps. 72:19; Isa. 6:3), the whole earth can thereby be regarded as a temple. The restoration of the cosmos begins, then, *in Christ*, in his resurrected humanity, and extends outward by the Spirit through the church to encompass, as St. John envisions it, a new heaven and a new earth. The presence and good order of God, symbolized in the language of temple, now extends, one could say, to infinity and beyond.

The Many Senses of "Temple"

Before proposing two lines of continuity that derive from our exposition of a temple theology as it relates to Calvin's thinking on materiality and worship, it might be helpful to take a brief account of the data. First, while the notion of temple continues throughout Scripture, it is identified in a wide variety of ways: with the garden, the minitemples of the patriarchal era (e.g., Bethel, Ai, Hebron, Moriah), the movable tabernacle of the Mosaic and juridical era, Solomon's temple, Ezekiel's temple, Herod's temple, and, in the New Testament, with Jesus, the church, human bodies, and the new cosmos.[32]

Second, and in light of the former, it is important that we distinguish clearly three categories of temple:

1. person as temple (Yahweh, Christ, church),
2. environment as temple (garden, Jerusalem, human bodies, new creation), and
3. cultic system as temple (the form, content, and activities of public worship).

When these categories are not clearly differentiated, problems of interpretation ensue. For example, when Beale argues that Jesus fulfills the "substantial essence" of the Jerusalem temple and that the new creation fulfills the "intended design" of Israel's temple,[33] two very different notions of temple are at work: temple as personal locus for God's presence and temple as cosmological witness to God's good order. The former points to a hypostatic reality (the tripersonal God), while the latter points

---

32. Cf. Moltmann, *The Spirit of Life*, 45–49.
33. Beale, "Eden, the Temple, and the Church's Mission in the New Creation," 28, 26.

to an environmental quality (the cosmos in a state of shalom). The means by which God accomplishes shalom include, for Israel, material symbols of worship, and it is over this point that disagreements in church history become pronounced.

Third, while in Beale's reading the Jerusalem temple performs hefty theological work, reordering Israel's relationship to the world by way of material-symbolic liturgical aids, his tentative remarks about New Testament worship seem to find these aids as perhaps accidental rather than integral to the church's formation.[34] While some contemporary theologians may regard the relationship of Israel's liturgy to the church's liturgy as "merely" analogous (whatever that means), others have perceived a stronger sense of continuity. Peter Leithart, for instance, contends that key biblical passages "demonstrate that Paul not merely employs the 'imagery' of the temple, but applies the whole theology of holy space and sacrilege to the new temple of the church. Paul's teaching here should be called a 'temple ecclesiology' rather than simply a literary employment of temple imagery."[35] What Leithart calls a temple ecclesiology, I prefer to call a temple theology in order to take account of the polysemic idea of temple in Scripture.[36]

Fourth, while the New Testament employs the category of temple in largely typological rather than literalistic manner, these various temples (Jesus, church, human bodies, new cosmos) remain thoroughly material instantiations.[37] Whatever contrasts are at play in the New Testament, the

34. Chapters 12 and 13 in Beale's *The Temple and the Church's Mission* are particularly disappointing on this account.

35. Peter J. Leithart, "Synagogue or Temple? Models for the Christian Worship," *Westminster Theological Journal* 63 (2002): 131, referring to 1 Cor. 3:16–17; Eph. 2:19–22; 1 Pet. 2:5; Heb. 4:12; 13:15; Matt. 26:28; 1 Cor. 10:18–22. So also Vernon H. Kooy, "The Apocalypse and Worship: Some Preliminary Observations," *Reformed Review* 30.3 (1977): 201. Leithart and Kooy would stand over against the judgment of Floyd V. Filson, "The Significance of the Temple in the Ancient Near East IV: Temple, Synagogue, and Church," *Biblical Archaeologist* 7 (1944): 77–88. See also Donald D. Binder, *Into the Temple Courts: The Place of the Synagogues in the Second Temple Period*, SBLDS 169 (Atlanta: Society of Biblical Literature, 1997); Paul F. Bradshaw and Lawrence A. Hoffman, eds., *The Making of Jewish and Christian Worship* (Notre Dame, IN: University of Notre Dame Press, 1991).

36. Similarly, Wright, "Worship and the Spirit in the New Testament," 6. While the argument of this chapter does not hinge on the need to establish any given liturgical form (low vs. high, "classic" vs. "free"), I suggest that a temple theology offers an especially cogent way to read the co-inherent relation of creation and worship.

37. Cf. John W. Cooper, *Body, Soul, and Life Everlasting: Biblical Anthropology and*

material shape of public worship is never regarded as problematic per se. And whatever "shadowy" may indicate for a new-covenantal liturgy, it signifies neither a theological nor an existential problem with materiality as such, nor necessarily a prescription for moderation. What the New Testament *does* find problematic for public worship is corrupt minds, false imaginations, idolatrous hearts, forgetful memories, and warped passions.[38]

The Way of "Shadowy" Worship?

How, then, ought we to think of "shadowy" worship? How do we regard the continuity and discontinuity that obtains between Israel's worship and the church's worship? For starters, where, with Israel, God is worshiped as Yahweh, the God of Abraham, Isaac, and Jacob, he is now worshiped as the God and Father of our Lord Jesus Christ, whom the Spirit makes real to the disciples—still the God of the patriarchs and prophets but now whose name is disclosed as triune.[39] Furthermore, the Jerusalem temple, as the one near-exclusive place where God meets his people, now becomes only one of many places across the face of the earth where God may be acceptably worshiped.

What was once singularly fixed now becomes ambulatory, as the church scatters to the four corners of the earth, dispersed to every tongue, tribe, and nation. Additionally, the particular activities of the temple, which rehearse the redemptive history of God to Israel, now become the particular activities of the church, oriented around Word and Table. Put differently, where the Jerusalem temple rendered Israel's salvation history, the church's liturgy now renders salvation history centered on the decisive revelation of Christ. And the temple, which served as the place of the people's encounter with the Shekinah of God, now becomes the

---

the Monism-Dualism Debate (Grand Rapids: Eerdmans, 2000), and Green, *Body, Soul, and Human Life.*

38. For detailed commentary on this issue, see, for example, David Peterson, *Engaging with God: A Biblical Theology of Worship* (Grand Rapids: Eerdmans, 1992); Edith M. Humphrey, *Grand Entrance: Worship on Earth as in Heaven* (Grand Rapids: Brazos, 2011), esp. "'That Your Prayers Not Be Hindered': Avoiding Pitfalls in Corporate Worship"; John Witvliet, "Calvin's Theology of Liturgical Sin," in *Worship Seeking Understanding*, 129–33.

39. Cf. Anthony C. Thiselton, *The Holy Spirit—in Biblical Teaching, through the Centuries, and Today* (Grand Rapids: Eerdmans, 2013), 122–29.

"temple of the Spirit," the people in whom the presence of God in Christ is made manifest.

With this reading of Scripture in mind, two lines of continuity can be proposed. With respect to the material symbols of worship, whether in an old- or a new-covenantal liturgy, I submit that creation is the necessary context of public worship and that the church's worship subsists in creation's ongoing worship. And I maintain that the aesthetic shape of public worship is ever and always caught up in the work of the Two Hands of God. I argue these lines of continuity over against Calvin, as well as with and beyond Calvin.

Contra Calvin: Continuity and Discontinuity

Over against Calvin, my argument is that the radical separation that he perceives between public worship and the material creation is unpersuasive, that the language of "weakness" to describe the material symbols of worship is not the preferred language of the New Testament, and that his habit of aligning material aids to worship with the language of slow, indolence, sloth, fickleness of human disposition, ignorance, frailty, lower, inferior, infirmity, and their capacity to keep humans bound to earth is largely foreign to the Gospels and the Epistles.[40] Calvin unnecessarily pits material over against spirit, mind, and heart (the alleged operations of the soul); to imply, as he does, that the operations of the body are less important to public worship than the operations of the soul is just as inapt as to say that the soul was less important to Israel's worship than the body.[41] The proper biblical contrast is not between mind and body but between, say, one object of contemplation (Yahweh) along with one set of liturgical activities (the Mosaic tabernacle), and another object of contemplation (the triune God) along with another set of activities (Word and Table).

Moreover, the primary theological language (as opposed to astronomical language) of the New Testament is of *heaven on earth*, not *heaven over against earth*, just as the language of ascent describes an existential movement from self to God, not a spatial movement away

---

40. Cf. Larry D. Harwood, *Denuded Devotion to Christ: The Ascetic Piety of Protestant True Religion in the Reformation* (Eugene, OR: Pickwick Publications, 2012), 73–74.

41. Thanks to Michael Farley for raising this point in personal correspondence.

from earth to heaven. With respect to the epistle to the Hebrews, which figures largely in Calvin's thinking on "shadowy" worship, an ethical-eschatological dualism governs the epistle's treatment of heaven and earth, not a metaphysical one.[42] And the promised inheritance of the saints is not "heaven," as in popular Christian imagination, but a renewed creation under the perfect rule of Christ: *on earth as in heaven*.[43] Put in liturgical terms, as the Swiss Reformed theologian Jean-Jacques von Allmen once remarked, there is no place on earth "which cannot be a witness of the presence of Christ and a prelude to the restoration of the Cosmos."[44]

Finally, Calvin confuses a temporary provision of material symbols during the present age with a concession to an unfortunate necessity in humans. The fact that few material symbols are explicitly commanded in the New Testament does not need to imply a pessimistic judgment on their material aspect, nor does the fact that the New Jerusalem is marked by the absence of certain material symbols entail a negative regard on their present use. This situation indicates only that certain symbols of worship will be appropriate to a given era of the church. If Calvin's first error is to separate what the Scriptures hold together, namely a positive regard for material symbols of worship in both new- and old-covenantal worship, his second error is one of omission, whereby he fails to identify the christological and pneumatological connections between creation at large and creation in the context of public worship.

---

42. David Moffitt, in *Atonement and the Logic of Resurrection in the Epistle to the Hebrews* (Leiden: Brill, 2011), 301, argues that the "dualism of Hebrews is not a dualism of flesh-and-blood body vs. spirit. Rather, it is the kind of dualism that blood sacrifice, at least as depicted in the Pentateuch, appears designed to address—a dualism that assumes the incommensurability of the sinful and impure human being (both at the level of the spirit and of mortal flesh) and the holy, pure realm of God's glorious presence. The latter realm is ultimately the highest heaven; the former is the earth." More critically to our thesis, "The 'coming world' of Heb 2:5 and the 'coming age' of 6:5 refer to the same eschatological reality—a new time *and* space" (81n83, emphasis original).

43. Cf. Wright, "Worship and the Spirit in the New Testament," 21.

44. Jean-Jacques von Allmen, "A Short Theology of the Place of Worship," *Studia Liturgica* 3.3 (1964): 156. Frank Senn adds, "This is precisely the eschatological dimension of the Christian liturgy that its celebrants exercise the priestly vocation of the redeemed world and thereby enact life in the new creation" (*New Creation: A Liturgical World View* [Minneapolis: Fortress, 2000], 62).

With and beyond Calvin: The Movement of Creation's Praise

The Church's Praise Correlative to Creation's Praise

With and beyond Calvin, I contend, first, that the church's praises subsist in creation's praise. This is the first movement in which the church is caught up. The work that Calvin perceives creation performing—as a mirror, chock-full of the insignia of God, capable of refreshing the faithful and inviting them to revel in the abundance of God's workmanship, as well as an occasion for cataphatic feasting and a stimulus to human praise in concord with the ongoing praise of irrational creatures—is the work that creation continues to perform in the life of the church *inasmuch as creation is the proper context for any creaturely praise*. Worship occurs in and through creation because it is God's continual pleasure to call forth praise in all his works, at all times and in all places. Calvin seems to believe as much when he comments on Genesis 1:11, "God acts through the creatures, not as if he needed external help, but because it was his pleasure."[45] It is God's pleasure, that is, as Calvin himself argues, to be found "in the clouds," not "above the clouds," in "the very beautiful fabric of the world," not "in his secret essence."[46] God does so "for our sake": not as an unfortunate requirement but as a way to honor human creatureliness.[47]

If it is true, as Calvin maintains, that human beings "cannot open their eyes without being compelled to see" God in creation, then this reality must also, in some sense, be true of the faithful who gather in spaces built out of the material of creation.[48] If it is right to say that both the sophisticated and the "untutored" are able to detect sparks of God's glory

45. *Comm.* Gen. 1:11.
46. 1.5.9. Cf. *Comm.* Gen. 3:8. Not only does creation function as a "living image"; for Calvin, so do the human creature, the Holy Scripture, and, supremely so, Christ Jesus. For this reason, we need no other images, certainly none made by human hands or of human imagination, certainly none that have not been ordained by God, all of which Calvin calls "false images." In a similar vein, Calvin explains the phrase "I am the bread of life" in *Comm.* John 6:48–51 as follows: "And thus [God] provides for our weakness, for He does not call us above the clouds to enjoy life, but exhibits it on earth just as if He were exalting us to the mysteries of His Kingdom."
47. *Comm.* Ps. 104:1.
48. *Comm.* Rom. 1:19; 1.5.1, 14–15; *Comm.* 1 Cor. 10:1, "Throughout the Scriptures the cloud is called the sign of his presence." Cf. Lukas Vischer, "Reich, bevor wir geboren wurden: Zu Calvins Verständnis der Schöpfung," *Evangelische Theologie* 69 (2009): 142–60.

in creation,[49] then it is theologically implausible to argue that the stone, metal, glass, wood, and light that compose a space of worship do not also participate in the sparkling evocation of God's glory—even to ravish the faithful. In his comment on Hosea 6:6-7, Calvin writes, "Some ornaments consistent with divine worship are not useless in church if they incline the faithful to practice holy things with humility, devotion and worship."[50] While we readily concur with Calvin, must it be said only in restrained terms? Might it also be said in capacious terms? Might the material and aesthetic ornaments of public worship induce the faithful to rapturous delight because they find themselves, here too, in the "beauteous theater" of creation?[51]

The Praise of Rational and Irrational Creatures

A second sense in which the church's praise subsists in creation's praise is *by bringing side by side, in noncompetitive fashion, the praise of "rational" and "irrational" creation.*[52] Calvin notes in his comment on Isaiah 1:3 that "irrational creatures" give instruction to human beings.[53] Under the tuition of creation, all people without distinction receive profit "at the mouth of the same teacher."[54] Even if creatures of earth and heaven do not possess a human tongue, they nonetheless act as "eloquent heralds of the glory of God." Both old and new covenants bear witness to this fact, no less poignantly than in Job 38:7, which tells of a time "when the morning stars sang together, and all the sons of God shouted for joy" (ESV). Job 12:7-8 adds, "But now ask the beasts, and let them teach you; and the birds of the heavens, and let them tell you. Or speak to the earth, and let it teach you; and let the fish of the sea declare to you" (NASB).

---

49. 1.5.2.

50. *Comm.* Hosea 6:6-7. Cf. *Comm.* Ps. 9:11 and *Comm.* Jer. 7:21.

51. Cf. *Comm.* Ps. 104:31.

52. "All creatures bring glory to God simply by being themselves and fulfilling their God-given roles in God's creation. . . . Here all creatures, including ourselves, are simply fellow-creatures expressing the theocentricity of the created world, each in our own created way, differently but in complementarity. In the worship of God there can be no hierarchy among the creatures" (Richard Bauckham, "Joining Creation's Praise of God," *Ecotheology* 7 [2002]: 47-49).

53. *Comm.* Isa. 1:3.

54. *Comm.* Ps. 19:3.

Jesus says much the same, when, in his exchange with the Pharisees in Luke 19:40, he refers to the admonitory role of creation: "I tell you, if these become silent, the stones will cry out!" (NASB). Much better, of course, one might suppose, is the willing acclamation of both human and nonhuman creation.

While we concede that the biblical authors here describe nonhuman creation in anthropomorphic terms, there is still a sense, in Scripture and in Calvin, that creation intelligibly communicates *in its own way* to God and to the human creature. If the church's praise can be said to be ontologically inseparable from creation's praise, then the praise of the faithful will be complemented and enriched by what we might call the suprarational language of creation. The purpose of the kinesthetic shape of worship, on this thinking, will not be to "get out of the way" but rather to serve the multiple purposes of the liturgy in its own sensory, metaphoric, and symbolic ways.[55] The work that artists perform will be to offer "articulate" voice to creation's praise, while never seeking to replace creation's own praise.[56] And the work of the church will be to welcome the familiar and strange voice of creation, whose purpose is to train the faithful to taste and see that the Lord is good, but without any sense that they will have comprehensively tasted the mystery of the triune life, neither presently nor in the age to come.

With and beyond Calvin: The Movement of the Two Hands of God

Along with my first contention that the church's praise is caught up in the movement of creation's praise, my second contention is that the church's praise is caught up in the movement of the Two Hands of God. The kinesthetic condition of worship is to be thought of as a christologically oriented and pneumatologically ordered space, caught up in the work of Christ and the Spirit to command, sustain, judge, redeem, empower, complete, and present creation's praise as a gift to the Father. Because the place of public worship involves the worship of creatures, it will always be

---

55. More on this point in chap. 6.

56. Cf. Jeremy S. Begbie, "Christ, Creation, and Creativity," in *Voicing Creation's Praise: Towards a Theology of the Arts* (Edinburgh: T&T Clark, 1991), 169–85; also Begbie, "Faithful Feelings: Music and Emotion in Worship," in *Resonant Witness: Conversations between Music and Theology*, ed. Jeremy S. Begbie and Steven R. Guthrie (Grand Rapids: Eerdmans, 2011), 323–54.

a Christ-centered, Spirit-enabled place fit for creatures. Eight assertions are to be drawn from this.

Creation "in Christ"

First, we can know what the material creation is about only "in Christ." No generic affirmation will suffice. In Christ, the firstborn of creation, we learn where creation is headed: "the complete restoration of a sound and well-constituted nature."[57] In Christ, the beloved Son of the Father, we learn what creation is for: for fellowship with the triune God. And it is only because of the Holy Spirit that we have epistemological and ontological access to this work of Christ. Calvin writes, "For Christ is that image in which God presents to our view, not only his heart, but also his hands and his feet. I give the name of his *heart* to that secret love with which he embraces us in Christ: by his *hands* and *feet* I understand those works of his which are displayed before our eyes."[58] The biblical cosmology bears witness to the fact that, in Christ, the earth and heaven are discovered as "good and beloved by God; that this life is the theater of sin and grace, death and life; that history matters and moves in a direction; that the structures of things, including the stars, had a beginning and may have an end; and that all creatures—animate and inanimate—stand before God."[59] Because Christ stands at the center of the cosmic order, the created realm can be properly regarded as the beloved world of God.[60]

This is something that Calvin could eagerly affirm. From the beginning of creation, he argued, Christ "already truly was mediator, for he always was the head of the Church, had primacy over the angels, and was the firstborn of every creature."[61] As the firstborn of creation, it is in him

---

57. *Comm.* Gen. 3:14. *Comm.* John 16:11, "But when Christ despoils [Satan] of his tyranny the world is restored and a well-tempered order appears."

58. *Comm.* Gen., "The Argument."

59. Gordon Lathrop, *Holy Ground: A Liturgical Cosmology* (Minneapolis: Fortress, 2004), 45.

60. Karl Barth, *Church Dogmatics*, III/1, trans. J. W. Edwards, O. Bussey, and Harold Knight (Edinburgh: T&T Clark, 1958), 346: "It is our duty . . . to love and praise the created order," Barth exclaims, "because, as is made manifest in Jesus Christ, it is so mysteriously well-pleasing to God." Or as St. Thomas Aquinas beautifully says it: "In [God's] hand were all the ends of the world. . . . When his hand was opened by the key of love, the creatures came forth" (cited in Robert W. Jenson, *Systematic Theology*, vol. 2: *The Works of God* [Oxford: Oxford University Press, 1999], 14).

61. In Joseph Tylenda, "Christ the Mediator: Calvin versus Stancaro," *Calvin Theo-*

that all creatures are created, so that Christ might be "the substance or foundation of all things."[62] And again, "What comparison is there between creature and the Creator, without the interposition of a Mediator?"[63] Because Christ is the mediator of "the whole world,"[64] the author of creatures both visible and invisible,[65] "the lawful heir of heaven and earth, by whom the faithful recover what they had lost in Adam,"[66] and the one who cares and keeps "all of creation in its proper state,"[67] creation discovers itself in motion: from the Father who has caught up the cosmos in the beloved life of his Son by the power of his Spirit.[68] However else we think of the kinesthetic shape of public worship, in short, it is *in Christ*.

The Praise of the Firstborn of Creation

Second, in public worship, we join the praise of the Firstborn of all creation, who, by virtue of his Spirit-enabled resurrection and ascent to the right hand of the Father, is able to announce and enact the praise of the age to come. In public worship we join the praise of the chief Leitourgos, as Calvin says. Commenting on Hebrews 12:2, Calvin writes, "It is a truth, which may serve as a most powerful stimulant, and may lead us most fervently to praise God, when we hear that Christ leads our songs, and is the chief composer of our hymns."[69] Creation's praise therefore *means* something in Christ. As the incarnate temple of God, Christ grounds, orients, and gathers up all of creation's praise in a gift of love to the Father. Christ's praise, transposed in the church's praise and in this light, becomes an actual and symbolic prelude to the restoration of creation's perfect praise. The church functions therefore as a *partner* of Christ's praise and a *poet*

---

logical Journal 8 (1973): 12. This is a translation of Calvin's *Responsum ad fratres Polonos, quomodo mediator sit Christus, ad refutandum Stancaro errorem* (1560); *CO* 9:333–42. Cf. Canlis, *Calvin's Ladder*, 55–57; 2.6.4.

62. *Comm.* Col. 1:15.

63. *Comm.* Eph. 1:10.

64. *Comm.* Col. 1:17.

65. *Comm.* Col. 1:16, 18.

66. *Comm.* Ps. 8:6.

67. *Comm.* Heb. 1:3. Christ is the one "who upholds the whole world by His will alone."

68. On the question of Calvin's views of immediate and mediate creation, see John Murray, "Calvin's Doctrine of Creation," *Westminster Theological Journal* 17 (1954): 21–43.

69. *Comm.* Heb. 12:2.

to creation's praise: on the one hand, joining Christ's praise for all of the Father's marvelous works, as well as offering praise *of* and *through* Christ, while, on the other, joining the praise of the cosmos but also translating that praise through the language of its liturgical life, whether enacted in its cultic activities or solidified in its material forms.

The Spirit-Empowered Creation

Third, by the power of the Holy Spirit the material creation obtains its life and order. "For it is the Spirit," Calvin writes, "who, everywhere diffused, sustains all things, causes them to grow, and quickens them in heaven and in earth."[70] The Spirit's work to animate creation is what Calvin called the Spirit's "universal grace"[71] or "universal action."[72] The Spirit is the one who gives and the one who takes life.[73] The prerogative of creaturely life, then, whether earthly or heavenly, belongs properly to the "secret efficacy of the Spirit."[74] It is also the Spirit who maintains creation's order. "Unless the Spirit of the Lord upholds everything," Calvin comments, "it all lapses back into nothingness" or chaos.[75] It is the "secret inspiration," "hidden support," "hidden instinct," and "secret virtue" that constitute the Spirit's work to counter the "subversion of all equity and well-constituted order," which Adam's rebellion incurred for creation.[76] But if the Spirit is responsible for creation's order, as Calvin rightly contends, it is important not to think of this order like that of a military or factory assembly line. It is instead a creative order, capable of surprising and enthralling.[77] It is an irrepressibly dynamic order, yielding new configurations of life and prompting praise to a God whose goodness is revealed through such beautiful fecundity.[78]

---

70. 1.13.14.
71. *Comm.* Isa. 44:3.
72. *Comm.* Rom. 8:14.
73. *Comm.* Isa. 40:7.
74. Cf. *Comm.* Gen. 1:2; see also 3.1.2; 2.2.13.
75. *Comm.* Isa. 40:7; cf. 1.13.14. See also his comments on Nah. 1:5 and Deut. 5:9–14.
76. Cf. *Comm.* Gen. 2:2; 3:1; *Comm.* Rom. 8:20; *Comm.* Ezek. 10:8; *Comm.* Isa. 40:22; *Comm.* Ps. 104:29. See also Schreiner, *The Theater of His Glory*, 22, 30, 34.
77. Cf. Thiselton, *The Holy Spirit*, 8.
78. For Calvin, the beauty of the world owes its strength and preservation to the power of the Spirit (1.13.14). He adds in *Comm.* Gen. 1:14, "Let us admire this wonderful Ar-

The Spirit-Empowered Creature

Fourth, it is the Spirit's office to enable the human creature to take "pious pleasure" in creation, as well as to make something of it. Three basic conditions, according to Calvin, are essential for the creature to enjoy creation rightly: humility, the lens of Scripture, and faith.[79] The Spirit is responsible for all three. The Spirit governs not only our pleasure in creation in general but also our pleasure in the gifts of science and art in particular. As Calvin remarks on Genesis 4:22:

> Now, although the invention of the harp, and of similar instruments of music, may minister to our pleasure, rather than to our necessity, still it is not to be thought altogether superfluous; much less does it deserve, in itself, to be condemned. Pleasure is indeed to be condemned, unless it be combined with the fear of God, and with the common benefit of human society. But such is the nature of music, that it can be adapted to the offices of religion, and made profitable to men; if only it be free from vicious attractions, and from that foolish delight, by which it seduces men from better employments, and occupies them in vanity. . . . Finally, Moses, in my opinion, intends to teach that that race flourished in various and pre-eminent endowments, which would both render it inexcusable, and would prove most evident testimonies of the divine goodness.[80]

Calvin believes that God "has destined all the riches, both of heaven and earth," for the use of the human creature.[81] But our pleasure in this abundance, he cautions, must be governed by the virtue of temperance. "As God bountifully provides for us, so he has appointed a law of temperance, that each may voluntarily restrain himself in his abundance."[82] It is the Spirit, Calvin explains, who daily corrects "the inordinate desires of the flesh" so that the faithful might ordinately enjoy the manifold gifts

---

tificer, who has so beautifully arranged all things above and beneath, that they may respond to each other in most harmonious concert."

79. As Calvin maintains in his "Argument" of Genesis: if profit is to be had in the meditation of God's works of creation, people must bring with them "a sober, docile, mild, and humble spirit." See also *Comm.* John 14:19; 20:23; 3.1.4; 4.14.8.

80. *Comm.* Gen. 4:22.

81. *Comm.* Ps. 8:6.

82. *Comm.* Ps. 104:15.

of God.[83] And it is with just such a confidence in the effective work of Christ's Spirit, we might argue, that the faithful become freed both *from* undue anxiety over creation's "excesses" and *for* righteous pleasure in this theater of abundance.[84] Because the Spirit, then, is poured out upon creation, upon Christ, and upon the faithful, creation can become a sphere of delight and work, of rest and celebration.

The Spirit as the Go-Between

Fifth, the Spirit is the Go-Between, who, through the Son, takes the gifts of the Father and offers them to creation, while at the same time taking the gifts of creation and, through the Son, offering them back to Father.[85] Calvin says simply: "What was his own he makes to be ours."[86] He adds, in book 3 of the *Institutes*, that without the Spirit "no one can taste either the fatherly favor of God or the beneficence of Christ."[87] Indeed, every action of the Holy Spirit "ends up to our blessedness."[88] Or more boldly: "Nothing but good comes from the Holy Spirit."[89] This good, for creation, is not only to be made a partaker of the life of God in Christ; it is also to be given a "space to be itself," to borrow Karl Barth's language.[90] Calvin remarks that God "fills, moves, and quickens

---

83. *Comm.* Rom. 8:2ff.

84. Calvin takes a christological turn in his argument on *Comm.* 1 Tim. 4:5: "Commonsense does indeed hold that the riches of the earth are naturally intended for our use, but, since our dominion over the world was taken from us in Adam, every gift of God that we touch is defiled by our stains and it on its side is unclean to us, till God graciously helps us and, by incorporating us into the Body of His Son, makes us anew lords of the earth, so that we may legitimately enjoy as our own all the wealth He supplies."

85. The language of go-between is taken from John V. Taylor, *The Go-Between God: The Holy Spirit and the Christian Mission* (Philadelphia: Fortress, 1973). Thiselton, *The Holy Spirit*, 21, 402, chap. 24, calls the Spirit "the Beyond Who Is Within." Cf. Vladimir N. Lossky, *The Mystical Theology of the Eastern Church* (New York: St. Vladimir's Seminary Press, 1988), 100–101; Moltmann, *The Spirit of Life*, 3–5.

86. *Comm.* Ps. 104:29.

87. 3.1.2.

88. *Comm.* Rom. 8:26.

89. *Comm.* Gal. 5:22. Calvin expresses a similar thought in 1.13.14, where he contends that "all good gifts proceed" from the Spirit alone.

90. Barth develops the idea in *Church Dogmatics*, III/3, trans. G. W. Bromiley and R. J. Ehrlich (Edinburgh: T&T Clark, 1960), §49. Noteworthy is his observation that, against all degenerative movement toward homogeneity, the work of God "has nothing

all things by the power of the same Spirit, and does so according to the character that he bestowed upon each kind by the law of creation."[91] And again, God "by the power of his Word and Spirit created heaven and earth" and "distinguished an innumerable variety of things [and has] endowed each kind with its own nature, assigned functions, appointed places and stations."[92]

What particular qualities or "goods" does creation uniquely exhibit? We recall here the work that Calvin believes the created realm is about: epiphanic, by revealing the invisible God through sensory media; pedagogical, by schooling the church in the "school of the beasts"; aesthetic, by awakening desire in the human creature through the beautiful forms and functions of the cosmos; admonitory, by rebuking humanity of its ingratitude and pride in light of such divine munificence; and doxological, by enacting and summoning the faithful to the praise of God. If creation is able to perform this work at all, it is only because the Holy Spirit enables it to. Or to press the matter toward theological precision, it is not so much that creation in itself possesses an inherent capacity to perform these functions, whether to represent God or to nourish and form the human creature. Rather, as Daniel Hardy rightly argues, "God makes the material capable of representing God."[93] It is *God the Spirit* who makes this function possible. And if Calvin, in his comment on Genesis 1:16, is right to say that, in Genesis, the Spirit "opens a common school for all," where the faithful are able to discover this manifold activity of creation, then it is plausible that the faithful will also discover this kind of activity in the aesthetic condition of public worship.

The Particularity of a Place of Worship

Sixth, the material condition of public worship bears witness to creation's particularity.[94] In the care and delight of our places of worship, we join God

---

whatever to do with a leveling down and flattening out of individuals and individual groupings. . . . To each of them He gives its own glory, its lasting worth, its definite value" (168).

91. 2.2.16; this is said with particular reference to Bezalel and Oholiab.

92. 1.14.20.

93. Daniel W. Hardy, "Calvinism and the Visual Arts: A Theological Introduction," in *Seeing beyond the Word*, ed. Finney, 5.

94. The language of creation's particularity features prominently in Colin Gunton, *The One, the Three, and the Many: God, Creation, and the Culture of Modernity* (Cambridge:

in his own affirmation of creation's "endlessly remarkable quiddity." We take pleasure, as Richard Bauckham offers, in the "strangeness, intricacy and difference" that God has entrusted to his creatures.[95] One of the purposes of the liturgical arts in this view would be to accent the particularity of our respective places of worship. It is not that art and architecture take creation's "own praise onto some higher plane," as Bauckham rightly insists; rather, they give creation's praise "a place within our own praise in addition to its entirely adequate place apart from us."[96] Our places of worship might thereby bear witness to the goodness of this space, this geography, this culture, along with the privileges and responsibilities that God has entrusted to this people, whom he has "implaced" here and now.[97] Our places of worship might also bear witness to a culturally contextual aesthetic excellence (to that which is well-crafted and beautifully formed), where this people, like the Israelites in anticipation of the construction of the tabernacle, take advantage of an opportunity to bring forward their particular artistic gifts—whether ornate or simple, extravagant or humble—on behalf of this particular place of God's meeting with his people. It is not too much of a stretch to believe that Calvin might agree with this line of thought.[98]

The Place of Worship as a Symbol of Salvation History

Seventh, going beyond anything Calvin ever imagined, the place of worship may serve to symbolize salvation history. While creation bears witness to its own distinctive characteristics, creation will take on a second, especially crucial task within a liturgical context, which is to bear witness to the salvific work of God. In this way, creation makes salvation history dynamically sensible. The place of public worship will be seen, then, not

Cambridge University Press, 1993). Amos Yong, in "Ruach, the Primordial Chaos, and the Breath of Life: Emergence Theory and the Creation Narratives in Pneumatological Perspective," in *The Work of the Spirit: Pneumatology and Pentecostalism*, ed. M. Welker (Grand Rapids: Eerdmans, 2006), appeals to "the dynamic, particularizing, relational, and life-giving presence and activity of the Spirit of God" (198–99) to ground his assertion.

95. Bauckham, "Joining Creation's Praise of God," 52. On this question, see also Gunton, *The Triune Creator*, 197–98.

96. Bauckham, "Joining Creation's Praise of God," 53.

97. On this point, see Edward S. Casey, *Getting Back into Place: Toward a Renewed Understanding of the Place-World*, Studies in Continental Thought (Bloomington: Indiana University Press, 2009).

98. E.g., see *Comm.* Ps. 24:7.

as a static place, a neutral placeholder for the operation of verbal and intellectual activities, but rather as a symbolically charged place *headed* somewhere—namely, toward the fulfillment of the new creation. Nor will this place simply "be" (as if that were even possible). It will be *for* something: for the Spirit's work of sanctification, shaping the way in which the faithful perceive their identity and vocation, their comings and goings, their resting and working, their kneeling and standing, their sense of God's presence with *them* in the descent of Christ by the Spirit and of their presence with *God* in their ascent with Christ through his Spirit. The place of worship will also be a contextualized place of memory and anticipation, where a settled community bears witness to their unsettled status as citizens of God's kingdom, awaiting and even enacting the final consummation of God's good future for all creation.[99]

The Place of Worship as Cataphatic Witness

This is perhaps another way of saying that, eighth, the place of worship witnesses not apophatically to the essential nature of God but rather cataphatically to the economy of God.[100] The purpose of a place of worship is fundamentally to capture not an invisible reality but a visible one, namely, the history of the work of God in Christ by his Spirit. The aim is not to get beyond the story of God's salvific work in history in order to penetrate the "holy otherness" of the Godhead. Put otherwise, in Scripture, the invisibility of God is never a problem as such that must be protected, nor is it the distinctive trait which Israel was to stress in its construction of tabernacle and temple. The chief issue is that God cannot not be manipulated

99. Hélène Guicharnaud, "An Introduction to the Architecture of Protestant Temples Constructed in France before the Revocation of the Edict of Nantes," in *Seeing beyond the Word*, ed. Finney, 134n1, notes the curious habit of French Protestants in the sixteenth and seventeenth centuries labeling their houses of worship as "temples." She writes, "The designation was an unambiguous way for Calvinists to distinguish their buildings from those of Catholic rivals." See also Matthew Koch, "Calvinism and the Visual Arts in Southern France, 1561 to 1685," in *Seeing beyond the Word*, ed. Finney, 180–81.

100. Calvin's remark in *Comm.* 2 Cor. 3:18 is especially noteworthy: "Our present knowledge of God is indeed obscure and feeble in comparison with the glorious vision we shall have at Christ's last appearing. At the same time [God] does offer Himself to us now, to be seen and openly beheld to the extent *that our salvation requires and our capacity allows.* Thus the apostle speaks of progress which will be perfection only when Christ appears" (emphasis added).

by human beings; he cannot be contained under creaturely lock and key. An aesthetically minimalist place of worship, which begrudges materiality or seeks to "neutralize" it, as a way to accent the apparently preferable "invisible" world over against the so-called visible world, is no more faithful to the revelation of God than an aesthetically maximalist place that invites its people to escape the material world into an allegedly more exciting immaterial world. A place of worship is faithful instead when it enables the church to learn how to live as both settlers and strangers in the world, while it awaits a home that is yet to come, and to "read" the meaning of the world in light of the redemptive and re-creative activity of the triune God, played out in the drama of the liturgy.

Conclusion

As Calvin sees it, God descends through the material symbols of worship so that the human creature might in turn ascend to him, yet there is scant evidence in Calvin's reasoning that the material creation might participate in that ascent. Nor is there a sense in which the ascent to heaven orients the church's worship on earth, our creaturely domain. Creation's fundamental dynamism is transferred to the domain of heaven, upward and away from earth, while the center of liturgical gravity is relocated from the whole of humanity to the internal regions of the soul. While exceptions exists, it is generally true that the material symbols of worship are perceived, at best, as an unfortunate necessity and, at worst, as inert powers whose chief function is to activate the faculties of the invisible soul.

While Calvin's original instincts about creation are the right ones, I believe he fails to carry them far enough. And while I leave the implications of our findings for the liturgical arts to the conclusion of the book, I raise here the question of the relation between the material creation and the human body as it concerns corporate worship. In what sense does the human body, as a material thing, participate in the purposes of the material creation? In what sense does the body perform a distinctive work in public worship? And how might Calvin's idea of "spiritual" worship both open up and close down possibilities for the human body in the *leitourgia*?

CHAPTER 6

Calvin's Theology of the Physical Body

The flesh [caro] is the very hinge [cardo] on which salvation turns.

Tertullian, *On the Resurrection of the Flesh*

Since God created our bodies as well as our souls, and nourishes and maintains them, this is good enough reason why he should be served and honored with our bodies. And furthermore, we know that the Lord honors us by calling not only our souls his temples, but also our bodies.

Calvin, *Against the Nicodemites*

Having explored Calvin's understanding of "shadowy" worship, I here turn to his treatment of "spiritual" worship. As I noted in chapter 1, for Calvin to reintroduce musical instruments into a new-covenantal liturgy encourages the faithful to cling to "earthly" things and to be drawn down by the gravity of a weak and infirm physical body rather than to be drawn up into the "spiritual" worship of God in heaven.[1] Together, these emphases set the agenda for the sort of public worship that the church should enact. I also raised the question whether a complex of meanings might be discovered in Scripture and in Calvin himself that could open up a more integral role for the physical body in worship.

---

1. Cf. *Comm.* Heb. 12:8; 1.13.1.

Calvin scholars will be the first to acknowledge that the frail condition of physical life provoked in Calvin a tendency to lurid rhetoric.[2] Calvin describes human bodies as "dust and a shadow,"[3] "dung,"[4] a "reformatory" (*ergastulum*),[5] a "putrid carcass" (*charongue*), a frail lodging (*loge caduque*), a house of mud (*maison de fange*), and a poor hut (*tabernaculum*).[6] The faithful, Calvin lamented, were condemned to live in "this unstable, defective, corruptible, fleeting, wasting, rotting tabernacle of our body," waiting (often miserably) for the redemption of the human body as we know it.[7] The "sparks of glory" notwithstanding,[8] the human body was all too often experienced, Calvin felt, as a "prison" (*carcer*)[9] and an "abyss of infection."[10]

With such a view of the human body, it is not surprising that Calvin failed to imagine a prominent role for corporeality in public worship. In a manner similar to the material symbols of worship, the embodied condition of the faithful presented an acute temptation to confuse the object of worship with the material forms themselves, so that the restricting of the "organs of the body" rather than the reordering of the body became the dominant priority in his prescriptions for "spiritual" worship.[11] Yet, tempting as it is to label Calvin as hopelessly pessimistic toward the body, this judgment would fail to reckon with a more complex story.

The Human Body Ktisiologically Considered

In commenting on Genesis 1:26, Calvin writes, "If you rightly weigh all circumstances, man is, among other creatures, a certain pre-eminent specimen of Divine wisdom, justice, and goodness, so that he is deservedly called by the ancients *microcosmos*, 'a world in miniature.'" Upon this

restrictive vs. reordered [margin annotation]

---

2. On this point, see esp. Charles L. Cooke, "Calvin's Illnesses and Their Relation to Christian Vocation," in *Calvin Studies IV*, ed. John H. Leith and W. Stacy Johnson (Davidson, NC: Colloquium on Calvin Studies, 1988), 41–52. Cf. 1.17.10.

3. *Comm.* 1 John 3:2.

4. *CO* 49:333.

5. 1.15.2.

6. Cited in Engel, *John Calvin's Perspectival Anthropology*, 169.

7. 3.9.5.

8. 3.20.31.

9. 3.9.4.

10. *Sermons on Job* 34; *CO* 35:202.

11. Cf. Canlis, *Calvin's Ladder*, 169.

human creature, the "exquisite workshop" of divine labor, "God looks upon himself, so to speak, and beholds himself in man as in a mirror."[12] While God beholds himself chiefly in the human soul, it is not improper to say that the human body bears certain "sparks" of God's glory.[13] Calvin reasons that the human body is "an image of God," as it were, perhaps no less so than the cosmos itself.[14]

The Glory of the Human Body

Calvin eloquently details the glory of the human body in his exposition of Psalm 139:15:

> When we examine [the body], even to the nails on our fingers, there is nothing which could be altered, without felt inconveniency, as at something disjointed or put out of place; and what, then, if we should make the individual parts the subject of enumeration? Where is the embroiderer who—with all his industry and ingenuity—could execute the hundredth part of this complicate and diversified structure? We need not then wonder if God, who formed man so perfectly in the womb, should have an exact knowledge of him after he is ushered into the world.

What is to be admired is not simply the detail with which God constructs the human body—from the "tip" of our fingers to the "human skin"—but that God gives "shape and beauty to a confused mass."[15] In the very structure of the body, "one must have the greatest keenness in order to weigh, with Galen's skill, its articulation, symmetry, beauty, and use. But yet, as all acknowledge, the human body shows itself to be a composition so ingenious that its Artificer is rightly judged a wonder-worker."[16] Like the universe itself, then, all the body's parts are rightly ordered: nothing is missing, nothing is out of place, neither in itself nor in relation to the soul.[17] The body at the original creation is a purposeful, beautiful work of God, dynamically related to its Maker.

12. *Sermons on Job* 10:7.
13. 1.15.3.
14. 2.12.7; 1.15.3. See also Engel, *John Calvin's Perspectival Anthropology*, 45.
15. CR 61:481–88; *Sermons on Job* 10:7–15.
16. 1.5.2.
17. 1.15.3.

Through this body, "fresh and lively,"[18] Calvin states that the human creature is to employ itself in pleasant, fulfilling, and fruitful work "and not to lie down in inactivity and idleness."[19] To each man or woman God has entrusted goods—indeed, the very "riches of heaven and earth"[20]—which he or she is to steward well, leaving to subsequent generations the fruits of their labors in better condition than they had found them. While God has endowed humanity with physical abundance, this provision gives no license to abuse or to hoard it. Calvin comments: "In lavishing upon us a more abundant supply of good things than our necessities require, [God] puts our moderation to the test. The proper rule with respect to the use of bodily sustenance, is to partake of it that it may sustain, but not oppress us," to enjoy but not to be mastered by "the multiplied bounties of God," to use them with gratitude and not in greed, and to engage in artistic and scientific ventures for the common good.[21]

The Body and the Soul

While the body bears its own peculiar glory, it is nothing without the soul. "Add the soul to the body," Calvin writes, "and you have a living man endowed with understanding and perception and fitted for all the activities of life, but remove the soul from the body and there will remain a useless corpse devoid of all perception."[22] As an immortal yet created essence, the soul is humanity's "nobler" or "principal" part.[23] It is that gift in which "the divine especially shines."[24] More strongly even, "Our souls are more precious to [God] than our bodies."[25] Calvin further explains, "For although God's glory shines forth in the outer man, yet there is no doubt that the proper seat of his image is in the soul."[26] The *imago*, in this sense, is primarily an internal and spiritual reality.

Inasmuch as it is an *internal*, or nonmaterial, reality, Calvin sees

[handwritten margin note: Calvin sees image being primarily of the soul.]

18. *Comm.* Gen. 2:9.
19. *Comm.* Gen. 2:15.
20. *Comm.* Ps. 8:6.
21. *Comm.* Ps. 104:15.
22. *Comm.* 1 Cor. 3:17.
23. 1.15.2.
24. 3.25.6.
25. *Sermons on Job* 37; *CO* 35:320.
26. 1.15.3.

here the distinctive quality of humans over against the rest of creation.[27] The soul is immortal, the body is mortal; the soul experiences fear of divine judgment, while the body does not; and the soul is able to search out heaven and earth, past and future, things hidden to sensory perception, which "clearly shows that there lies hidden in man something separate from the body."[28] The nonmaterial nature of the *imago* is something that humans share with the angels.[29] Inasmuch as the soul is "set in the body," dwelling there "as in a house," it animates the whole body, rendering its organs "fit and useful for their actions," while also holding "the first place in ruling man's life, not alone with respect to the duties of his earthly life, but at the same time to arouse him to honor God."[30] For all these reasons, "God's image is properly to be sought within him, not outside him, indeed, it is an inner good of the soul."[31]

Insofar as it is a *spiritual* reality, the soul is regarded as the seat of both spiritual corruption and spiritual restoration.[32] This spiritual dimension of the soul is thus seen most clearly from a soteriological perspective. "Since the 'animal nature,' which we have first of all, is the image of Adam, so we will conform to Christ in His heavenly nature; and when that happens our restoration will be complete. For we now begin to bear the image of Christ, and we are daily being transformed into it more and more; but that image depends upon spiritual regeneration."[33] The soul is spiritual in a second sense. Since humanity reflects something of God, that resemblance cannot be found in the physical body, which God does not possess. As Calvin argues in his *Psychopannychia*, "These expressions [after his image and likeness] cannot possibly be understood of [Adam's] body, in which, though the wonderful work of God appears more than in all other creatures, his image nowhere shines forth. God Himself, who is a Spirit . . . cannot be represented by any bodily shape."[34]

27. 1.15.3.

28. 1.15.2.

29. 1.15.3, "We ought not to deny that angels were created according to God's likeness, inasmuch as our highest perfect, as Christ testifies, will be to become like them."

30. 1.15.6.

31. 1.15.4. In his *Psychopannychia*, 422–23, Calvin uses rather strong language: "Nothing constitutes this image in the flesh of man"; "it [the body] does not represent any image of God"; "the image of God is outside the flesh"; "the soul of man is not of the earth."

32. 1.15.4. See also *Comm.* 2 Cor. 5:17; 1.15.1, 4; *Comm.* John 1:4.

33. *Comm.* 1 Cor. 15:49. He makes a similar comment in *Comm.* 1 John 3.

34. In *Psychopannychia*, 3:422–25.

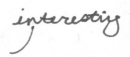

While Calvin repeatedly places the body in a subordinate relation-ship to the soul, he also goes to great lengths to emphasize the *integrity of the human creature*.[35] Adam bore the true image of God when he "was endued with a right judgment, had affections in harmony with reason, had all his senses sound and well-regulated, and truly excelled in every-thing good."[36] Again, this understanding is more plainly perceived from the perspective of Pentecost. "For how is the whole man entire, except when his thoughts are pure and holy, his affections all honorable and well-arranged, and when too his body itself devotes its energies and service to good works alone?"[37] The whole person is healed and holy, then, when soul and body are consecrated to God.[38] Conversely, the whole person is vitiated by sin, corrupt, and diseased, "from head to foot," in both body and soul.[39]

The Body Frail and Fallen

Mary Engel Potter suggests that, for Calvin, human infirmity is registered as both fragility and corruption.[40] Human life is inconstant, requiring the providence of God to keep it from reverting to chaos, and subject to per-verse forces, requiring the salvific intervention of God.[41] Yet, while the body suffers the consequences of sin as much as the soul,[42] there is a sense in which the body signifies an especially frail and fallen quality.[43] Even prior to the fall, Calvin believes that the "dusty" constitution of humans seems to imply an inferior quality: "Let foolish men now go and boast of the excellency of their nature!" Calvin notes that the body of Adam is formed of clay "to the end that no one should exult beyond measure in his flesh. He must be excessively stupid who does not hence learn humil-

35. 2.14.1; "Brief Confession of Faith," in *Tracts and Treatises*, 2:131.

36. *Comm.* Gen. 1:26.

37. This viewpoint figures largely in Calvin's *Sermons on Job*, e.g., Job 14:6; 35:8.

38. *Comm.* Rom. 6:13; 6:6; cf. *CR* 60:81.

39. 2.1.9; 2.3.1; 3.19.4; 3.14.1.

40. Engel, *John Calvin's Perspectival Anthropology*, 17.

41. Cf. Calvin's comment on Gen. 2:7.

42. *Comm.* Rom. 8:10, "The word *body* signifies the more stolid mass as yet unpu-rified by the Spirit of God from earthly defilements, which delight only in what is gross. It would be absurd otherwise to ascribe to the body the blame for sin."

43. 1.17.10, "Innumerable are the evils that beset human life; innumerable, too, the deaths that threaten it."

ity."[44] The dusty, earthy quality of humans does not, then, express a commendable connection to the rest of creation; rather, it is a defect of sorts. Though Adam possessed an immortal soul and in this way was "crowned with glory," he nonetheless "smacked of the earth."[45]

In the fall the human creature experiences a "mournful and wretched overthrow" of all that was good.[46] Here the *imago* becomes thoroughly marred; here the creature becomes "confused, mutilated, and disease-ridden";[47] here humanity becomes alienated from God, from itself, and from its own body.[48] In the primordial rebellion against God, depravity is thus diffused through all parts of the soul as well as of the body. The whole self is maimed: "The mind is smitten with blindness, and infected with innumerable errors; [namely,] that all the affections of the heart are full of stubbornness and wickedness; that vile lusts, or other diseases equally fatal, reign there; and that all the senses burst forth with many vices."[49] The physical body, however, has its own way of bearing sin or being "consumed with rottenness."[50] Borrowing St. Paul's language, Calvin concludes: "The groaning of believers arises from their knowledge that here they are exiles from their native land and are shut up in the body as in a work-house (*ergastulo*), and so they count this life a burden because in it they cannot obtain true and perfect happiness because they cannot escape the slavery of sin except by death and so they wish to be elsewhere."[51]

This "body of sin" or "body of death," however, is not to be equated with physicality as such. Ever the careful exegete, Calvin describes these phrases as instances of synecdoche, by which the New Testament authors denote the physical body under the condition of sin. Explaining Romans 7:24, he writes, "By *the body of death* he means the mass of sin, or the constituent parts from which the whole man is formed, except that in his case alone the remnants of sin were left, which held him captive."[52] To describe

44. *Comm.* Gen. 2:7. The equation of lowliness with dustiness is not to be confused with the same idea in Paul of the "lowly body" in Phil. 3:21.
45. *Comm.* 1 Cor. 15:47.
46. *Comm.* Ps. 8:7–9.
47. 1.15.4; *Comm.* Gen. 1:26.
48. *Comm.* Gen. 2:16; 3:1.
49. *Comm.* Gen. 3:6. Cf. Calvin's comments on John 3:6; 6:63; Ps. 97:7; Rom. 8:7; and Isa. 40:6, 22; *CR* 61:486.
50. 3.25.3.
51. *Comm.* 2 Cor. 5:4.
52. *Comm.* Rom. 7:24, emphasis original.

the feeling of being trapped in this sin-ridden body, Calvin uses the graphic language of "prison." As he preaches in a sermon on Job 13, "We see that we are held here as in a prison, as long as this body envelops us we are slaves to sin."[53] He develops this line of thought in a comment on 2 Corinthians 5:4: "[Paul] explains the metaphor [of "tent"] further by saying, *that what is mortal may be swallowed up of life.* Since flesh and blood cannot inherit the kingdom of God, what is corruptible in our nature must die so that we may be thoroughly renewed and restored to a state of perfection. That is why our body is called a prison in which we are held captive."[54]

This image of prison recurs in Calvin's sermons, commentaries, tracts, and *Institutes* and seems to capture something definitive about the physical body of this age. It signals physical weakness.[55] It confirms the idea of the immortal soul,[56] illumines the nature of faith,[57] explicates the nature of Christ's incarnation and his experience at the cross,[58] and describes the right way to perceive death.[59] Finally, the image of prison highlights the basic differences between body and soul.

the image of
a prison

Both in the body and out of the body we labor to please the Lord. . . . We shall perceive the presence of God when we shall be separated

53. *CO* 33:627–28.

54. *Comm.* 2 Cor. 5:4, emphasis original.

55. 3.6.5, "But no one in this earthly prison of the body has sufficient strength to press on with due eagerness, and weakness so weighs down the greater number that, with wavering and limping and even creeping along the ground, they move at a feeble rate." Cf. *Comm.* Matt. 22:30.

56. 1.15.2, "Besides, unless souls survive when freed from the prison houses of their bodies, it would be absurd for Christ to induce the soul of Lazarus as enjoying bliss in Abraham's bosom, and again, the soul of the rich man sentenced to terrible torments." The language of "prison" appears explicitly in 1 Pet. 3:19 (cf. Rev. 2:10; 20:7), from which Calvin infers that Christ appears to the spirits of the dead. On this account, in *Psychopannychia*, 429, 449, he makes an appeal to 4 Esd. 3–4.

57. 3.25.1, "Since we hope for what we do not see, and, as is elsewhere stated, 'faith is the indication of things unseen,' so long as we are confined in the prison house of the flesh, 'we are away from the Lord.'" See also *Des Libertins, CO* 7:204.

58. 4.17.31, "In this manner, he is said to have descended to that place according to his divinity, not because divinity left heaven to hide itself in the prison house of the body, but because even though it filled all things, still in Christ's very humanity it dwelt bodily, that is, by nature, and in a certain ineffable way." See also 1.15.2.

59. 3.9.4, "If departure from the world is entry into life, what else is the world but a sepulcher? And what is it for us to remain in life but to be immersed in death? If to be freed from the body is to be released into perfect freedom, what else is the body but a prison?" Cf. *Comm.* John 11:26.

from this body . . . [and] we will no longer walk by faith but by sight, since the load of clay by which we are pressed down acts as a kind of wall of partition, keeping us away from God. . . .

. . . The body, which decays, weighs down the soul, and confining it within an earthly habitation, greatly limits its perceptions. If the body is the prison of the soul, if the earthly habitation is a kind of fetters, what is the state of the soul when set free from this prison, when loosed from these fetters? Is it not restored to itself, and as it were made complete, so that we may truly say, that all which it gains is so much lost to the body?[60]

Such strong language raises the question whether there is anything more positive to be said about human bodies? Is there no sense that, while Christ will surely "make our vile body conformable to his glorious body," rescuing it from slavery to "the prison of our flesh," the physical body is invested *today* with resurrection life because of the Spirit's work?[61]

The Human Body Christologically Considered

If more is to be discovered about Calvin's anthropology, it will be by examining his understanding of the relation of Christ's body to the human bodies of the faithful. What does Christ's body tell us about human bodies? What benefits are transmitted to the faithful through Christ's body? And how exactly does the Christian receive these benefits, "such that whatever is [Christ's] may be called ours"?[62] For Calvin, the phrase that captures this experience for the faithful is the *mirifica commutatio*, the wonderful exchange.[63] This is the idea that everything that humanity has lost in Adam may be restored in Christ.[64] This restoration is a gift, not a possession, a grace imputed to those who receive it in faith by the Spirit's power, not an endowment, like sin, which obtains automatically.[65] In Christ, the

60. *Psychopannychia*, 405–6.
61. Cf. *Comm.* 1 John 3:2.
62. 4.17.2.
63. See his comments on John 13:31; 16:14; Heb. 11:1; and 2.12.2. Cf. Zachman, *Image and Word*, 108.
64. See his comments on Gen. 3:6, 14; Ps. 8:5–6; 1 Cor. 15:21, 27; Heb. 1:2.
65. Cf. 2.1.7; 2.1.8; *Comm.* 1 Cor. 15:45; *Comm.* Rom. 5:17. Adam's relationship to the rest of humankind, for Calvin, is to be seen as a radical one rather than a representative

faithful "enjoy so much of the fragments of the good things which they lost in Adam, as may furnish them with abundant matter of wonder at the singularly gracious manner in which God deals with them."[66] Calvin eloquently articulates the "wonderful exchange" as follows:

> This is the wonderful exchange which, out of his measureless benevolence, he has made with us; that, becoming Son of man with us, he has made us sons of God with him; that, by his descent to earth, he has prepared an ascent to heaven for us; that, by taking on our mortality, he has conferred his immortality upon us; that, accepting our weakness, he has strengthened us by his power; that, receiving our poverty unto himself, he has transferred his wealth to us; that, taking the weight of our iniquity upon himself (which oppressed us), he has clothed us with his righteousness.[67]

By taking on a mortal body in "the likeness of sinful flesh," Christ bestows an immortal, incorruptible body upon the faithful in the resurrection of the dead. It is noteworthy that this statement in the *Institutes* appears in his commentary on the Lord's Supper, for it is here that Christ's "flesh" plays a crucial role in the believer's sanctification.[68] Commenting on Colossians 1:18, Calvin writes, "For in the resurrection there is the restoration of all things, and thus it is the beginning of the second and new creation, for the former had fallen in the ruin of the first man."[69] Christ's resurrection "is the foundation [*hypostasis*] and pledge of ours," and it is his resurrected body that constitutes "the reward of the spiritual life."[70] To know what the human body is destined for, then, we must first look at Jesus's body.

> For we know that the body of Christ was subject to death, and that it was delivered from corruption, not by some inherent property of its own . . . but by the providence of God and nothing else. Therefore not

---

one. On this point, see Aaron Denlinger, "Calvin's Understanding of Adam's Relationship to His Posterity: Recent Assertions of the Reformer's 'Federalism' Evaluated," *Calvin Theological Journal* 44 (2009): 226–50.

66. *Comm.* Ps. 8:7–9.

67. 4.17.2.

68. Cf. *Comm.* John 6:55.

69. The idea of restoration is key in Calvin's thinking: see, e.g., *Comm.* Gen. 3:14; *Comm.* Isa. 65:25; *Comm.* 1 Cor. 15:46; *Comm.* Acts 3:21; 3.9.5.

70. *Comm.* 1 Cor. 15:21.

only, as regards the substance of His body, was He earthy, but for a time He also shared in our earthy condition. For before the power of Christ could show itself by conferring the life of heaven on us, it was necessary for Him to die in the weakness of the flesh. But it was in the resurrection that this heavenly life first appeared, that He might give life to us also.[71]

Significantly, the language of "body" (*corpus*), "earth" (*terrenus*), and "flesh" (*carnis*) is used synonymously here to describe Christ's physical self. Christ takes on a common body in order to transform it into an uncommon body: a resurrected body.[72] As such, Christ's resurrected body functions as a proleptic sign of all rightly ordered bodies. As Calvin explains in the *Institutes*, "God's natural Son fashioned for himself a body from our body, flesh from our flesh, bones from our bones, that he might be one with us. Ungrudgingly, he took our nature upon himself to impart to us what was his, and to become both Son of God and Son of man in common with us."[73] Christ takes upon himself the "very flesh" of weak humanity, not only to confer a "quickened" body, but also to sympathize with the "weakness" characteristic of embodied humanity.[74]

Furthermore, the hope of a resurrected body is intimately related to Christ's body in the sacraments. Christ's baptism prefigures the union of the faithful to Christ's bodily life: "For [Christ] consecrated and sanctified baptism in his own body, that he might have it in common with us as the firmest bond of union and fellowship which he deigned to form with us."[75] Similarly, in view of the Lord's Supper, Calvin asserts: "If you want to have anything in common with Christ you must especially take care not to despise His flesh."[76] Only through Christ's "humbled flesh" and through partaking of Christ's flesh, therefore, do the faithful have access to life immortal for the sake of fellowship with the Father.[77]

---

71. *Comm.* 1 Cor. 15:47.

72. *Comm.* 1 Cor. 15:35, 53.

73. 2.12.2.

74. See esp. *Comm.* John 11:33–35, where Calvin discusses godly emotion (which Christ exhibits) and disordered emotion (which humans regularly exhibit). About Jesus weeping publicly at Lazarus's tomb, Calvin writes, "He proved Himself to be our brother, so that we might know that we have a Mediator who willingly excuses and is ready to help those infirmities which He has experienced Himself."

75. 4.15.6.

76. *Comm.* John 6:56.

77. *Comm.* John 14:28.

The Human Body Pneumatologically Considered

How exactly do the faithful partake of Christ's resurrected body? By the Spirit of Christ.[78] Indeed, the Holy Spirit not only continually urges "us to hope for the resurrection of our flesh"[79] but also engrafts the faithful into Christ's own flesh. For Calvin, union with Christ is not merely a matter of imitation or example,[80] nor is it simply a future reality; it is a matter of a mystic union with Christ by his Spirit.[81] As he explicates Romans 6:5, "Our ingrafting signifies not only our conformity to the example of Christ, but also the secret union by which we grow together with Him, in such a way that He revives us by His Spirit, and transfers His power to us." The result of this union is a new creation. As the firstfruits of that new creation, Christ makes it possible for the faithful to experience *now* this new-creation life on account of the eschatological Spirit. Moreover, in the same way that the Holy Spirit constitutes the humanity of Christ, so the Spirit constitutes all renewed humanity, "spiritually" renewing both body and soul, now in part, later in full.

Commenting on John 14:16, Calvin writes, "Christ's proper work was to appease the wrath of God by atoning for the sins of the world, to redeem men from death and to procure righteousness and life. That of the Spirit is to make us partakers not only of Christ Himself, but of all His blessings."[82] Apart from participation in the Spirit, it is impossible to "taste either the fatherly favor of God or the beneficence of Christ."[83] For Calvin, the "sacred and mystic union" with Christ is strictly a pneumatological bond. To stress this point, Calvin claims this union is not an "inflowing of substance" that the faithful receive but rather the "grace and power of the Spirit."[84] Equally important, the believer's participation in the Spirit is a christologically oriented reality. Calvin writes, "The Spirit bestows on us nothing apart from Christ; but He takes from Christ what he sheds on us."[85]

---

78. *Comm.* 1 Cor. 15:50.

79. 3.25.8.

80. *Comm.* Rom. 8:29.

81. Todd Billings, in *Calvin, Participation, and the Gift: The Activity of Believers in Union with Christ* (New York: Oxford University Press, 2008), provides a helpful entryway into the idea of participation in Calvin.

82. See also his comments on John 16:14; 1 Cor. 15:27, 57; and Col. 1:20.

83. 3.1.2; cf. 3.1.1, 4.

84. 1.15.5.

85. *Comm.* John 16:14. "For as soon as the Spirit is severed from Christ's Word, the door is open to all sorts of craziness and impostures."

With regard to the renewal of humanity, for Calvin, the Christian bears the image of Christ in two stages: now in part, in the eschaton in full. The Christian also experiences the renewal of the *imago* at two levels: in the soul and in the body. On the first point, Calvin observes: "For we now begin to bear the image of Christ, and we are daily being transformed into it more and more; but that image depends upon spiritual regeneration. But then, it will be restored to fullness, in our body as well as our soul; what has now begun will be brought to completion, and we will obtain in reality what as yet we are only hoping for."[86]

While "the blessed state of the soul after death is the beginning of this building" (i.e., the "heavenly tent" conformable to Christ's image), its completion is the glory of the final resurrection.[87] The human body will share in the glory of God, "but only after it has been renewed and restored to life by the Spirit of Christ."[88] As believers advance in faith, "they continually aspire to new increases of the Spirit, so that the firstfruits with which they are imbued suffice for the continuance of eternal life."[89]

Unquestionably, Calvin believes that the renovating work of the Spirit concerns itself chiefly with the "faculties" of the soul.[90] Since the *imago* resides chiefly in the soul, so Calvin's reasoning goes, it constitutes the chief domain of the Spirit's work: to bring the heart, mind, and will under the dominion of Christ.[91] Yet Calvin's christological commitments do not allow him to keep the body too far from the purview of the Spirit's work. Even as the Spirit constitutes Christ's whole life, so the Spirit conforms the whole life of the redeemed. Calvin pulls all the theological strands together in the following comment on 1 Corinthians 6:15: "We should note that the spiritual union which we have with Christ is not a matter of the soul alone, but of the body also, so that we are flesh of His flesh etc. (Eph. 5:30). The hope of the resurrection would be faint, if our union with Him were not complete and total like that." And it is precisely because Christ's own body, his "flesh," as St. John names it (John 1:14), is quickened by the Spirit, that the faithful experience *even now* a quickening of their bodies by the power of Christ's Spirit.[92]

[handwritten margin note: Calvin was emphatic in his writing]

86. *Comm.* 1 Cor. 15:49. Cf. 3.3.9.
87. *Comm.* 2 Cor. 5:1.
88. *Comm.* 1 Cor. 15:50.
89. *Comm.* John 7:38; cf. *Comm.* Rom. 8:23.
90. Calvin's comments on Rom. 7:18 and 1 Cor. 15:44 are noteworthy.
91. *Comm.* Col. 3:10. Cf. Calvin's comments in 1.15.4; 3.1.4; *Comm.* Phil. 2:13; *Comm.* John 3:5; *Comm.* John 1:13.
92. *Comm.* John 6:63.

With respect to the human body, Calvin perceives a dual task in the Spirit's work: arousing hope for the resurrection of the body *and* investing the body of this age with a foretaste of the body of the age to come.[93] To experience spiritual renewal is first and foremost to experience the Spirit-enabled mortification of the body under the condition of sin and the Spirit-enabled vivification of the body under the dominion of Christ.[94] "As, however, Christ's kingdom is spiritual, this change must take place chiefly in the Spirit, and hence it is with propriety that he begins with this."[95] The term "spirit," as often as not in Calvin's commentaries, stands for the Spirit of regeneration, not for the soul. "This passage also teaches us that by the word *Spirit* Paul has not up to this point meant the *mind* or the *understanding*, which the advocates of free will call the superior part of the soul, but the gift of heaven. He explains that it is those whom God governs by His Spirit who are spiritual, and not those who obey reason on their own impulse."[96]

While there remains a proclivity in Calvin to want to restrict the Holy Spirit's "spiritual" work to the sphere of the soul, his Christology yet again opens up a more holistic picture of the Spirit's ministry. Following Paul's line of thought in 1 Corinthians 6, Calvin contends that, since God has made the bodies of the faithful "members of Christ," it matters what they do with their bodies now: "Since God the Father has united us to His Son, what a disgraceful thing it would be to tear our bodies away from that sacred union, and give them over to things quite unworthy of Christ." For this reason, holiness is now to be played out in the body, no less than "in the whole of our life."[97] An additional reason why it matters what the faithful do with their physical bodies involves the relation between the present body and the resurrected body. Calvin questions his imagined interlocutor: "What of the fact that [the bodies of the faithful] are also members of Christ? Or that God commands all their parts to be sanctified to him? Or that it is his will that his name be praised with men's tongues, that pure hands be lifted to himself, that sacrifices be offered? What mad-

---

93. 3.1.2: The Spirit "arouses hope of a full renewal 'because he who raised Christ from the dead will quicken our mortal bodies, because of his Spirit that dwells in us.'" See also 3.25.8.

94. Calvin pursues this line of argument in his discussion of the ascension (4.17.28) and of the Lord's Supper (4.17.33).

95. *Comm.* 2 Cor. 5:7. Cf. *Comm.* 1 Cor. 15:44; 2.3.1.

96. *Comm.* Rom. 8:9, emphasis added.

97. *Comm.* Rom. 12:1.

[handwritten margin note: Calvin defined spirit as a gift of heaven]

[handwritten margin note: CONFLICTED]

ness is it for that part of man, deemed by the Heavenly Judge worthy of such shining honor, to be by mortal man reduced to dust beyond hope of restoration?"[98]

Not only must the mind and the heart be enlisted in the work of sanctification. The body too must play its part. "Our members, too, are to be dedicated and consecrated to His will so that all our powers of soul and body may aspire to His glory alone."[99] Even before the last resurrection, then, the human body experiences the renewing operation of the eschatological Spirit because of its union to Christ.[100]

Critical Questions

As we transition now to a critical examination of Calvin's theology of the human body, certain questions need to be asked. To what extent does a Platonic mind-set dominate Calvin's approach? How exactly ought we to construe such a mind-set? Is he in fact a pessimist, or is he simply inconsistent in his thinking? Has his rhetoric on the physical body in some way distorted his theological and liturgical proposals? Is there another way to read the relation of the body to the *imago*? Do the interior activities of the soul sum up the meaning of the image of God in the human creature and thus also the priorities of public worship? And does "spiritual" worship in a new-covenantal era necessarily reduce the body to a minimalist role? Contextual, rhetorical, and exegetical questions figure largely in our answers to these questions.

Contextual Questions

As Calvin scholars have widely noted, Calvin's anthropology must be carefully set within its proper historical context.[101] Much like St. Paul's anthropology, Calvin's writing has an occasionalist quality about it, shap-

98. 3.25.7.

99. *Comm. Rom.* 6:13; cf. Calvin's comments in 1 Thess. 5:23 and 1 Cor. 6:13–20.

100. *Comm. Rom.* 8:11.

101. See, for example, Parker, *Calvin's New Testament Commentaries*; David C. Steinmetz, *Calvin in Context* (Oxford: Oxford University Press, 2010); Heiko Oberman, "The Pursuit of Happiness: Calvin between Humanism and Reformation," in *Humanity and Divinity in Renaissance and Reformation*, ed. John O'Malley (Leiden: Brill, 1993), 252.

ing the terminology and the uses of terms. With respect to his contemporary interlocutors, Anabaptists, humanists, Libertines, Nicodemites, and Rome serve as foils to his own thinking on the human body.[102] Over against the Libertines, for example, Calvin stresses the created nature of the soul, while over against the Anabaptists he emphasizes the soul's immortality. With regard to the church fathers, both Augustine and Chrysostom function as conceptual backdrops for Calvin's arguments.[103] Beyond these conversation partners, it is important to keep in mind that the *Psychopannychia* represents Calvin's early thinking, whereas his sermons on Job, which include extensive commentary on human nature, appear toward the end of his career. In an evaluation of Calvin's anthropology, caution is required in order not to make too much or too little of any given text. Each text, in turn, must be read both contextually and stereoscopically to discern points of continuity and discontinuity with the received tradition, as well as the places where Calvin makes his distinctive mark on the tradition.[104]

The more controverted question is Calvin's relation to Plato. Is Calvin substantially influenced by Platonic philosophy, or is it simply a matter of occasional linguistic affinity?[105] Charles Partee is an especially helpful guide here. The first thing to understand is that there is no one, homogenous Plato. There is instead a development in Plato's thinking on the soul, determined by the literary and historical context.[106] Partee explains: "It is true that Calvin's doctrine of the immortality of the soul has some 'points of contact' with the early, religious aspect of Plato's doctrine

---

102. Engel, *John Calvin's Perspectival Anthropology*, 154.

103. On the patristic background for Calvin's thinking, see Brian E. Daley, "A Hope for Worms: Early Christian Hope," in *Resurrection: Theological and Scientific Assessments*, ed. Ted Peters, Robert John Russell, and Michael Welker (Grand Rapids: Eerdmans, 2002), 136–64.

104. On the conflicting judgments of scholars about the place of the *Psychopannychia* in Calvin's thought, see Engel, *John Calvin's Perspectival Anthropology*, Appendix V: "Calvin's *Psychopannychia*," 213–19.

105. N. T. Wright, *The Resurrection of the Son of God* (Minneapolis: Fortress, 2003), 47–55, helpfully explains the Hellenistic background for the idea of the body as prison of the soul.

106. Charles Partee, "The Soul in Plato, Platonism, and Calvin," *Scottish Journal of Theology* 22 (1969): esp. 285; 287: "It is not so remarkable that Calvin was indirectly influenced by the common 'theological Platonism' of so much of Christian thought from the Greek fathers through Augustine to the Renaissance Platonists, or that aspects of Calvin's doctrine 'resemble' the Platonic view. In this 'weak' sense Calvin is not alone in being influenced by Platonism."

[handwritten note in left margin: still grounded in the biblical text.]

and its transmission in Neoplatonism, but even there the differences are more fundamental than the similarities."[107] The second thing to understand, Partee persuasively argues, is that, although resemblances exist between Calvin's language and Renaissance Platonism, Calvin's argument remains biblically rooted rather than philosophically resourced.[108] Rhetoric alone does not automatically signify theology, and careful attention must always be given to the function of language in particular contexts and to the pattern of language across contexts.[109]

Rhetorical Questions

Calvin, no less than St. Paul, employs strong, variable rhetoric to describe the human body in ways that may lead the reader to believe inconsistent thinking is at work.[110] Said differently, any inconsistencies in Calvin's anthropology may simply reflect biblical inconsistencies, actual or apparent.[111] Robert Jewett concedes as much about Paul: "The seemingly erratic pattern of development [of Paul's anthropology] has been shown to correlate quite closely with the argumentative situation in each letter. New connotations and technical usages of the terms emerged in each instance in response to some heretical

---

107. Partee, "The Soul in Plato, Platonism, and Calvin," 279. "If all men are either Platonists or Aristotelians (Coleridge)," Partee concludes, "then in this general, historical sense Calvin was a Platonist," no more, no less.

108. Partee, "The Soul in Plato, Platonism, and Calvin," 293. Cf. 3.25.7; *Psychopannychia*, 420. See also Davis, "Not 'Hidden and Far Off,'" 407n7; Roy Battenhouse, "The Doctrine of Man in Calvin and Renaissance Platonism," *Journal of the History of Ideas* 9 (1948): 447-71.

109. Davis, "Not 'Hidden and Far Off,'" 417, argues that "it is only by looking beyond rhetoric to the actual function of body in Calvin's thought that one can appreciate its role." See also James C. Goodloe IV, "The Body in Calvin's Theology," in *Calvin Studies V*, ed. John H. Leith (Davidson, NC: Colloquium on Calvin Studies, 1990), 106-7.

110. For a summary of the charge of inconsistent thinking in Calvin's anthropology, see Engel, *John Calvin's Perspectival Anthropology*, "Introduction." Cf. Richard Prins, "The Image of God in Adam and the Restoration of Man in Jesus Christ: A Study in Calvin," *Scottish Journal of Theology* 25 (1972): 34; Brian A. Gerrish, "The Mirror of God's Goodness: Man in the Theology of Calvin," *Concordia Theological Quarterly* 45 (1981): 221.

111. Green, *Body, Soul, and Human Life*, 46: "The biblical writers do engage questions regarding the nature of humanity, but they do so implicitly." On the variety of terms that the Old Testament uses to describe the human person, see Robert A. Di Vito, "Here One Need Not Be Oneself: The Concept of 'Self' in the Hebrew Scriptures," in *The Whole and Divided Self*, ed. David E. Aune and John McCarthy (New York: Crossroad Publishing, 1997), 49-88.

tendency or movement in a Pauline congregation. . . . Despite the occasional correlation of Hellenistic categories to the Judaic term 'heart,' Paul did not in general evince any interest in producing a truly consistent anthropology."[112]

Additionally, alleged inconsistencies might also indicate a complex idea.[113] While the Scriptures, for example, describe the human creature as a crown of God's glory (Ps. 8:5) or as a "factory" of inestimable treasures,[114] the Scriptures also describe humanity in language that Calvin appropriates in his own colorful way: as a "poor worm of the earth, unhappy creature, miserable swine," and an "abyss of infection,"[115] a "factory of idols,"[116] a "five foot worm,"[117] a "monster,"[118] "grubs crawling upon the earth,"[119] and unfit to be ranked with "worms, lice, fleas, and vermin."[120] Does such language make Calvin a pessimist? If by pessimism is meant a dim view of things, then three possibilities can be suggested: a pessimism with respect to human pride over against God, a pessimism when humans are considered in their corrupted condition, and a pessimism about the role of the human body in public worship.[121] In light of the data, I would call Calvin a pessimist in all three senses. I also contend that his pessimism is warranted in the first two senses but not in the third.

Where Calvin more obviously fails to persuade is in his handling of the terms "flesh," "body," and "body as prison." In Scripture the term *sarx* signifies two basic realities: the human creature in its creaturely status (Rom. 4:1; 9:3; 11:14; Gal. 4:23, 29; 1 Cor. 9:11, 15–50; Ps. 142:2 LXX) and in its fallen condition, or what is often termed "carnal man" or "sinful man" (Rom. 7:14; 8:5, 9–11; 2 Cor. 10:2–3).[122] Calvin readily accepts both

112. Robert Jewett, *Paul's Anthropological Terms: A Study of Their Use in Conflict Settings*, AGJU 10 (Leiden: Brill, 1971), 447.

113. N. T. Wright, "Mind, Spirit, Soul, and Body: All for One and One for All; Reflections on Paul's Anthropology in His Complex Contexts" (paper presented at the Society of Christian Philosophers: Regional Meeting, Fordham University, March 18, 2011).

114. Cited in T. F. Torrance, *Calvin's Doctrine of Man* (Grand Rapids: Eerdmans, 1957), 26.

115. *CO* 35:202.

116. 1.11.8.

117. *CO* 33:662; cf. Ps. 22:6.

118. *Sermons on Job* 33:29.

119. 2.6.4.

120. Cited in Gerrish, "The Mirror of God's Goodness," 212.

121. 1.17.10, "We need not go beyond ourselves: since our body is the receptacle of a thousand diseases."

122. *Comm. Rom.* 6:12; 2.3.1; 3.19.4; 3.14.1. Cf. Robert H. Gundry, *Sōma in Bibli-*

senses, and he repeatedly stresses that the soul cannot be excluded from "the flesh" in the latter sense,[123] which points to a corruption of human nature in toto.[124] "But if flesh is contrasted to the Spirit as something corrupt to what is sound, the crooked to what is straight, the defiled to the holy, the polluted to the pure, we may readily conclude that the whole of man's nature is condemned in one word. Christ is therefore saying that our understanding and reason are corrupted because they are carnal and that all the affections of the heart are depraved and wicked because they too are carnal."[125]

Yet, as often as Calvin affirms that the whole human person suffers the damaging effects of sin, his rhetorical habit is to place the body, more often than the soul, on the problematic side of "flesh." "The spirit takes the place of the soul in man, but the flesh, which is the corrupt and polluted soul, that of the body."[126] And again, "Our souls are fixed to the earth, and so enslaved to our bodies that they have fallen from their proper excellence."[127] To put the point crudely: there is more language in Calvin about the physical body as a problem to the salvific, sanctifying work of God than as integral to this divine work.[128] Where there is an appropriate judgment of the body in its complicity to the "deeds of the flesh," there is all too often a failure to commend the body as a blessed instrument of God's glory on earth.

Perhaps this tendency is in response to the biblical habit of placing the body in linguistic proximity to rebellious *sarx*.[129] Perhaps this rhetor-

---

cal Theology, with Emphasis on Pauline Anthropology (Cambridge: Cambridge University Press, 1976), 58.

123. *Comm.* Rom. 6:6; 7:18; 8:7; *Comm.* Gen. 3:6; *Comm.* Ps. 97:7; *Comm.* Isa. 40:6, 22; *Comm.* John 6:63. On the fallen mind (see 2.2.13–25), Calvin says that "an immense crowd of gods flow forth from the human mind" (1.5.12). On the fallen will: 2.2.26–27; 2.3; 2.5; esp. 2.2.12. See Paul Helm, "John Calvin, the 'Sensus Divinitatis,' and the Noetic Effects of Sin," *International Journal for Philosophy of Religion* 43 (1998): 87–107.

124. *Comm.* Rom. 7:24; *Comm.* Ps. 8:7–9; *Comm.* Gen. 3:1; 1.15.4.

125. *Comm.* John 3:5.

126. *Comm.* 2 Cor. 5:8.

127. *Comm.* Rom. 6:12. More bluntly, *Sermons on Job* 37, "Our souls are more precious to [God] than our bodies."

128. See also *Comm.* Col. 2:11.

129. Conversely, there is no corresponding language in Paul about a "mind of sin" or a "heart of death" or a paradoxical "carnal soul." As Jewett, *Paul's Anthropological Terms*, 297, rightly argues, however, in Romans the body is "dead" on account of sin, not on account of its materiality.

ical habit is mitigated by Calvin's positive discourse on the resurrected body. But the consistently negative cast that marks Calvin's rhetoric on the physical body generates a potential for a distorting perspective.[130] His repeated use of the term "prison" to describe the physical body departs from the strictly technical, intertextually nuanced language of Scripture (e.g., "body of sin" or "body of death") and introduces philosophical baggage that (potentially) sends his readers in the wrong direction.[131] As the case may be, the notion of a prison engenders a certain prejudicial view of the physical body that fails to reckon fully with the bodily basis of redemption to which the Scriptures bear witness.[132]

[handwritten marginal notes: "IL. ★" in left margin; "Misuse of language" in right margin]

Exegetical Questions: Part 1

In contrast to Calvin's diminished role for the human body in the redemptive and liturgical work of God, the body (Gk. σῶμα, *sōma*) plays a more prominent role in the New Testament picture, to the extent that it represents the concrete place for life "in Christ" to be worked out, quite literally.[133] Udo Schnelle writes that St. Paul "uses σῶμα as the comprehensive expression of the human self" or as a technical term to denote the whole person in its corporal relations.[134] For the biblical writers this is the normative way to enact human life before God, publicly and privately.[135] The problem of the human body is not materiality; its problem, like the mind or heart as well, is its enslavement to sin. Its fundamental need, conversely, is transformation, not an escape from the material order.[136] In

[handwritten note: "transformation not escape."]

130. On this point, see Selinger, *Calvin against Himself*, 2–3.

131. Cf. *Psychopannychia*, 440–44. Calvin also uses the language of "celestial soul" (444), which rather confuses things. J. Faber's claim (*Essays in Reformed Doctrine* [Neerlandia, AB: Inheritance Publications, 1990], 243) that, when Calvin describes body and soul from the angle of creation, he employs the language of "inn" and "guest" rather than "prison," does not seem to be borne out by the evidence.

132. Cf. Udo Schnelle, *The Human Condition: Anthropology in the Teachings of Jesus, Paul, and John* (Minneapolis: Fortress, 1996), 56–57.

133. Gundry, *Sōma in Biblical Theology*, 35.

134. Schnelle, *The Human Condition*, 57.

135. Jewett, *Paul's Anthropological Terms*, 261. See also Bill T. Arnold, "Soul-Searching Questions about 1 Samuel 28: Samuel's Appearance at Endor and Christian Anthropology," in *What about the Soul? Neuroscience and Christian Anthropology*, ed. Joel B. Green (Nashville: Abingdon, 2004), 78.

136. Wright, *The Resurrection of the Son of God*, 231.

that light the Christian, in view of the eschaton, seeks to live well "in the flesh" but not "according to the flesh" (2 Cor. 10:2–3), in this way imitating its Master, who tabernacled in the world as "flesh" but not "according to the flesh" (John 1:14; 8:15). Jewett helpfully summarizes: "Unlike the word 'flesh,' σῶμα can be used to depict the whole scope of salvation including the resurrection (Rom. 8:11) and redemption (Rom. 8:23) of the body and the bodily worship in the world (Rom. 12:1), which is the form of ethical activity the new aeon inaugurates and requires. The agent of this somatic salvation is the 'body of Christ' (Rom. 7:4) whose death and resurrection marked the turning of the aeons."[137]

In Calvin's emphasis on the soul as the seat of the "image of God," as well as the special locus of God's redemptive work, along with a corresponding diminishment of the "dusty" quality of human life, he fails to perceive the constitutive role of the physical body in sanctification, and as it concerns the public worship of the church, he ascribes the human body, at best, a subordinate or supplemental role, at worst, a problematic or worrisome role. This position is in contrast to the holistic picture of the human person that the earliest pages of Scripture envision.[138] While we cannot treat the technical complexity that surrounds the historical-critical and theological discussions of the *imago* in Genesis, we draw attention here to the corporeal aspect of the image of God.

Exegetical Questions: Part 2

Starting in 1901 with the publication of Hermann Gunkel's critical work on Genesis, biblical scholars have largely moved away from a "substantialist" reading of Genesis 1:26–27, and along with a greater understanding of the relational and royal dimensions of the *imago* has also come an emphasis on the corporeal dimension of the *adam*, which in turn has led to a greater stress on the holistic nature of the human creature. Claus Westermann comments representatively: "Gen 1:26f. is concerned neither with

137. Jewett, *Paul's Anthropological Terms*, 457.
138. Joel B. Green, "Eschatology and the Nature of Humans: A Reconsideration of Pertinent Biblical Evidence," *Science and Christian Belief* 14 (2002): 33–50, argues that this holistic picture carries through right to the end, implicating our understanding of the so-called intermediate state of the human person between death and resurrection, which he believes will be embodied, our present experience of "space and time" notwithstanding.

the corporeal nor with the spiritual qualities of people; it is concerned only with the person as a whole."[139] This interpretation is underscored by a consideration of ancient Near Eastern literature. In a comparative study of Egyptian and Babylonian literature, the language of "image" and "likeness" is used to illumine the role of the king as the embodied image of the divinity. Wherever the king was, *in his very person*, there also was the god; and as the image of that god, the king mediated the rule of the god in the created sphere. While the *imago* is radically "democratized" in Genesis, the language of 1:26–27 functions in similar fashion: to point to the human creature as a "moulded three-dimensional embodiment" of the one, true God.[140]

This reading of the Genesis narrative is strengthened, among other ways, on philological grounds. While comparatively rare in the Old Testament, a translation of the preposition *beth* in Genesis 1:27 as "as" (*a beth essentia*, "of essence"), not "in," is possible and commonly accepted by grammarians.[141] Such a translation matters because it opens up a different way of understanding the phrase commonly rendered "in the image of God." The point is not that the human is made *in* the image of God, nor does the human *have* the image of God; instead, the human is created *as* God's image.[142] The function of the *imago*, then, is not to depict something in God but rather to express the character of God in the world.[143]

139. Westermann, *Genesis 1–11: A Commentary*, trans. John J. Scullion (Minneapolis: Augsburg, 1984), 150. So too T. C. Vriezen, *An Outline of Old Testament Theology* (Newton, MA: Charles T. Branford, 1970), 49, and Gerhard von Rad, *Old Testament Theology*, vol. 1, trans. D. M. G. Stalker (New York: Harper & Row, 1962), 58.

140. P. Humbert, *Études sur le récit du paradis et de la chute dans la Genèse* (Neuchâtel: Secretariat de l'Université Neuchâtel, 1940), 157; cited in David Clines, "The Image of God in Man," *Tyndale Bulletin* 19 (1968): 56. For an excellent summary of ancient Near Eastern background literature, see Werner H. Schmidt, *Die Schöpfungsgeschichte der Priesterschrift* (Neukirchen-Vluyn: Neukirchener Verlag, 1964), 127–49; see also H. Wildeberger, "Das Abbild Gottes," *Theologischer Zeitschrift* 21 (1965): 245–59.

141. So, for example, Exod. 6:3; Ps. 118:7. Cf. Emil Kautzsch, ed., *Gesenius' Hebrew Grammar*, trans. A. E. Cowley (Oxford: Clarendon, 1976, 1910), 379; M. O'Conner and Bruce K. Waltke, *An Introduction to Biblical Hebrew Syntax* (Winona Lake, IN: Eisenbrauns, 1990), 198; Cyrus Gordon, "'In' of Predication or Equivalence," *JBL* 100 (1981): 612–13.

142. Clines, "The Image of God in Man," 80, see also 72–79. So too Schmidt, *Schöpfungsgeschichte*, 143n1. Contra this view, Phyllis A. Bird, "'Male and Female He Created Them': Gen 1:27b in the Context of the Priestly Account of Creation," *HTR* 74.2 (1981): 138n 22, and Westermann, *Genesis*, 145.

143. Corporeality in Israel extended to temple activities (1 Kings 6–7), feasts (Lev. 23;

As God's image, the whole human creature represents the life of God in its own native sphere: creation.[144] Put otherwise, in the creature's life as a whole, formally and functionally, God was to be reflected "on earth, as in heaven."[145]

With this perspective in mind, it is not surprising to discover in the New Testament a concern for the entire *anthrōpos* (human being). Whenever the Scriptures speak of one dimension of human life, it is usually done to emphasize not a part but the whole from a certain point of view. While *psychē* (life, soul), for instance, may refer to the whole person in terms of its "inner life" or even simply a "human creature," and the creature's *pneuma* (spirit) may point to the center of human personality, where the encounter with God takes place, *sōma* "is the whole person seen in terms of public, space-time presence."[146] Though the *sōma* does not play the same role in the creative and redemptive work of God as either the *psychē* or the *pneuma*, it nonetheless plays its own crucial role.[147] N. T. Wright argues, rightly I believe, that Paul's fundamental concern is for the whole creature:

> May the God of peace sanctify you wholly, *holoteles*, and may your spirit, soul and body be preserved (*tērētheiē*) whole and entire (*holoklēron*) unto the royal appearing of our Lord Jesus the Messiah. . . . When Paul thinks of human beings he sees every angle of vision as contributing to the whole, and the whole from every angle of vision. All lead to the one, the one is seen in the all. And, most importantly, each and every aspect of the human

Esther 9:18–32), land (Gen. 12:7; Deut. 1:8; Josh. 1:1–4), nationhood (Gen. 15:5), sacrificial cult (Lev. 1–7, 16–17), eschatological vision of the new creation (Isa. 2:1–4; 65:17), hands (Pss. 47:1; 63:4), eyes (Pss. 119:18; 141:8), feet (Ps. 119:105), tongue (Pss. 51: 14; 71:24); bowing (Ps. 95:6; 2 Chron. 29:29), dancing (Ps. 149:3; 2 Sam. 6:14), kneeling (2 Chron. 6:13; Ps. 95:6), lifting arms (Ps. 28:2; Neh. 8:6), neighbor love (Isa. 59:9–16; cf. 64:6), holiness (2 Chron. 3:8–14; cf. Luke 1:8–11), and uncleanliness as both physical and moral (Lev. 14:1–32; 15:1–33; Pss. 24:4; 51:7; Isa. 6:5).

144. Lawson G. Stone, "The Soul: Possession, Part, or Person? The Genesis of Human Nature in Genesis 2:7," in *What about the Soul?*, ed. Green, 49. Contra Calvin, *Psychopannychia*, 449, 452.

145. See Meredith G. Kline, "Creation in the Image of the Glory-Spirit," *Westminster Theological Journal* 39 (1977): 268.

146. Wright, *The Resurrection of the Son of God*, 283. Cf. Marc Cortez, *Theological Anthropology: A Guide for the Perplexed* (London: T&T Clark, 2010), 69–70.

147. See F. LeRon Shults, *Reforming Theological Anthropology: After the Philosophical Turn to Relationality* (Grand Rapids: Eerdmans, 2003), 164.

being is addressed by God, is claimed by God, is loved by God, and can respond to God.[148]

Conclusion

Whatever else Calvin may affirm about the human body, he underemphasizes its constitutive role in human life before God. And while a case could be made that Calvin exhibits a positive regard for the physical body equal to that in the Scriptures, the language that marks his discussions of public worship and the exegetical and theological warrants that he employs to exclude or reduce the role of the body in that particular context fail to do justice to the richly corporeal, kinetic vision of worship that God in Christ enables the church to enact by the power of his Spirit.

148. Wright, "Mind, Spirit, Soul, and Body," 14. Wright identifies seven types of dualism that might be compatible with ancient Jewish thought: heavenly, theological, moral, eschatological, epistemological, sectarian, and psychological. A duality, however, is not to be readily equated or confused with a dualism. While Calvin, in his comment on 1 Thess. 5:23, acknowledges Paul's concern for the "whole man," the dominant theological accent lies on the soul over against the body.

CHAPTER 7

A Trinitarian Theology of the Physical Body

For Calvin the capacity of the soul to affect the body is not matched by any capacity of the body to affect the soul. The body remains "motion devoid of essence."

Margaret Miles, "Theology, Anthropology, and the Human Body"

But there is no doubt that meeting and weeping and fasting, and like activities, apply equally to our age whenever the condition of our affairs so demands. For since this is a holy exercise both for the humbling of men and for their confession of humility, why should we use it less than the ancients did in similar need?

Calvin, *Institutes*

In a comment on Romans 6:5, Calvin writes that, because God requires us "to worship Him in a spiritual manner, so we most zealously urge men to all the spiritual sacrifices which He recommends."[1] What Calvin means by "spiritual" here is a simple ceremonial apparatus and a concentration on "the pure exercises of faith."[2] This emphasis corresponds to the subjective side of public worship: that which concerns human activity. The objective

---

1. Wright, "Mind, Spirit, Soul, and Body," 147.
2. Wright, "Mind, Spirit, Soul, and Body," 151–53. See also Calvin's commentary on Mic. 6:6–8; 1 Pet. 2:5; John 4:23–24; Pss. 50:23; 51:17; and Mal. 1:11.

side of worship corresponds to the nature of God. The faithful ought to avoid entanglement in "petty carnal observances" because it contravenes the "spiritual" and therefore "lawful" worship of an invisible God.[3] When too many physical activities are introduced into public worship, moreover, it tends to provoke a desire to cling to "earthly" things or to confuse earth and heaven. Where the body proves useful, however, is in its subordinate cooperation to the activities of the heart and mind.

Calvin, of course, is not as straightforward as the preceding paragraph might indicate. While he stresses the pivotal need to "pray within ourselves,"[4] he also commends the practical value of liturgical ceremonies as a way for the body to be "exercised."[5] The faithful err when they exercise their bodies in a "mindless" fashion, yet acts of kneeling can serve as excellent "exercises whereby we try to rise to a greater reverence for God."[6] And though the believer is shut up in "prison," this is no reason not to give the physical body its due care. Why? Because it is *God* who maintains it.[7] Grounded in the work of the Spirit, this "spiritual" union is both a future and a present reality for the faithful, living in light of the future resurrection and of their present incorporation in the divine life. In their participation in Christ, moreover, the faithful *now* find "life in their own flesh"; the human body *now* is a member of Christ, and the body *now* is a temple of the Spirit—for this reason, "outward actions" matter *now*.[8]

Yet, as positively as we might wish to paint the picture, Calvin's affirmations of the constitutive role of the human body in the exercises of Christian faith occur only rarely. His rich insights on the human body here fail to be developed in any comprehensive manner. And although it is possible to find in Calvin commendations of the physical body in the context of public worship, those commendations are the exception. More common is a concern for the "spiritual" requirements of worship in the new-covenantal era, which prioritizes the interior activities of the soul in correspondence to the *theo*-logical priority of God's nonmaterial essence.[9] Where Calvin hints at a christological and pneumatological read-

---

3. 2.8.17, with reference to the second commandment.

4. 3.20.29, 30.

5. Calvin, "On the Necessity of Reforming the Church," in *Tracts and Treatises*, 1:127.

6. *Institutes* (1536), 9.27.

7. 2.8.40, 41; 3.20.44; see also Engel, *John Calvin's Perspectival Anthropology*, 164.

8. 4.17.8; *Comm.* 1 Cor. 6:15–20.

9. 1.13.1. Cf. 1.2.2.

ing of the human body, this chapter argues for a more comprehensive Trinitarian treatment of the physical body in the context of the church's public worship.

The Human Body Christologically Constituted

To know what human bodies are for, we do not go back to the beginning in Genesis. We go to Christ's ascended body in glory, in heaven.[10] His body, born of the Virgin Mary, suffering death, resurrected, and ascended to the right hand of the Father, is *the* paradigmatic body.[11] What does Christ's body tell us about all human bodies?

The Body as sarx

First, this body, as the beloved apostle testifies, is *sarx* (John 1:14). In canonical perspective, this body recalls the flesh that Adam beholds in his counterpart, Eve: "flesh of my flesh" (Gen. 2:23 LXX). Made from the *adamah* (ground, land), this is a body that is embedded in creation. Through this body, conditioned by the rhythms of creation—of waking/sleeping, working/resting, fullness/emptiness, presence/absence—a psychosomatic, sensory-aesthetic knowledge of the world is acquired.[12] Upon this original flesh God pronounces a definitive benediction (Gen. 1:31) and enables it to bear his glory. In the definitive flesh of Christ, which appeared "full of grace and truth" (John 1:14), God's glory is supremely witnessed. Or in Paul's language, "In [Christ] all the fullness of Deity dwells in bodily form [*sōmatikōs*]" (Col. 2:9).[13] And as Calvin rightly suggests, it is through

10. James D. G. Dunn, "1 Corinthians 15:45—Last Adam, Life-Giving Spirit," in *Christ and the Spirit in the New Testament: Studies in Honor of C. F. D. Moule*, ed. Barnabas Lindars and Stephen S. Smalley (Cambridge: Cambridge University Press, 1973), 140–41.

11. *Comm.* Phil. 3:21, "We see, even in life, but chiefly in death the present meanness of our bodies; but the glory which they will have, conformably to Christ's Body, is incomprehensible."

12. On this point, see Mark Johnson, *The Body in the Mind: The Bodily Basis of Meaning, Imagination, and Reason* (Chicago: University of Chicago Press, 1990); Joel B. Green, *In Search of the Soul: Perspectives on the Body-Soul Problem* (Eugene, OR: Wipf & Stock, 2010).

13. In *Comm.* Col. 2:9, Calvin translates this term (= Lat. *corporaliter*, "physically") as

this flesh that the faithful experience the firmest bond of fellowship with God.[14] This flesh is seen and touched (1 John 1:1), and by its touch, it heals other bodies (Luke 13:13). It is positively a *fleshy* flesh: "It is I myself! Touch me and see, for a ghost does not have flesh and bones as you see that I have" (Luke 24:39).[15] Take these physical properties away, Calvin argues, "and flesh now ceases to be."[16]

Through this flesh, moreover, the purpose of all flesh is apprehended: communion with God. Calvin points to this fact in his comment on John 14:28, "Let us therefore learn to view Christ humbled in the flesh, that He may lead us to the fount of blessed immortality. For he was not appointed our leader just to draw us to the sphere of the moon or the sun, but to make us one with God the Father."[17] For Calvin, as Canlis rightly observes, "communion is the groundwork of creation, the purpose of anthropology, and the *telos* toward which all creation strains."[18] The key factor, then, is not the "substance" or "essence" of the body, its properties or potential, but rather its "orientation." As Heiko Oberman notes, in Calvin's thinking the body exists either in fellowship with God or alienated from God.[19] And in Christ's body the disorientation that all fallen bodies suffer is reversed. The human body is thus reoriented to its Maker, no longer "bewildered" but reconciled.[20] While Calvin worries at times about our need for physical manifestations of God's presence to his people,[21] it remains generally true that Christ's flesh is "the locus of human salvation."[22]

---

substantialiter ("substantially") or *essentialiter* ("essentially"); cf. *Comm.* Col. 2:17. Schnelle, *The Human Condition*, 57: flesh "is the very place where faith acquires visible form."

14. 4.15.6; 2.12.2.

15. It is noteworthy that the term *sōmata* of Rev. 18:13 carries with it the connotation "human beings."

16. 4.17.29, "He proves himself no specter, for he is visible in his flesh."

17. 2.12.3, "Our common nature with Christ is the pledge of our fellowship with the Son of God."

18. Canlis, *Calvin's Ladder*, 54.

19. Oberman, "The Pursuit of Happiness: Calvin between Humanism and Reformation," *Studia Historiae Ecclesiasticae* 19 (1993): 17.

20. Oberman, "The Pursuit of Happiness," 17.

21. See Calvin's comments on Acts 2:2.

22. Canlis, *Calvin's Ladder*, 101.

A Particular Body

Second, Christ's body is constituted by race, culture, history, and tradition.[23] This is another way of saying that it is a particular body. His is a Jewish body, "born of a woman, born under the law" (Gal. 4:4). Through this body, Jesus in his earthly ministry accomplishes not everything that ever could have been done but, more important, the will of the Father, the God of Abraham, Isaac, and Jacob. In Calvin's words, "He has achieved [salvation] for us by the whole course of his obedience."[24] Although, according to Richard Prins, Calvin never explicitly states exactly in what respects the "image of Christ" differs from the "image of Adam," nevertheless "by inference it is possible to conclude that Christ's image does involve his suffering, his humility, his marvelous works, his death and glorious resurrection, and certainly his possession of the life-giving Spirit, since in all these Christ shows forth the glory of his Father."[25] Even if Calvin fails to stress this fact sufficiently, there is still a sense that Christ's particular human life is seen as the definitive stage for God's redemptive work[26] and that the integrity of his mission is inseparable from the Jewishness that marked his particular body (as a synecdoche for his life).[27]

As a particular body, Christ's body is also strictly localized. During his earthly sojourn Jesus goes to this town but not that town, healing this person but not that one, embracing some but not all.[28] He comes to Israel, for the sake of the nations, yet he restricts his ministry to an astonishingly small geographic space. In his ascension, Christ's body remains a localized, particular body. This fact was of special concern to Calvin. "Let them not, then, ascribe this property to Christ's glorious body—that it is in many places at once and not held in any space." Christ's body is "seated" at the right hand of the Majesty on high, he argued, not ubiquitous; it is emplaced in the heavenlies, not ontologically diffused, for "it is the true nature of a body to be contained

---

23. Cf. Willie James Jennings, "'He Became Truly Human': Incarnation, Emancipation, and Authentic Humanity," *Modern Theology* 12 (1996): 239–55.

24. 2.16.5.

25. Prins, "The Image of God in Adam and the Restoration of Man in Jesus Christ," 43.

26. Calvin hints at this possibility in *Comm.* John 17:22.

27. See, in particular, N. T. Wright, *Jesus and the Victory of God* (Minneapolis: Fortress, 1996), 85.

28. Cf. Günter Thomas, "Resurrection to New Life: Pneumatological Implications of the Eschatological Transition," in *Resurrection: Theological and Scientific Assessments*, ed. Ted Peters, Robert John Russell, and Michael Welker (Grand Rapids: Eerdmans, 2002), 270.

in space, to have its own dimensions and its own shape."[29] The problem with the advocates of Christ's ubiquity in the Lord's Supper, Calvin insists, is that they wish to "make a spirit out of Christ's flesh." Yet, what stood "at the right hand of the Father" was not a "specter" but the concrete body of Christ.[30] To insist on the integrity of Christ's corporeality in heaven, then, was, for Calvin, to preserve the particularity of all human bodies.[31]

A Body Marked by Continuity and Discontinuity

Third, Christ's body is marked by continuity and discontinuity. In the Gospels, Christ's wounds serve as a locus of continuity between his crucified body and his resurrected body. According to John's Gospel, Jesus takes the initiative to exhibit his wounds, "his hands and his side" (John 20:20). This act comes not in response to doubt but rather to the word of "peace" (John 20:19); it is a positive act, not a conciliatory one; a commendation of his body, not a concession to weak faith. When Thomas realizes that he has missed out on this exchange, he demands the same affirmative witness.[32] "Believing" in Jesus is, for John, believing in something visceral, somatic (John 20:27), and to recall Christ's wounds is a way for the church to remember Christ rightly.[33] More strongly even, it is this wounded body that constitutes the identity of the Second Person of the Trinity. Following a similar exchange in the Lukan narrative (Luke 24:38–40), Jesus requests of his disciples something to eat. Calvin supposes that Jesus's postresurrection act of eating functioned as pantomimed acts of condescension.[34] The disciples' weak faith required, Calvin believed, what could only be regarded as a sign of corruption in the present age.[35] To be free from the need for food, conversely, pointed to a discontinuity in Jesus's body.

---

29. 4.17.29. "But how weak and fragile that hope would be, if this very flesh of ours had not been truly raised in Christ, and had not entered into the Kingdom of Heaven!"

30. 4.17.29. Cf. *Comm.* Acts 1:9.

31. 4.17.12–19. Cf. David H. Kelsey, "Human Being," in *Christian Theology: An Introduction to Its Traditions and Tasks*, ed. P. Hodgson and Robert King (London: SPCK, 1998), 144.

32. On this point, see Marianne Meye Thompson, *The God of the Gospel of John* (Grand Rapids: Eerdmans, 2001), 115.

33. Thomas, "Resurrection to New Life," 263–64.

34. *Comm.* Luke 24:42; *Comm.* Matt. 22:30.

35. Cf. *Psychopannychia*, 451, where Calvin describes food, drink, and sleep as "signs of corruption" and a kind of defect of the soul in the present age. See also *Comm.* 1 Cor. 15:44.

However, as Joel Green argues, these "earthy" eating episodes mark a significant point of continuity in the person of Jesus. He is "not only capable of eating, but actually initiates a resumption of the table fellowship that had characterized Jesus's ministry in Galilee and en route to Jerusalem. Hence, the post-resurrection persistence of Jesus's identity is established, first, with reference to his physicality and, second, with reference to relationality and mission."[36] Yet, in Jesus's receiving the gift of a *sōma pneumatikon* (1 Cor. 15:44; see also Rom. 8:11, 23), this new body exists in sharp discontinuity with the body that bore the "likeness of sinful flesh" (Rom. 8:3). While the substance of his body remained the same, Calvin writes, Christ's resurrected body possessed a different, "quickened" quality.[37] The Spirit fashions for Christ an incorruptible body, "a body for the realm of the Spirit,"[38] that is not simply alive, a *nephesh hayah*, but "hyperalive, excessively alive," as Jeremy Begbie describes it.[39] And it is such a body, "animated and controlled by the Holy Spirit," that the faithful can anticipate in their incorporation in Christ's glorified life.[40]

A Broken Body

Fourth, in Christ we discover the true extent of the body's brokenness. Calvin writes, "Clothed with our flesh [Christ] vanquished death and sin together that the victory and triumph might be ours. He offered as a sacrifice the flesh he received from us, that he might wipe out our guilt by his act of expiation and appease the Father's righteous wrath."[41] In Christ the present body is seen to be a "body of death." It is not simply a body caught up in the forces of entropy; instead, it is categorically a "body of

36. Green, *Body, Soul, and Human Life*, 168.

37. *Comm.* 1 Cor. 15:39; 3.25.3; *Comm.* 1 Pet. 3:18; *Comm.* Rom. 1:4 and 8:11; *Comm.* Eph. 1:19–20.

38. Anthony C. Thiselton, *The First Epistle to the Corinthians: A Commentary on the Greek Text*, NIGTC (Grand Rapids: Eerdmans, 2000), 1276–81. See also Alan G. Padgett, "The Body in Resurrection: Science and Scripture on the 'Spiritual Body' (1 Cor 15:35–58)," *Word and World* 22 (2002): 155–63.

39. Jeremy S. Begbie, "Looking to the Future: A Hopeful Subversion," in *For the Beauty of the Church: Casting a Vision for the Arts*, ed. W. David O. Taylor (Grand Rapids: Baker Books, 2010), 198n6.

40. Thiselton, *The Holy Spirit*, 80.

41. 2.12.3.

sin," under the judgment of sin. This is the good news, Calvin maintains, because it is a form of truth-telling that human self-deception desperately requires. Ours is a body marked by infirmity (and therefore vulnerable to disease and entropy) as well as stained by sin (and therefore susceptible to rebellious and disordered passions). For Calvin, a proper Christology requires a sober realism about the effects of sin on the body. This truth is liberating, rather than depressing.

Although Calvin's rhetoric may degenerate into an obsession with the frail and fallen quality of creaturely life, we need to remember that there is a good purpose to this rhetoric. "Calvin's emphasis on creaturely frailty and sin," Canlis explains, "is not to stress the distance from God but to stress that it is God who takes the initiative with us—not we with him."[42] In Christ's initiative, to become "flesh from our flesh, bones from our bones,"[43] we discover not only the comprehensive corruption of the body but also its destiny to be hale and holy, capable of fellowship with God.[44] This is the good news. In assuming a body "in the likeness of sinful flesh," Calvin argues, Christ thereby experiences our common infirmities "in order that He might be more inclined to sympathy."[45] In Christ, then, we discover the one who in the flesh empathizes with weak and bewildered bodies, which groan for their full redemption (Rom. 8:23).[46]

The only way that other human bodies can attain this Christomorphic telos is by being made a member of the body of Christ, which is possible only by the Holy Spirit.[47]

The Human Body Pneumatologically Constituted

The double entendre expressed in the phrase "the body of Christ" points to the somatic and ecclesial nature of the redemptive work that the Spirit of Christ accomplishes in God's people. The human body in its most fundamental sense is both a *corpus Christi* and a *corpus ecclesiasticus*: a body

---

42. Canlis, *Calvin's Ladder*, 64–65.

43. 2.12.2.

44. Cf. Wendell Berry, "The Body and the Earth," in *The Art of the Commonplace: The Agrarian Essays of Wendell Berry* (Berkeley, CA: Counterpoint Press, 2002), 98–99.

45. *Comm.* Rom. 8:3. See also *Comm.* 1 Cor. 15:47.

46. 4.17.9; cf. *Comm.* John 11:33–35: Christ clings to his people, Calvin writes, "wholly in spirit and body."

47. *Comm.* Eph. 3:17.

of Christ and an ecclesial body.[48] In Pauline terms, "there is no crucified One (Rom. 7:4) or exalted One (Phil. 3:21) without his body, just as conversely participation in the body of Christ is not imaginable without the glorification of God in the σῶμα of the believer."[49] How does the Holy Spirit enable human bodies to become partakers of Christ's body and thereby achieve their God-given end?

An Incorporated Body

First, the Scriptures make clear that there is no salvation apart from the physical body of Christ, crucified and resurrected, nor apart from the body of Christ that is his church, which in both cases is a gift of the Holy Spirit.[50] To be "in Christ" is to be "with Christ," which in turn is to be integrated into the body of Christ in both senses.[51] This idea is especially vivid in Calvin's sacramental writings. To partake of Christ's flesh, he maintains, is to experience the infusion of Christ's life into us, "as if it penetrated into our bones and marrow."[52] This flesh of Christ is effective now: "Such, I say, is the corporeal presence which the nature of the sacrament requires, and which we say is here displayed in such power and efficacy, that it not only gives our minds undoubted assurance of eternal life, but also secures the immortality of our flesh, since it is now quickened by his immortal flesh, and in a manner shines in his immortality."[53]

In the quickening of the human body, which occurs when the redeemed partake of the eucharistic elements, a material thing feeds them with the material body of Christ by the Spirit's power.[54] "[Christ] shows that in his humanity there also dwells fullness of life, so that whoever has partaken of his flesh and blood may at the same time enjoy participation

---

48. This phrase intentionally plays off of Robert W. Jenson's language from his essay "*Anima Ecclesiastica*," in *God and Human Dignity*, ed. R. Kendall Soulen and Linda Woodhead (Grand Rapids: Eerdmans, 2006), 59–71.

49. Schnelle, *The Human Condition*, 59.

50. Steven R. Guthrie, *Creator Spirit: The Holy Spirit and the Art of Becoming Human* (Grand Rapids: Baker Academic, 2011), 69.

51. Jewett, *Paul's Anthropological Terms*, 301. Canlis, *Calvin's Ladder*, 117.

52. 4.17.10. See also *Comm.* Luke 24; *Comm.* 1 Cor. 10:16; *Comm.* John 6:51.

53. 4.17.32, Beveridge translation.

54. Cf. Davis, "Not 'Hidden and Far Off,'" 415.

in life. . . . In like manner, the flesh of Christ is like a rich and inexhaustible fountain that pours into us the life springing forth from the Godhead into itself."[55] This is a Spirit-ual work, Calvin insists.[56] The faithful partake of the "proper substance" of the body of Christ by way of the "secret and miraculous power of God," that is, the Holy Spirit, which is another way of saying, for Calvin, a "spiritual" participation.[57] Always this partaking of Christ's flesh is for the sake of communion.[58]

Not only is the physical body of Christ necessary for the faithful, so too is their incorporation into the church, the embodied presence of Christ in the world. "By the grace and power of the same Spirit," Calvin writes, "we are made [Christ's] members, to keep us under himself and in turn to possess him."[59] Apart from our participation in the "spiritual and mystical body of Christ,"[60] it is impossible to experience "any forgiveness of sins or any salvation."[61] Calvin adds that Paul "takes it for granted that in the person of Christ there had been exhibited a specimen of the power which belongs to the whole body of the Church."[62] To be in Christ is to be in Christ's body: this too is a Spirit-ual work. "Though every one of us is said to be the temple of God and is so described, yet all must be united together in one, and joined together by mutual love, so that one temple may be made of us all. Since it is true that each one is a temple in which

55. 4.17.9. Canlis, *Calvin's Ladder*, 102, points to a possible weakness in Calvin's sacramental theology here, where the language of "channel" can give the impression that God acts *through* a man, not *as* a man.

56. 3.1.2; cf. 3.25.3. The pneumatological source of life in Christ's flesh is less explicit in *Comm.* John 6:51.

57. "Short Treatise on the Lord's Supper," in *Tracts and Treatises*, 2:198. *Comm.* Rom. 6:5, "In spiritual ingrafting . . . we not only derive the strength and sap of the life which flows from Christ, but we also pass from our own nature into His. The apostle desired to point quite simply to the efficacy of the death of Christ, which manifested itself in putting to death our flesh, and also the efficacy of His resurrection in renewing within us the better nature of the Spirit."

58. In *Comm.* John 6:35, commenting on the meaning of the phrase "I am the bread of life," Calvin writes, "For faith does not look at Christ merely from afar, but embraces Him, that He may become ours and dwell in us. It causes us to be united in His body, to have life in common with Him and, in short, to be one with Him."

59. 3.1.3. *Comm.* John 7:38, "For the chief glory of Christ's Kingdom is that He governs the Church by His Spirit."

60. *Comm.* 1 Cor. 12:12.

61. 4.1.4. For Calvin there is no enjoyment of "God's fatherly favor" apart from participation in the visible church, or "mother."

62. *Comm.* Rom. 8:11.

God dwells by His Spirit, so all ought to be so fitted together, that they may form the structure of one universal temple."[63]

A Body as Temple

Second, the human body achieves its telos by conducting itself as a "temple of the Holy Spirit." As with the phrase "body of Christ," this phrase also carries a double sense. The first is corporate; the second is corporeal. In 1 Corinthians 3:16 Paul asks the believers, "Do you not know that you are the temple of God and that the Spirit of God dwells in you?" The "you" here is plural. What once described the physical Jerusalem temple now describes the people of God: they are an *embodied* counternarrative to the pagan temples that characterized the city of Corinth. Calvin, rightly, I believe, contends that the *kai* should be translated "because" rather than "and."[64] The believers are the temple of God precisely because the Spirit dwells in them. Like a human body, the community of Christ is constituted by the Holy Spirit in order that they might be many-in-one. Paul argues a similar line of thought in 1 Corinthians 6:19: "Do you not know that your body is a temple of the Holy Spirit who is in you?" (once again, plural "you[r]"). The corporate is now seen to be inseparable from the corporeal. The faithful, Calvin writes, are united to Christ not only in "spirit" but also in "flesh": "Christ is so joined to us, and we to Him, that we are united in one body with Him."[65] The faithful are, quite literally, "flesh of his flesh," which is what Paul has in mind when he describes the union that the Spirit accomplishes between human bodies, the body of Christ, and the church as the body of Christ.

The ramifications of this reality are several. For one, as a temple of the Spirit, the body now experiences the power of the age to come. The Spirit *today* infuses the life of the age to come in bodies that paradoxically (mysteriously?) are subject to the decay of a fallen cosmos. To be members of Christ's body, "of his bones and of his flesh," as Calvin argues, means that we belong to another, not ourselves.[66] Because the human body is Christ's, it ought to be consecrated to Christ. And because of the

63. *Comm.* 1 Pet. 2:5.
64. *Comm.* 1 Cor. 3:16.
65. *Comm.* 1 Cor. 6:15.
66. *Comm.* Eph. 5:30.

Spirit who indwells it, the human body belongs to the realm of Christ's resurrected body and therefore again should be consecrated in anticipation of its full participation in that realm. Put otherwise, to the extent that the eschatological Spirit infuses the human body with a taste of the age to come, so the faithful are to behave corporeally, "in Christ," *as if* they were already citizens of the New Jerusalem.[67] Calvin comments: "With the same end in view [Paul] asserted in verse 19 that not only our souls, but also our bodies are temples of the Holy Spirit, so that we may be under no delusions about acquitting ourselves well towards Him, for we can only do that when we yield ourselves to His service, wholly and completely, so that He may also direct the outward actions of our lives by His Word."[68]

While Calvin may muddle things by needlessly stressing the fact that the soul is a temple—when Paul nowhere makes that point, nor need he under the circumstances—and by using the language of "the filth of the earth" to describe what Paul would more likely identify technically as rebellious flesh, still Calvin rightly identifies the place of the human body in the economy of God as belonging to Jesus as a gift of the Father through the Spirit, rather than as a "property" that we "own" to do with as we please.

A Pneumatologically Particular Body

Third, the Holy Spirit gives the gift of particularity to human bodies. In the same way that the Spirit particularizes Jesus's body, so the Spirit particularizes all human bodies.[69] Calvin underscores the ministry of the Spirit in Jesus's life in his comment on John 3:34: "And indeed it is right that the Spirit should dwell in Him without measure, that we may all draw from His fullness, as we have seen. . . . The Father has poured out upon

---

67. Again Canlis, *Calvin's Ladder*, 242, puts her finger on the theological dilemma: "Calvin failed to see how our participation in the ascended Christ, the center of the new creation, brings our present materiality into this new eschatological reality. The Ascension does not merely locate Christ in heaven; rather, the risen, *human* Jesus also sends his Spirit to accomplish in creation what was accomplished first in him. By doing so, he transforms the physical from serving as a barrier to participation into becoming the very means by which we enjoy Christ in the Spirit."

68. *Comm.* 1 Cor. 6:20.

69. Adriana Destro and Mauro Pesce, "Self, Identity, and Body in Paul and John," in *Self, Soul, and Body in Religious Experience*, ed. Albert I. Baumgarten, J. Assmann, and G. G. Stroumsa, SHR 78 (Leiden: Brill, 1998), 192–93.

[Christ] an unlimited wealth of His Spirit."[70] Christ was sinless at birth not because of his divine nature but "because he was sanctified by the Spirit."[71] It is the Spirit who empowers Jesus to accomplish the mission of the Father, but it is also Jesus who gives the Spirit to his disciples so that they too, renewed by that same Spirit, may accomplish the Father's mission. "For the fullness of the Spirit was poured out upon Him so that He might bestow it upon each one in a definite measure."[72] This gift of the Spirit is for the sake ultimately of communion. Canlis helpfully summarizes: "Participation is nuanced with communion, for the Spirit acts to affirm creation's particularity and freedom even as it is shepherded toward its *telos* of Trinitarian communion."[73]

The Spirit is active at every point of Jesus's life: overshadowing Jesus at his birth (Luke 1:35), moving Simeon to visit the Christ child in the temple (Luke 2:27), descending upon Jesus at his baptism (Mark 1:10), driving him into the desert to be tempted (Matt. 4:1), empowering his teaching (Luke 4:18; John 3:34), as well as his works of healing and exorcism (Matt. 12:28; Luke 4:14–21), superintending his death (1 Pet. 3:18), raising him from the dead (Rom. 1:4; 8:11; cf. 1 Cor. 15:42–49), and partnering with him in the summons of the heavenly bride of Christ (Rev. 22:17).[74] At Pentecost, Jesus gives instructions to his apostles *by* the Holy Spirit (Acts 1:2). At Christ's ascension a cloud hides him from his disciples' sight (Acts 1:9). This cloud recalls the cloud that enveloped (*epeskiazen*) Jesus at his transfiguration (Luke 9:34), an event that uses the same language of Luke 1:35, which states that the Spirit will envelope (*episkiasei*) Mary at her conception.[75] The Spirit, then, is the one who enables Jesus not only to be a particular person but also to possess a particular body.[76] The particularity of all human bodies is derivative of the particular body that Jesus enjoys on account of the Spirit's work.

70. See also *Comm.* 1 Cor. 15:46–47 and *Comm.* Rom. 6:9.
71. 2.13.4.
72. *Comm.* John 20:22.
73. Canlis, *Calvin's Ladder*, 60. Cf. *Comm.* 1 Cor. 15:45.
74. Cf. Eugene J. Rogers, *After the Spirit: A Constructive Pneumatology from Resources outside the Modern West* (Grand Rapids: Eerdmans, 2005), 75–208.
75. Rogers, *After the Spirit*, 54: "In the New Testament, the Spirit leads, follows, or accompanies the Son into the most intimate places: not, instructively, into his 'mind' or 'heart,' but into much messier places, paradigms of the physical: the womb, the wilderness, the garden, the grave."
76. Cf. Gunton, *The One, the Three, and the Many*, 198–204.

Again: A Body Marked by Continuity and Discontinuity

Fourth, like Christ, the bodies of the faithful experience both continuity and discontinuity. John Barclay observes that Paul's use of the term *pneumatikos* "describes people not through analysis of their human constitution but in relation to their new status as graced by the Spirit of God."[77] *Pneumatikos* in Pauline Christianity, that is, designates an eschatological rather than an anthropological reality, and thus a *sōma pneumatikos* points to an eschatological tension for the Christian. Insofar as they will receive a "Spirit-ual body" to replace their *sōma psychikon*, the redeemed shall enjoy a radically different bodily life in the age to come. But inasmuch as the human body is a temple of the Holy Spirit, the faithful are to live now in continuous relationship to the final fulfillment of God for the human body.[78] For this reason Calvin emphasizes the Pauline requirement for believers to "present" their members to righteousness (Rom. 6:13), to "offer" their bodies as living sacrifices (Rom. 12:1), and to "glorify" God with their bodies (1 Cor. 6:20). Even though the physical body suffers the rot and decay caused by entropic forces, it nonetheless remains, even till death, the site for holiness to be played out in all spheres of life.[79]

One implication of this eschatological tension is the way in which bodily freedom is regarded. Put simply, the renewing work of the Spirit implies for the physical body a freedom *from* and a freedom *for*. Reworking Karl Barth's language, while God frees the body to "be itself," this freedom is to be seen as a bounded rather than an unbounded freedom.[80] It is a freedom to be a certain kind of body, not any kind of body. It is to be a body "within its limits": limits to its possibilities, capacities, development, and place.[81] The human body is also free, not when it lives as it

---

77. John M. G. Barclay, "Πνευματικός in the Social Dialect of Pauline Christianity," in *The Holy Spirit and Christian Origins: Essays in Honor of James D. G. Dunn*, ed. Graham N. Stanton, Bruce W. Longenecker, and Stephen C. Barton (Grand Rapids: Eerdmans, 2004), 161.

78. On this point, see Oberman, "The Pursuit of Happiness," 24.

79. The fact that our bodies are betrayed by advanced age, regularly disappoint us, unexpectedly fall ill, repeatedly break down, or fail to live up to our expectations, as Calvin knew quite well, is no reason for the Christian to yield to despair or to acts of bodily sabotage.

80. Barth, *Church Dogmatics*, IV/4:22 (hereafter *CD*).

81. Barth, *CD* III/3:87.

pleases, but when it lives before the face of God.[82] To be just this kind of physical body is Christ's glory and the creature's too.[83] "It has freedom to experience and accomplish that which is proper to it, to do that which it can do, and to be satisfied."[84] We are in good hands, after all.[85] God preserves the creature to live fully *in* God, *for* God, and thus also fully *for* others rather than in the imprisoned walls of a solipsistic pursuit of "self-realization." What preserves the creature in this freedom? For both Barth and Calvin, the answer is the Holy Spirit, for it is the Spirit who gifts the faithful with a freedom to offer their bodies as unceasing living sacrifices.

A Mortified and Vivified Body

Fifth, the Spirit is the one who gives the faithful power to mortify their rebellious flesh and to live in their bodies in Christlike fashion. The remedy for the debilitating frailty and corruption that mark human bodies is the empowering presence of the Spirit. Calvin highlights this point repeatedly. The Spirit corrects "the inordinate desires of the flesh,"[86] which include all "weaknesses" that characterize the "infirmity of our nature and all the outward signs of humiliation."[87] Not only does the Spirit empower the faithful, the Spirit also suffers with them. "The Spirit itself takes part of the burden which oppresses our weakness, and not only gives us help and succor but lifts us up, as though it itself underwent the burden with us."[88] The Spirit trains all bodily desires, enabling the faithful to "steadfastly persevere in choosing what is good."[89] Calvin stresses that the mortifying and vivifying work of the Spirit obtains a gradual sanctification for the faithful. While gradual, it is nonetheless a certain renewal of the believer.[90] "This restoration does not take place in one moment or one

---

82. Barth, *CD* III/3:92.

83. Barth, *CD* III/3:149, 168.

84. Barth, *CD* III/3:185.

85. Barth, *CD* III/3:123, 130, 132.

86. *Comm.* Rom. 8:2; see also his comments on Rom. 6:6 and 8:13.

87. *Comm.* 2 Cor. 12:10.

88. *Comm.* Rom. 8:26.

89. 3.10.1; *Comm.* 2 Cor. 5:5.

90. *Comm.* Rom. 8:11: "[Paul] is not speaking of the last resurrection . . . but of the continual operation of the Spirit, by which He gradually mortifies the remains of the flesh and renews in us the heavenly life." Cf. *Comm.* John 17:17.

day or one year; but through continual and sometimes even slow advance God wipes out in his elect the corruptions of the flesh, cleanses them of guilt, consecrates them to himself as temples renewing all their minds to true purity that they may practice repentance throughout their lives and know that this warfare will end only at death."[91]

As confident as Calvin is about the Spirit's effective work in the believer, it is curious that this kind of language fails to factor in any kind of substantial way in his worries over the disordered passions of the body in a liturgical context. A proper pneumatology would need to retain a confidence in the sanctifying power of the Spirit in all domains of Christian life, including the liturgical. In his anxiety about bodily temptations in worship, Calvin misses out on an opportunity to commend the reordering power of the Spirit in this central context for Spirit-ual formation.[92]

A Christomorphic Body

Sixth, the fundamental thrust of the New Testament is to understand the "spiritual" work of God as the work of the Spirit to conform the whole human person to the life of Christ. This is a comprehensive reality. No sphere of life is left untouched by the Spirit-ual work of God. Calvin summarizes the Christian life as follows:

> Ever since [Christ] engrafted us into his body, we must take especial care not to disfigure ourselves, who are his members, with any spot or blemish. Ever since Christ himself, who is our Head, ascended into heaven, it behooves us, having laid aside love of earthly things, wholeheartedly to aspire heavenward. Ever since the Holy Spirit dedicated us as temples to God, we must take care that God's glory shine through us, and must not commit anything to defile ourselves with the filthiness of sin. Ever since both our souls and bodies were destined for heavenly incorruption and an unfading crown, we ought to strive manfully to keep them pure and uncorrupted until the Day of the Lord. These, I say, are the most auspicious foundations upon which to establish one's life.[93]

91. 3.3.9. Cf. *Comm.* Rom. 8:1; *Comm.* John 7:38.
92. Cf. Canlis, *Calvin's Ladder*, 170.
93. 3.6.3.

For Calvin, both internal and external dimensions of human life fall under the governance of the Holy Spirit. This becomes especially clear in his anti-Nicodemite writings.[94] Human beings owe God a dual honor, "which is comprised of the spiritual service of the heart, and of external adoration."[95] Because "the Lord has rescued our body and soul from death, he has secured the one as well as the other, in order to be their master and ruler. Therefore, after both body and soul in man have been consecrated and dedicated to God, it is necessary that his glory shine forth just as much in one as it does in the other."[96] While true "religion and sanctity" do not hinge on external matters, there is still value in an external service, "adoring God with the eyes, hands, or feet," which functions as "an appendage and accessory of spiritual service."[97]

The accent in Calvin's use of the term "spiritual" clearly falls on the person of the Spirit.[98] At its best, as Canlis observes, "Calvin saw the Spirit's work as that of transposition: taking what was the realm of physicality and moving it to the Trinity's domain."[99] The material realm follows the gravitational pull of the Spirit's work to bring all things into fellowship with God. There is never *mere* materiality; it is materiality always *headed somewhere*. Yet, at its worst, in Calvin, the physical body fails to receive a thoroughgoing pneumatological treatment. And because Calvin regards public worship as first and foremost a set of exercises of the interior life, the physical exercises that he commends remain in subordinate relation to the so-called soulish ones. Canlis again captures the problem well: "Calvin's great strength lay in his rich and consistent emphasis on the necessity of human participation in Christ. His weakness lay in his inability (or polemical reticence?) to reflect on the fittingness of the material realm for just such a relation. This reticence resulted in a suspicion of material things as unable to bear the weight of spiritual reality. That the Spirit does

94. See, in particular, Calvin's letter of 1537 to his fellow believers in France, "On Shunning the Unlawful Rites of the Ungodly and Preserving the Purity of the Christian Religion," in *Tracts and Treatises*, 3:359–411, esp. 372–73.

95. *CO* 24:387; cited in Eire, *War against the Idols*, 256, 258. See also *CO* 11:328.

96. In Calvin's *Petit Traicté, CO* 6:580, cited in Eire, *War against the Idols*, 258.

97. *Response à un Holandois, CO* 9:597, cited in Eire, *War against the Idols*, 259.

98. Philip W. Butin repeatedly makes this point in his writings on Calvin. See, for example, his "Constructive Iconoclasm"; "John Calvin's Humanist Image of Popular Late-Medieval Piety and Its Contribution to Reformed Worship," *Calvin Theological Journal* 29 (1994): 419–31; and *Revelation, Redemption, and Response: Calvin's Trinitarian Understanding of the Divine-Human Relationship* (New York: Oxford University Press, 1994), esp. chap. 6.

99. Canlis, *Calvin's Ladder*, 116.

not lead us 'up and away' to God but creates in material things God's divine reality is something from which Calvin tends to shy away."[100]

The Human Body Liturgically Constituted

Calvin's hesitations notwithstanding, one of the central places where the faithful learn how to view their bodies rightly and to live a bodily righteous life is in public worship. It is here that the faithful learn what it means to disciple the human body. This too is a work of the Two Hands of God. In what way, then, does the church's liturgical context contribute to the attainment of the physical body's telos?

An Ecclesially Incorporated Body

First, to worship well corporeally requires that the faithful worship well corporately. Calvin asserts: "Whoever refused to pray in the holy assembly of the godly knows not what it is to pray individually, or in a secret spot, or at home."[101] Public worship is a central place for the believer's formation. Apart from this exercise of right praise, the conditions in which right confession might take place are jeopardized.[102] Indeed, the "whole substance of Christianity" consists firstly in "the mode in which God is duly worshipped."[103] Central to right worship is, as always, communion with God. As Calvin comments on Psalm 24:7, "What is the design of the preaching of the word, the sacraments, the holy assemblies, and the whole external government of the church, but that we may be united to God?" This communion is "through Christ," where all "ceremonies, to be exercises of piety, ought to lead us straight to Christ."[104]

---

100. Canlis, *Calvin's Ladder*, 170. Canlis adds that Calvin's "mistrust of the physical realm left him tongue-tied over its *downward* implications for the material realm (whether in the form of the sacraments, the church, or elements of our humanity)" (168; emphasis original).

101. 3.20.29.

102. *De Fugiendis, CO* 5:244: "Genuine piety begets genuine confession."

103. "The Necessity of Reforming the Church," 126. In his reply to Sadoleto, *CO* 5:392, Calvin adds, "Nothing is more dangerous to our salvation than a twisted and perverse worship of God."

104. 4.10.29; cf. *Comm.* 1 Pet. 2:5. See also Calvin's "Catechism of the Church of Geneva," 85.

While Calvin persists in seeing "the infirmities of our flesh" as an impediment to the ability of external aids to lift the faithful up "even to God," the biblical narrative keeps Calvin returning to the importance of corporeal practices in corporate worship.[105] In fact, one could go so far as to argue, on Calvinian terms, that to know what a physical body is requires participation in the body of the Christ, where public worship functions as a fundamental orientation for this embodied life in Christ. If the human body discovers its right orientation by being conformed to the (individual) body of Christ, then the (church) body of Christ in worship becomes a primary locus where physical bodies are rightly formed.

A Disciplined Body

Second, the primary corporeal activities of public worship include training or discipling of the human body. Not only do the faithful learn what bodies are for through the practices of worship, it is also through the members of the church that the faithful receive the help to live rightly in their own bodies. Ministries of singing, prayer, healing, counseling, friendship, and community, among others, are key here. Calvin offers this commendation of the sacraments: "The purpose of the mysteries [i.e., the sacraments] is to give us practice in devotion and love."[106] "The prayers," he continues, "also ought to be effective for doing all those things. Besides all this, the Lord works efficaciously by His Spirit, because He does not want the things which He has appointed to be fruitless," but instead that all would "be made better men as a result of them."[107] To offer up our bodies is, for Calvin, to offer "not only our skin and bones, but the totality of which we are composed."[108] It is the whole human person, in all liturgical activities, which is to be offered as a living sacrifice. A sacrifice, significantly, is something that is not only used but also used up, yet here in public worship the body remains living, not dead. And in being consumed by the Spirit, it becomes even more alive with the life of Christ, not diminished.[109]

Training the faithful, in practical terms, takes place through physical

105. *Comm.* Ps. 24.
106. Cf. *Comm.* Eph. 4:16.
107. *Comm.* 1 Cor. 11:17.
108. *Comm.* Rom. 12:1.
109. See Rom. 12:1 and 2 Cor. 4:10, 13; 1 Cor. 9:24–27; 1 Thess. 5:23.

gestures and movements such as kneeling, lifting holy hands, passing the kiss of peace, standing, bowing, walking, and such. For Calvin, however, only those physical expressions that the New Testament commands or exhibits in practice are worthy of commendation.[110] To include only the descriptive instances that appear in the New Testament, however, is to underestimate the power of the whole body, in a range of postures and actions, to form the whole person. In a sense Calvin endows the body with too anemic a capacity to form the soul. Though the body bears the sparks of God's glory, for Calvin it does not possess the same constitutive capacity as the heart or the mind. Against Calvin's worries over the body's errant passions, I argue that the body positively contributes to the Spirit's work of sanctification, namely, to counter the idols of the mind, the forgetfulness of memories, a will that is bent against God, the disordered affections, and the distorted passions of the body itself. The body is hereby invited to participate in the Spirit's work to reorder the human body to Christ's order, animating it with new life, for the sake of *this* body's worship in *this* local body of Christ.[111]

An Exercised Body

Third, the aim of public worship ought to be the discipleship of the whole human person through a set of holistic "exercises." In light of their adoption by the Spirit and reception of Christ's grace, as Calvin comments on 1 Timothy 2:8, Paul invites the church to pray with the faithful lifting their hands. Liturgical activities, for Calvin, are a logical function of theological realities. He writes: "We should learn therefore that this practice is in keeping with true godliness, provided that the truth it represents also accompanies it; firstly, knowing that God is to be sought in heaven, we should form no earthly or carnal conception of Him, also that we should lay aside fleshly affections so that nothing may prevent our hearts from rising above this world."[112]

While idolaters shut God up in wood or stone, and hypocrites offer something with their bodies that contradicts the condition of their hearts,

110. Cf. Old, "John Calvin and the Prophetic Critique of Worship," 82.

111. Steven R. Guthrie, "Temples of the Spirit: Worship as Embodied Performance," in *Faithful Performances: Enacting Christian Tradition*, ed. Trevor A. Hart and Steven R. Guthrie (Aldershot, UK: Ashgate, 2007), 104.

112. *Comm.* 1 Tim. 2:8.

the faithful are to offer their bodies to God with integrity.[113] When done in this way, such practices strengthen the often-weak soul.[114] They must never, of course, become attempts to manipulate God, nor should they be practiced in "heart-less" fashion. Yet, when the Christian sings, this activity serves to exercise "the mind in thinking of God and keeps it attentive—unstable and variable as it is, and readily relaxed and diverted in different directions, unless it be supported by various helps."[115] The faithful are also to lift their hands.[116] In doing so, the Christian indicates his or her desire to be "diligent in the exercise" of supplication and thanksgiving.[117] Kneeling is also recommended, though not necessarily commanded. Calvin summarizes his liturgical ethos as follows:

> But because [God] did not will in outward discipline and ceremonies to prescribe in detail what we ought to do (because he foresaw that this depended upon the state of the times, and he did not deem one form suitable for all ages), here we must take refuge in those general rules which he has given, that whatever the necessity of the church will require for order and decorum should be tested against these. Lastly, because he has taught nothing specifically, and because these things are not necessary to salvation, and for the upbuilding of the church ought to be variously accommodated to the customs of each nation and age, it will be fitting . . . to change and abrogate traditional practices and to establish new ones. Indeed, I admit that we ought not to charge into innovation rashly, suddenly, for insufficient cause. *But love will best judge what may hurt or edify; and if we let love be our guide, all will be safe.*[118]

The pastoral wisdom exhibited in this remarkable statement will eventually make it possible for both minimalist and expansive uses of the human body in the liturgy to appear in the Reformed tradition. Yet what is missing in his recommendations for physical expression in worship is

---

113. Calvin stresses the holistic aspect of sanctification in *Comm.* Rom. 6:11.

114. Cf. Old, "John Calvin and the Prophetic Critique of Worship," 78. In 3.20.29 Calvin notes that Christ's example of the regular exercise of prayer serves to remind human beings how "unsteady" their minds are.

115. 3.20.31.

116. 3.20.16.

117. *Comm.* Ps. 63:4.

118. 4.10.30, emphasis added.

the kind of expressly christological and pneumatological rendering of bodily activities that appear in his 1 Timothy comments. The terms on which he construes "spiritual" worship make it nearly impossible for him to read activities like kneeling or hand-raising as *proper human activities* in response to God's nature. Physical aids to worship, for Calvin, are principally coordinated to the needs of the soul. All too rarely are they tied to the constitutive work of Christ and the Spirit.

A Formative Body

Fourth, public worship is chiefly a matter not of self-expression but of formative expression. Just as Christian worship ought to make space for spontaneous expressions of prayer and praise, it ought also to encourage ritualized and symbolic expression. A ritualized form of expression will involve repeated activities, as Calvin observed, that are performed for the good of the body, regardless of one's temperament or the feelings of the moment.[119] A symbolic form of expression will take seriously the Christomorphic shape of all of worship, in which the physical body is invited to take part. In this sense we might say that Christians in corporate worship are *informed* in Christ, *transformed* by the Spirit, and *re-formed* by embodied practices, both free and *preformed*. To put the point in practical terms, the church does not do everything that could be done with the physical body in the context of public worship. While Christians may use their bodies in playful ways, perhaps by dancing during a song, they will not play sports with them. They will do only certain things with the body, some of them repeatedly, some occasionally. These things will remind them that they do not perceive their bodies rightly simply by moving them about throughout the week. They perceive them rightly by being gathered in their own *bodies*, as Christ's *Body*, around *Christ's* body.

A Worshiping Body

Fifth, in public worship the human body enters into creation's ongoing praise. If the human body is made from the *adamah*, the earthy stuff of creation, then it is not unreasonable, on Calvinian terms, to believe that

---

119. *Comm.* 1 Cor. 11:17.

it too participates in creation's ongoing praise. It too is, in fact, already at praise. It too will in some way reveal the invisible God through its tangible presence. It too will school the church in the "school of the beasts." It too will awaken in the heart of the faithful a delight in God through the beauty of its form and functions. It too, in some fashion, will be able to admonish the human heart concerning its ingratitude and pride in light of such divine munificence. It too, finally, will enact and summon the communion of believers to the praise of God. Whether the Christian acknowledges or cooperates with creation's praise is another matter. Humility would be required here, where the faithful are continually offered the opportunity to lift up their bodies *coram Deo,* while also learning how the human body might lead the faithful in a praise that resonates with the doxology of the entire cosmos.[120]

Conclusion

Reformed minister Richard Ray argues that Calvin's liturgical theology is intimately linked to an "eschatology of invisibility." In this view, a kind of bodily humility needs to be preserved in worship before a transcendent God.[121] If this chapter's analysis has been accurate, Ray's judgment is an overstatement of a more complex set of ideas. Calvin is at his most persuasive when he interprets the meaning of the physical body in light of Christ's body—in its physical, sacramental, and ecclesial senses. He similarly persuades when he traces out the logical implications of the body as a "temple of the Spirit." And when faced with what he regarded as the hypocritical conduct of the Nicodemite believers, Calvin brings body and soul into an intimate, mutually determinative relation. If a telos for the human body is discernable in Calvin's theology, it will point to both its beautiful order and its tragic disorder, both its hope in Christ's resurrected body and the power it obtains from the Holy Spirit to enable the church to live in faithful obedience to God.

The weakness of Calvin's thinking involves a failure to reckon more comprehensively with the body's *Spirit*-ual condition, a tendency to indulge in rhetoric (such as "prison of the body") that pulls the body closer

---

120. See Gunton, *The Triune Creator,* 200.

121. Richard A. Ray, "John Calvin on Theatrical Trifles in Worship," in *Calvin Studies VI,* ed. John H. Leith (Davidson, NC: Colloquium on Calvin Studies, 1992), 108.

toward the sorts of problematic Platonic thinking that he himself wished to avoid, and a proclivity to restrict himself to the express examples of embodied worship in the New Testament rather than hewing closely to his christological reading of the human body, which, in turn, would open up a wide range of liturgically fitting bodily postures and expressions. When, in the following chapter, we consider the material condition of public worship, here too we discover a tension in Calvin between the more general language of "spirit" and the more specific language of the Holy Spirit to enable material things to bear Christ's glory. Here too we discover that "spirit and truth" play a far more interesting role in both Scripture and Calvin's theology than we might at first glance suspect.

CHAPTER 8

The "Simple" Worship of God

In the name of a deeper spiritualism . . . Calvin's systematic removal of the regenerate Christian away from materialism, obscure complexity, and over-sensuous involvement in the earthly arts receives its seminal inspiration from a reading and interpretation of several key scriptural models.

Peter Auksi, *Christian Plain Style*

And here again it must be observed that truth is not contrasted to falsehood but to the outward addition of the figures; so that it is, as they say, the pure and simple substance of spiritual worship.

Calvin, *Comm.* John

In his exegesis of John 4:23–24, Calvin infers a mutually determinative relation between the ideas of "spiritual" and "simple" worship, both of which, he maintains, point to the reality that the church has left behind the "shadows" of Israel's worship. As I noted at the outset of this book, for Calvin, although God allows Israel to worship with musical instruments, a new-covenantal era requires a simple worship devoid of such "papist amusements." Calvin grants that Christians will have need of external aids to worship, but he insists that they be moderate and sober, in concord with the simplicity of Christ and his gospel.

Though the term "simplicity" (*haplotēs*) appears rarely in the New

Testament,[1] Calvin places the idea of simplicity at the center of his liturgical proposals, and similar to the tendencies that have been observed in preceding chapters, Calvin's emphasis on simple worship involves a diminished role for materiality in public worship.[2] How does Calvin arrive at his understanding of "simple" worship? And might there be trajectories in his theology that open up different possibilities for the material condition of worship? These two questions give shape to our present discussion.

The Polyvalence of "Simple" in Calvin

To understand why Calvin appealed to the notion of simplicity as a requirement for public worship, we need first to consider other uses to which he puts the idea. The term "simple" not only qualifies his convictions about musical instruments, it also describes his understanding of Jesus's speech habits, the priority of Paul's preaching, the Bible's rhetorical style, the requirements of doctrine, and the material and ceremonial shape of public worship. Especially noteworthy is Calvin's enlisting the language of simplicity to qualify his understanding of worship that occurs "in spirit and in truth." In the following section, I catalog Calvin's use of "simple" into three groups. In each of these groups, Calvin demonstrates a concern over things that might intrude upon the right worship of God.

Simple Doctrine

One arena where Calvin conscripts the language of simplicity is in relation to doctrine. Here the primary contrast stands between doctrine, or "the gospel" (biblically considered), and "human tradition" (pejoratively considered). Calvin's 1547 commentary on 2 Corinthians is pivotal. With Beza and Jerome, but against Erasmus, Calvin insists that the phrase *apo*

---

1. See Eph. 6:5; Col. 3:22; 2 Cor. 1:12; 11:3. Most English Bible translations render this Greek word "sincere" or "pure." NASB uses "simplicity" in 2 Cor. 11:3, while the KJV is one of the few translations to qualify Christ rather than the believer with the term. A different sense of the word appears in Rom. 12:8; 2 Cor. 8:2; 9:11, 13. A variant of the term appears in Matt. 6:22 and Luke 11:34.

2. Millet, "Art and Literature," 426, observes that the "art of simplicity" was paramount in all of Calvin's literary endeavors.

tēs haplotētos tēs eis ton Christon (11:3) should be translated "[that you may not be corrupted] from the simplicity that is in Christ." Calvin maintains that *simplicity* here should modify "Christ" rather than the Corinthian believers, whom Paul is addressing. What is being corrupted is the simplicity of Christ, not the simplicity of the Christian's devotion. The former points to the "pure simplicity of the gospel" or the "pure doctrine of Christ," which admits of "no foreign admixtures" or "profane and foreign contrivances."[3] Paul's fear for the Corinthian believers is that "they would turn aside little by little from the simplicity they had learnt" in the beginning of their faith.[4]

This basic conviction is played out in the rest of Calvin's writings. For the Pharisees and scribes, Calvin remarks, "the simple command of God" was insufficient. "It is quite clear that Christ was setting the word 'leaven' in opposition to the simple and pure Word of God." Appealing to 2 Corinthians 11:3, he argues that "faith is adulterated as soon as we are led away from the simplicity of Christ." The Father, furthermore, has appointed Christ to be the sole teacher of the church in order that Christ "might retain us in the simplicity of His Gospel." In his 1544 treatise "On the Necessity of Reforming the Church," Calvin urges Christians to a "simple and sincere obedience" to Christ. Similarly, in his "Confession of Faith," published nearly twenty years later, Calvin adds that "it is not for us to invent what to us seems good, or to follow what may have been devised in the brain of other men, but to confine ourselves simply to the purity of Scripture."[5]

Christ's style of speaking, Calvin believes, reflects and perhaps even establishes this characteristic of doctrinal simplicity. "For the preaching of Christ is bare and simple, therefore it ought not to be obscured by an overlying disguise of words." Indeed, it was for the sake of the uneducated and poor that Jesus displayed *une simplicité grande*. And what does one find in Scripture? "Complete simplicity"; in both manner and substance the Scriptures are "so simple that it seems to be only a doctrine for fools." This feature of Scripture emboldens Calvin "to fight [false] eloquence

3. *Comm.* 2 Cor. 11:3.
4. See Calvin's comments on Pss. 33 and 81. Against this reading, see Paul Barnett, *The Second Epistle to the Corinthians*, NICNT (Grand Rapids: Eerdmans, 1997), 496–502; Ralph P. Martin, *Second Corinthians*, WBC 40 (Waco, TX: Word Books, 1986), 333–38.
5. "Confession of Faith," 147. See also *Comm.* Matt. 15:2; *Comm.* Matt. 16:12; *Comm.* Col. 2:8; "On the Necessity of Reforming the Church," 148; "On Shunning the Unlawful Rites of the Ungodly," 371, 406; *Comm.* 1 Cor. 14:40.

with the simplicity of the gospel." What must be resisted, in every case, is the "outward brilliancy of words," the intoxication "with empty delights," "the tickling" of ears with jingles, or the attempt to cover up the cross of Christ with ostentation.[6]

Simple Ceremonies

What Calvin finds objectionable in "nonsimple" doctrine, he finds equally objectionable in "nonsimple" liturgical ceremonies. In this case Calvin posits a contrast between simple worship that arises out of an "inward sincerity of heart" and an excess of ceremonies that binds the conscience in an unconscionable fashion and that grounds true worship in a false trust of external aids. The chief error of the Pharisees, as Calvin reads Matthew 15, is that they made true religion consist in external ceremonies: "Only they thought nothing of true holiness, which consists of a genuine integrity of heart." Contrary to the Roman church, "the worship of God is spiritual and is not placed in sprinkling with water or in other ceremonies."[7] As he stresses in a comment on Matthew 16:6, "Neglecting spiritual worship, [they] bring in the traditions of men in their transitory disguises, as if God could be snared in such traps. For although external ceremonies may be impressive, before God they are childish trifles, save in so far as by their help we are trained in true godliness."

This concern for simple worship over against a bloated ceremonial worship directly informs Calvin's view of musical instruments. His comment on Psalm 81:1–3 is representative:

> With respect to the tabret, harp, and psaltery, we have formerly observed, and will find it necessary afterwards to repeat the same remark, that the Levites, under the law, were justified in making use of instrumental music in the worship of God; it having been his will to train his people, while they were as yet tender and like children, by such rudiments, until the coming of Christ. But now when the clear light of the gospel has dissipated the shadows of the law, and taught

---

6. *Comm.* 1 Cor. 1:17; cf. *Comm.* 1 Cor. 2:3. In *Comm.* 1 Cor. 1:17; in 1.7.2 he asserts that the Bible's power lies in its "unpolished simplicity, almost bordering on rudeness, [which] makes a deeper impression than the loftiest flights of oratory."

7. *Comm.* Matt. 15:7–8.

us that God is to be served in a simpler [*simplicem*] form, it would be to act a foolish and mistaken part to imitate that which the prophet enjoined only upon those of his own time.

Rome's error is to "burden the Church with an excess of ceremonies." While Israel benefited from an elaborate ceremonial system, as "wholesome exercises and aids to godliness," now God commands the church to worship in a ceremonially simple manner. Rome's liturgy is little more than a "theatrical show," utterly opposed to the dignified expression of pure worship that the New Testament enjoins. Instead of being "living exercises of piety," these excessive ceremonies are "frivolous and useless." The papists "pursue the shadow for the substance," turning God's worship into "fictitious worship," where superstition, hypocrisy, and idolatry abound. Against all this distortion, Calvin asserts: "We worship God more simply. That we have in no respect detracted from the spiritual worship of God, is attested by fact." The only kinds of ceremonies the church requires, in the end, are those that are "sober and suitable."[8]

Simple Material Shape of Worship

In contrast to a sensory-rich worship, Calvin defends a simple or minimal use of material media in worship. Similar to his concern for a ceremonially simple worship, he maintains that external exercises in public worship yield only a negligible benefit.[9] A pure conscience and a sincere heart, as emblematic of true godliness, are far more valuable. "This means that the man who has godliness lacks nothing, even though he does not have the small assistance these ascetic practices can afford. Godliness is the beginning, middle and end of Christian living and where it is complete, there is nothing lacking. Christ did not follow as ascetic a way of life as John the Baptist, and yet He was not for that reason any whit inferior."[10] Though "bodily exercises" may be of some value, as Calvin understands

8. See *Comm.* Gal. 4:5; *Comm.* Gal. 4:9; "On the Necessity of Reforming the Church," 131–33, 148, 151; "Short Treatise on the Lord's Supper," 192. The catalog of abuses, according to Calvin, includes the veneration of images and relics, turning the Mass into a spectacle, encouraging prayer to the saints and angels, forbidding the eating of meat on Friday, enjoining priestly celibacy, and requiring auricular confession.

9. *Comm.* 1 Tim. 4:7.

10. *Comm.* 1 Tim. 4:8; cf. *Comm.* 2 Cor. 4:16; *Comm.* Rom. 14:18.

"vigils, long fasts, lying on the ground and such like," the apostle Paul regards them as of "small and meager" profit.[11]

In addition, to bring musical instruments or other visual decorations into public worship is to engage in a "ridiculous and inept imitation of papistry," when all that is needed is "a simple and pure singing of the divine praises, coming from heart and mouth, and in the vulgar tongue."[12] This diminished role for material aids to worship is, at some level, consonant with Calvin's ambiguous regard for the sacraments as *tangible* media.[13] In question 24 of his "Confession of Faith," Calvin asks why the sacraments are necessary. He answers: human "ignorance and frailty" make such external signs necessary.[14] It is regrettable, in fact, that Scripture and preaching are not enough for the faithful.[15] If Christians were "wholly spiritual," like angels, he writes, they would not have need of them.[16]

Simple as a Correlate of "Spirit and Truth"

The idea that physical aids of worship involve an appeal to human "weakness" is fully at play in Calvin's association of "simple" with the notion of worship in "spirit and truth." In book 3 of the 1559 *Institutes*, Calvin insists that both Jews and pagans err by placing false confidence in their physical temples of worship. Since the faithful are themselves God's true temples, the locus of true worship lies in an interior, nonmaterial space, "for we have the commandment to call upon the Lord, without distinction of place, 'in spirit and in truth.'"[17] This wording follows logically, Calvin believes, from God himself being a "spirit."[18] Indeed, this has been God's way all along: "Nor from the beginning was there any other method of worshipping God, the only difference being, that this spiritual truth,

---

11. *Comm.* 1 Tim. 4:7-8. Calvin adds, "Thus even though the heart be pure and the motive upright, Paul finds nothing in outward actions he can value highly." Cf. *Comm.* Col. 2:22; 3.19.8.

12. Calvin makes this comment in relation to 1 Sam. 18:6; *CO* 30:259.

13. On this point, see also Selinger, *Calvin against Himself*, 66-68.

14. "Short Treatise on the Lord's Supper," 166.

15. "Confession of Faith," 152, 159.

16. "Catechism of the Church of Geneva," 84, 91. Cf. 3.20.30; 4.5.18.

17. 3.20.30.

18. "Catechism of the Church of Geneva," 71. From the 1545 Latin version: "Quandoquidem Deus spiritus est," *CO* 6:85-86; cf. *CO* 24:350.

which with us is naked and simple, was under the former dispensation wrapt up in figures."[19] In "On the Necessity of Reforming the Church," Calvin ties this assertion directly to John 4:23: "By these words he meant not to declare that God was not worshipped by the fathers in this spiritual manner, but only to point out a distinction in the external forms, viz., that while they had the Spirit shadowed forth by many figures, we have it in simplicity. But it has always been an acknowledged point, that God, who is a Spirit, must be worshipped in spirit and in truth."[20]

To affirm the simple worship of God "in spirit and in truth" is to reject external splendor and ceremonial ostentation, which is "agreeable to our carnal nature." The kind of worship that the Father seeks, Calvin maintains in his 1553 commentary on John's Gospel, "is the pure and simple substance of spiritual worship."[21]

To summarize, while Calvin employs the notion of "simple" in diverse settings, a common thread runs throughout. First, the gospel must remain unencumbered with spurious "traditions" and rhetorical pomposities that distort the Christian faith. And second, all sorts of liturgical ostentations and engorgements must be removed that draw the faithful away from the true worship of God. Inasmuch as Calvin regards "simple" as a logical and liturgical derivative of worship "in spirit and truth," it is necessary that we revisit his exegesis of John 4:23–24. Consistent with the patterns that have been observed thus far, materiality stands in a problematic tension to worship that occurs "in spirit and truth."

Calvin on John 4:23–24

Calvin sets the scene in John 4 by noting that the Samaritan woman's language in 4:20 signifies an interest in the nature of "pure worship." Calvin understands this phrase to mean public worship. From Jesus's statement in 4:22, Calvin deduces a contrast between "what God enjoins us in the Gospel," on the one hand, and, on the other, the shadow of ceremonies that include incense, lights, sacred vestments, and so forth. Once Calvin arrives at verses 23 and 24, a series of antonymous terms frame the shape of his argument. Worship "in spirit and truth" marks a contrast:

19. "On the Necessity of Reforming the Church," 127.
20. "On the Necessity of Reforming the Church," 128.
21. *Comm.* John 4:23.

spiritual	vs.	external figures
substance	vs.	shadows
inward faith of the heart	vs.	external obedience
pure worship	vs.	flavor of carnality and earthliness
nothing hidden	vs.	veil of temple
naked truth of Christ	vs.	outward ceremonies
age of maturity	vs.	age of childishness
moderate and sober	vs.	excessive and human inventions
handed down by Christ	vs.	the "doubly carnal show" of Rome
purity of worship	vs.	corruptions of worship
godly and true worship	vs.	perverted and hypocritical worship
bare and simple worship	vs.	swollen mass of ceremonies
truth	vs.	outward addition of figures
spiritual worship	vs.	the coverings of the ancient ceremonies
namely, with God's nature	vs.	outward ceremonies

On the left side of this contrast stand three key factors: (1) a new-covenantal era, (2) a stress on "soulish" activities in public worship, and (3) the need for a moderate form of worship. On the other side stand three corresponding factors: (1) an old-covenantal era, (2) a worry over a materially oriented public worship, and (3) the experience of a "swollen mass of ceremonies." Above it all stands a desire to remain faithful to the essence of God. When Calvin states that true worship "rests in the spirit," he means that it must remain consistent with God's being as nonmaterial, rather than, as ancient commentators had done, point to the work of the Spirit of Christ.[22]

Ceremonies, concomitantly, are to be regarded as adventitious and should be kept sober in order not to obscure the "naked truth of Christ." An excess of material symbols of worship not only belongs to the old age of the church, but their very materiality appeals to the cravings of human nature. God's nature "no more agrees with the flesh than fire does with water. . . . God is so unlike us that those things which please us most are to Him disgusting and boring." Only "plain and simple worship," oriented around the "inward faith of the heart," pleases God.[23]

While Calvin's anxiety about the material shape of worship cannot

22. *Comm.* John 4:24.
23. *Comm.* John 4:23.

be separated from the historical circumstances that set the content and rhetoric of his thought in a proper perspective, it is also necessary to ask whether he has rightly interpreted the meaning of John 4:23–24.[24] Does worship "in spirit and truth" demand a simple worship of the heart? Does "simplicity" require a minimal role for materiality in corporate worship?[25] To answer these questions, I reexamine Jesus's exchange with the woman at the well. I do so in considerable detail because of the pivotal role that this passage plays in Calvin's thinking about public worship.

Two Traditions on John 4:23–24

Two basic traditions of interpretation characterize the church's reading of John 4:23–24, with its decisive language on the character of worship with the advent of Christ and the gift of the Spirit. One tradition includes, among others, Calvin and those Reformed theologians who follow closely in his path.[26] In this tradition, the words of Jesus to the Samaritan woman are understood to point to the essential nature of God as "spirit" (*pneuma ho theos*), as well as to the interior condition of the human worshiper "in spirit and truth" (*en pneumati kai alētheia*). Here, materiality is regarded as negligible, irrelevant, or problematic to true worship. The comment of eighteenth-century English Presbyterian Matthew Henry is typical: "Christians shall worship God, not in the ceremonial observances of the Mosaic institution, but in *spiritual* ordinances, consisting less in *bodily exercise*, and animated and invigorated more with divine power and ener-

24. See, for example, Barbara Pitkin, "Calvin as Commentator on the Gospel of John," in *Calvin and the Bible*, ed. Donald K. McKim (Cambridge: Cambridge University Press, 2006), 164–98, esp. the bibliographic list at 176n49.

25. To argue for this sort of minimalism in worship is not uncommon in Reformed circles. So, for example, Ligon Duncan, "Traditional Evangelical Worship," in *Perspectives on Christian Worship: Five Views*, ed. J. Matthew Pinson (Nashville: B&H Academic, 2009), 115; Bryan Chappel, *Christ-Centered Worship: Letting the Gospel Shape Our Practice* (Grand Rapids: Baker Academic, 2009), 54, 67, 108–10; Don A. Carson, ed., *Worship by the Book* (Grand Rapids: Zondervan, 2002).

26. Others who follow this interpretative tradition include James D. G. Dunn, *The Parting of the Ways: Between Christianity and Judaism and Their Significance for the Character of Christianity* (London: SCM Press, 1991), 93; also James Montgomery Boice, *The Gospel of John* (Grand Rapids: Zondervan, 1985), 253; Ernst Haenchen, *John*, trans. Robert W. Funk, vol. 1 (Philadelphia: Fortress, 1984), 223; George Johnston, *The Spirit-Paraclete in the Gospel of John*, SNTSMS 12 (Cambridge: Cambridge University Press, 1970), 46.

gy."[27] The present-day Reformed Baptist pastor John Piper speaks force-fully: "What we find in the New Testament, perhaps to our amazement, is an utterly stunning degree of indifference to worship as an outward ritual, and an utterly radical intensification of worship as an inward experience of the heart."[28]

A second tradition of interpretation moves in a largely opposite direction.[29] Here the language of John's Gospel is understood to point to the activities of the triune God. Questions of location or materiality are not seen to stand in necessarily contrastive relation to the worship that Jesus announces. The Roman Catholic biblical scholar Raymond Brown, for example, writes, "Today most exegetes agree that in proclaiming worship in Spirit and truth, Jesus is not contrasting external worship with internal worship. . . . An idea of purely internal worship ill fits the NT scene with its Eucharistic gatherings, hymn singing, baptism in water, etc."[30] Marianne Meye Thompson, situated in a Reformed ecclesial context, adds: "That Jesus speaks of an alternative worship does not demonstrate that Christian worship of God renders irrelevant protected sacred space and holy places; precisely the opposite."[31]

While I am sympathetic to this second tradition of interpretation, and while I find Benny Thettayil's exegesis of this passage largely persuasive,[32] I wish to suggest the possibility that a more positive assessment

27. *Matthew Henry's Commentary on the Whole Bible*, vol. 5: *Matthew to John* (Old Tappan, NJ: Fleming H. Revell, 1986), 906, emphasis original. See also Andreas Köstenberger, "John," in *Commentary on the New Testament Use of the Old Testament*, ed. G. K. Beale and D. A. Carson (Grand Rapids: Baker Academic, 2007), 439.

28. John Piper, "Worship God!," sermon given on November 9, 1997, www.desiring god.org/ResourceLibrary/TopicIndex/60/1016_Worship_God.

29. See D. Moody Smith, "John," in *The Harper Collins Bible Commentary*, ed. James L. Mays (San Francisco: HarperSanFrancisco, 1988), 956-86; E. C. Hoskyns, *The Fourth Gospel* (London: Faber & Faber, 1947); Dorothy A. Lee, *The Symbolic Narratives of the Fourth Gospel: The Interplay of Form and Meaning*, JSNTSup 95 (Sheffield, UK: JSOT Press, 1994).

30. Raymond E. Brown, *The Gospel according to John*, vol. 1, Anchor Bible (Garden City, NY: Doubleday, 1966), 180.

31. Thompson, *The God of the Gospel of John*, 216-17. Similarly, Gary M. Burge, *The Anointed Community: The Holy Spirit in the Johannine Tradition* (Grand Rapids: Eerdmans, 1987), esp. 164. Rudolf Schnackenburg, *The Gospel according to St. John*, vol. 1 (New York: Seabury, 1968), 437; J. Ramsey Michaels, *The Gospel of John*, NICNT (Grand Rapids: Eerdmans, 2010), 253; Herman Ridderbos, *The Gospel of John: A Theological Commentary*, trans. John Vriend (Grand Rapids: Eerdmans, 1991), 163-64.

32. Benny Thettayil, *In Spirit and Truth: An Exegetical Study of John 4:19-26 and a*

of the material shape of worship, not simply the preclusion of an anti-material reading, might emerge from John 4:23–24.[33] More specifically, while John's Gospel may not yield clear directives regarding the material shape of worship, we may well discover specific orientations in the narrative that make certain conclusions more plausible than others and that problematize Calvin's assumptions about so-called simple worship. In the section that follows I engage a careful examination of the language of (1) *pneuma ho theos*, (2) *en pneumati kai alētheia*, and (3) *topos*.

"God Is Spirit"

Interpretation of the phrase *pneuma ho theos* in 4:24 has followed along two veins. One vein of interpretation has seen in Jesus's statement an assertion concerning the essential nature of God, what I call the "essentialist" reading.[34] Leon Morris, in this view, suggests that the Samaritan woman's attempt in verse 20 to steer the conversation in a new direction "serves to open up the way for Jesus to speak of the essential nature of God and of the worship that should be offered him."[35] Similarly, J. H. Bernard states, "It is the Essential Being, rather than the Personality, of God which is in question."[36] John H. Bennetch, following a line of thought reminiscent of Calvin's exegesis, believes that *ho theos* functions as a synonym for "the Father" and that Jesus's emphasis lies on the nonmaterial nature of God.[37]

A different vein of interpretation argues that 4:24 presents an "actualist" rather than an "essentialist" description of God. Jesus's language, that is, is intended to exhibit God's dynamic relation to humanity, rather than indicate a divine attribute. At stake here is God's relation to creation, not God in himself. Lesslie Newbigin well expresses this hermeneutical

Theological Investigation of the Replacement Theme in the Fourth Gospel (Leuven: Peeters, 2007).

33. C. K. Barrett, in *The Gospel according to St. John*, 2nd ed. (Philadelphia: Westminster, 1978), 238 (hereafter *St. John*), asserts: "This clause [4:23] has perhaps as much claim as 20:30f. to be regarded as expressing the purpose of the gospel."

34. So, e.g., Louis Berkhof, *Systematic Theology*, rev. ed. (Grand Rapids: Eerdmans, 1996), 42, 66.

35. Leon Morris, *The Gospel according to John*, rev. ed. (Grand Rapids: Eerdmans, 1995), 236.

36. J. H. Bernard, *Gospel according to St. John*, vol. 1, ICC (Edinburgh: T&T Clark, 1928), 150.

37. J. H. Bennetch, "John 4:24a: A Greek Study," *Biblioteca Sacra* 107 (1950): 80, 73.

tradition: "This action of the Father [to seek true worshipers] is the Father himself in action, for God is Spirit, and Spirit is action—the mighty action which is 'from above' and which, like the wind, is invisible and yet unmistakable in its presence and its powerful effects. God is not essence but action. His being is action, and the action is the seeking of true worshippers out of Jewry and out of Samaria and out of every nation."[38] Similar to such phrases as "God is light" and "God is love," the phrase "God is Spirit" can be seen hereby to describe an activity of God.[39] These are things God *does*; in doing them, we witness who God *is*. Four points can be adduced on behalf of an actualist reading of *pneuma ho theos*.

First, it is unlikely that God's nonmaterial nature would have been in serious doubt for faithful Samaritans or Jews.[40] Did this woman really need reminding that God has no physical body, that "God is invisible and unknowable," or that "the mystery of divine invisibility" was key?[41] Arguments such as these fail to persuade in light of the religious and historical context for John 4, especially if we are right in assuming a Jewish background rather than an exclusively Greek background for John's Gospel.[42]

Second, an essentialist reading is unwarranted from the narrative itself. What the woman needs is not a rebuke of anthropomorphic projections of God. What she needs, according to 4:7–15, is living water; what she gets, according to 4:25–30, is a revelation of the Messiah.[43] Jesus's answer to her question remains consistent with his answer to Nicodemus

38. Lesslie Newbigin, *The Light Has Come: An Exposition of the Fourth Gospel* (Grand Rapids: Eerdmans, 1982), 53. For actualist interpretations, see also, among others, Brown, *John*, 172, 180; Hoskyns, *The Fourth Gospel*, 244; Schnackenburg, *St. John*, 437–38; Smith, "John," 964; Michaels, *The Gospel of John*, 253; R. H. Lightfoot, *St. John's Gospel*, ed. C. F. Evans (Oxford: Clarendon Press, 1956), 134; Burge, *The Anointed Community*, 147; J. F. McHugh, *A Critical and Exegetical Commentary of John 1–4*, ICC (Edinburgh: T&T Clark, 2009), 306–15.

39. Thettayil, *In Spirit and Truth*, 124, identifies the various arguments surrounding the anarthrous use of *pneuma*. He reasons, rightly I believe, that the definite article is implied and that a definite Spirit, not any spirit, is in view.

40. Cf. Thettayil, *In Spirit and Truth*, 43–105.

41. Barrett, *St. John*, 238; Johnston, *The Spirit-Paraclete in the Gospel of John*, 15; Burge, *The Anointed Community*, 192, argues that "personal efforts and ambitions" might be seen to replace the power of God.

42. On this point, see W. D. Davies, "Reflections on Aspects of the Jewish Background of the Gospel of John," in *Exploring the Gospel of John: In Honor of D. Moody Smith*, ed. R. Alan Culpepper and C. Clifton Black (Louisville: Westminster John Knox, 1996), 43–64.

43. Cf. Isa. 55:1; Rev. 22:17.

(3:1–21): that the work of the Spirit, whom Jesus equates with "living water" in 7:37–39, is required in order to enter into God's kingdom.

Third, it is a strange move, as is often done, to assert that the nonmaterial nature of God (God *as* spirit) establishes the basis for right-hearted worship (humans *as* spirit).[44] In what way exactly does God's spiritual nature as such necessarily or logically *generate* heartfelt worship?

Fourth, the primary sense of "spirit" in John does not stand in opposition to matter.[45] Nor is it intended to describe the immanent activities of God, where the divine "spirit" communicates with the human "spirit."[46] Instead, the Johannine language of *pneuma* describes the sovereign activities of God over a dark and broken world.[47] For John, participation in life "from above" is possible only by the Spirit, whom the Father gives to those who believe in his Son (20:31).[48] It is God's Spirit who calls forth true worship and enables new birth to occur.[49] Frederick Dale Bruner puts the point well: "Worship is only secondarily and reflexively humans seeking *God*; it is, first of all and creatively, the divine Father, through Jesus the Truth, by the Fountain Spirit—the one God seeking humans and moving them upward to him."[50]

"In Spirit and Truth"

The meaning of the phrase "God is Spirit" is illumined by, and contextually related to, the phrase *en pneumati kai alētheia*. As with *pneuma ho theos* (4:24), so the interpretation of *en pneumati kai alētheia* (4:23) involves two divergent lines of thought. One view believes this phrase

44. See, for example, Terry Johnson, *Reformed Worship: Worship That Is according to Scripture* (Greenville, SC: Reformed Academic Press, 2000), 21.

45. This is an argument made by B. F. Westcott, *The Gospel according to John* (Grand Rapids: Eerdmans, 1958), 73.

46. James D. G. Dunn, *Jesus and the Spirit: A Study of the Religious and Charismatic Experience of Jesus and the First Christians as Reflected in the New Testament* (London: SCM, 1975), 353.

47. Instances of the language of "Spirit" alone include John 1:32, 33; 3:5, 6, 8, 34; 4:23, 24; 6:63; 7:39; the phrase "Holy Spirit" appears in 1:33; 14:26; 20:22.

48. See Thettayil, *In Spirit and Truth*, 128–30, 159.

49. Cf. Thiselton, *The Holy Spirit*, 138.

50. Frederick Dale Bruner, *The Gospel of John: A Commentary* (Grand Rapids: Eerdmans, 2012), 264, emphasis original. So also Stephen T. Um, *The Theme of Temple Christology in John's Gospel* (London: T&T Clark, 2006), 17.

describes a facet of human beings.[51] That is, it points to an internal and invisible condition of the rightly oriented worshiper. C. H. Dodd writes that "*alētheia* has in the Fourth Gospel in general its Hellenistic sense of reality, reality as apprehended, or knowledge of reality. Thus *pneuma* has some very close relation to reality, unseen and eternal."[52] George Johnston adds, "The outlook and mentality of John strongly indicate that we are to interpret 'worship in spirit' as inward worship, the offering of the heart, done out of love and not within a legal system like that of the Synagogue."[53] The concern, then, is for the "total orientation of one's life" toward God, as well as the "state of the heart" as the basis of right worship.[54]

Against this reading, I maintain that the phrase describes not something the worshiper does but something that happens *to* the worshiper.[55] Brown insists that the phrase has little to do with the inner recesses of the worshiper precisely because "the Spirit is the Spirit of God, not the spirit of man."[56] Central for John is not the heart of the worshiper but the work of Christ and the Spirit, who together enable one to enter the kingdom of God.[57] It is the Spirit, Jesus tells the woman, who makes worship possible "in the hour that is coming, and now is."[58] The Spirit who descends and

51. In this vein, Gordon Fee offers a perceptive analysis of the way in which English-language Bibles, starting with the KJV (1611) on through to the TNIV (2002), have translated the term *pneuma* in the NT, in "Translational Tendenz: English Versions and Πνεῦμα in Paul," in *The Holy Spirit and Christian Origins: Essays in Honor of James D. G. Dunn*, ed. Graham N. Stanton, Bruce W. Longenecker, and Stephen C. Barton (Grand Rapids: Eerdmans, 2004), 349–59.

52. C. H. Dodd, *The Interpretation of the Fourth Gospel* (Cambridge: Cambridge University Press, 1958), 223.

53. Johnston, *The Spirit-Paraclete in the Gospel of John*, 45. Similarly, Andreas J. Köstenberger, *John*, BECNT (Grand Rapids: Baker Academic, 2004), 157.

54. F. J. Moloney, *Experiencing God in the Gospel of John* (New York: Paulist Press, 2003), 129; Michaels, *The Gospel of John*, 255. See also Rodney Whitacre, *John*, IVPNTCS (Downers Grove, IL: IVP, 1999), 106, who sums up this interpretive tradition.

55. Cf. Rudolf Bultmann, *The Gospel of John* (Philadelphia: Westminster, 1971), 190, and David E. Aune, *The Cultic Setting of Realized Eschatology in Early Christianity* (Leiden: Brill, 1972), 104.

56. Brown, *John*, 180. To this point we might add that, in John, just as Jesus is the hypostasized *Logos* of God, so the Paraclete is the hypostasized *Pneuma* of God.

57. Explicit language of "heart" in John appears in few contexts, mainly related to emotional conditions, e.g., 14:27; 16:6, 22. In 12:38–41, citing Isa. 6:9–10, we have a description of the work of God on the human heart.

58. D. A. Carson, *The Gospel according to John* (Grand Rapids: Eerdmans, 1991), 225–26, comes close to this sense but muddles a Trinitarian reading with his choice of terms and

remains upon Jesus is the same Spirit who accomplishes the will of the Father in the ones who believe in the Son.[59] Thompson argues this case from the logic of the narrative, noting that the narratives both of Nicodemus and of the woman "point the reader away from the human being as self-sufficient actor to the human being as recipient of the activity and Spirit of God. It would then seem odd if, in conversation with the Samaritan woman, Jesus were to urge her to 'look within,' as it were, for the strength and capacity to offer true worship. Quite the contrary, one is brought into the eschatological hour by God's caring activity in Jesus and by the divinely sent Spirit of God."[60]

How, then, should the phrase be understood? Many view it as a hendiadys.[61] That is, by regarding the two terms in dynamic relationship, acceptable worship can be seen as that which occurs *in the Spirit who brings to bear the Truth, that is, Jesus,* upon the life of the worshiper.[62] In John's narrative, Jesus is presented as the fullness of truth (1:14), the revelation of the truth of God (5:25-33; 8:45-46; 17:17; 18:37), the truth himself (8:32; 14:6), and the one who bestows the Spirit of truth upon his disciples (15:26; 16:13). In John, it is *both* "the truth shall make you free" (8:32) *and* "if the Son makes you free, you will be free indeed" (8:36). The Spirit, in turn, is the one who bears witness to the Truth and who makes the presence of Jesus real to his disciples. The Spirit is the "other" helper, inasmuch as Jesus is seen to be the "first" helper (14:16-18).[63]

The kind of worship that the Father seeks, then, has a clear Christocentric and pneumatic shape: it is *in* the Truth, not merely *of* the truth; and it is by *the* Spirit, not by *any* spirit. New-covenantal worship arises out of a right orientation to the person of Jesus, rather than to "the way things really are,"[64] and it requires the work of the Spirit rather than the

---

irregular capitalizations, which render the Spirit in impersonal terms, while the Word is rendered in more personal ones.

59. J. Marsh, *Saint John,* Pelican Gospel Commentaries (Harmondsworth, UK: Penguin Books, 1968), 218.

60. Thompson, *The God of the Gospel of John,* 215, over against, say, R. C. H. Lenski, *The Interpretation of St. John's Gospel* (Minneapolis: Augsburg, 1961), 322.

61. Note "grace and truth" in John 1:14; "light" and "life" in 1:4.

62. Cf. Felix Porsch, *Pneuma und Wort: Ein exegetischer Beitrag zur Pneumatologie des Johannesevangeliums* (Frankfurt: Josef Knecht, 1974), 159; Dorothy A. Lee, "In the Spirit of Truth: Worship and Prayer in the Gospel of John and the Early Fathers," *Vigiliae Christianae* 58 (2004): 280.

63. Thiselton, *Holy Spirit,* 143; cf. Thettayil, *In Spirit and Truth,* 158.

64. C. John Collins, "John 4:23-24, 'In Spirit and Truth': An Idiomatic Proposal,"

sincerity of the human heart, as important as the latter may be, to orient the worshiper to the Father.[65] Over against *alētheia*, in John, stands not untruth but un-Jesus, as it were. The opposite of *pneuma*, likewise, is not hypocrisy but false spirits (see 1 John 4). The "hour," then, that Jesus discloses in his person invites an intimate relationship with God *as* Father, through Jesus *as* Truth, by the Spirit *as* Paraclete.[66]

Here, then, we begin to discern the *Trinitarian* shape of Jesus's exchange with the Samaritan woman.[67] Worship "in this new time" occurs in the Spirit, who bears witness to Jesus, the perfect Son of the Father, while the Son is the one who both mediates worship to the Father and is himself a proper object of worship.[68] These are not two poles around which the church's worship orbits: a "truth" pole and a "spirit" pole. Instead, it is the unified work of Son and Spirit, who together enable the faithful to offer acceptable worship to the Father. It is, as Thettayil rightly argues, "essentially God-centered, made possible by the gift of the Holy Spirit, and in personal knowledge of and conformity to God's Word-made-flesh, the one who is God's *alētheia*, the faithful exposition and fulfillment of God and his saving purposes."[69]

The Language of topos in 4:20–23

If the Trinitarian reading of John 4:23–24 is largely correct, what does it mean to worship God in the sphere of *pneumati kai alētheia*? And what

---

Presbyterion 21 (1995): 120–21. Collins believes that Jesus's statement to the Samaritan woman that "real" worshipers will worship in spirit indicates in the inner self, "that is to say, in reality."

65. A. Boyd Luter Jr., "'Worship' as Service: The New Testament Usage of *Latreuō*," *Criswell Theological Review* 2 (1988): 339–40.

66. McHugh, *John 1–4*, 315.

67. A Trinitarian reading of the text is far from new. Such a reading goes back to Athanasius, Basil, Hilary, Cyril of Alexandria, and Ambrose. Cf. McHugh, *John 1–4*, 312–14. See also Anthony J. Casurella's excellent treatment of the Paraclete passages in the writings of the church fathers: *The Johannine Paraclete in the Church Fathers: A Study in the History of Exegesis* (Tübingen: J. C. B. Mohr [Paul Siebeck], 1983).

68. Cf. Lee, "In the Spirit of Truth," 287–92. See also Smith, "John," 964; Wright, "Worship and the Spirit in the New Testament"; Burge, *The Anointed Community*, 197; Schnackenburg, *St. John*, 438–40; Thompson, *The God of the Gospel of John*, 214–16.

69. Thettayil, *In Spirit and Truth*, 163; cf. Bruner, *The Gospel of John*, 264; A. T. Lincoln, *The Gospel according to Saint John* (New York: Continuum, 2005), 182.

does this "sphere" imply for the material shape of worship in this new hour? Since the text itself does not provide a direct answer to this double question, it will be necessary to consider the nature of the contrast at play in Jesus's exchange with the nameless woman. Of particular import here is the language of *topos*, or place/space.

Consider Jesus's reference to place in John 4:20–23:

> Our fathers worshiped on this mountain but you say that in Jerusalem is the place where it is necessary to worship. Jesus said to her: "Believe me, woman, that the hour is coming when neither on this mountain nor in Jerusalem shall you worship the Father. You worship what you do not know; we worship what we know, for salvation is from the Jews. But an hour is coming, and now is, when the true worshipers shall worship the Father in Spirit and Truth. For indeed the Father seeks such as these to worship him."

In looking at the immediate backdrop to the text, we see a heightened rhetorical interplay existing between the language of place and the language of worship. Does this interplay imply a negative estimation of "place"? Is there an indifferent view of materiality at work here? Are place and materiality set in oppositional relationship to worship in this eschatological hour? To answer these questions we must consider the nature of the contrast at work in Jesus's response to the Samaritan woman. In verse 20 the woman uses three key terms: *on this mountain, in Jerusalem,* and *topos*. Two initial observations can be offered.

First, all three terms function as semantic equivalents. Worship for both Samaritan and Jew took place on a mountain—Gerizim, or what is presently called the Judean mountains, and Jerusalem. While both mountains could be regarded as geographic places, the term *topos* in the New Testament often serves as a euphemism for "the temple."[70] Thus *topos* here should be viewed, inter alia, as both an actual place and a symbolic place.[71] A second observation is that Jesus's answer is far from straightforward. Where the woman makes reference to a geographic place, Jesus answers

70. George R. Beasley-Murray, *John,* 2nd ed., WBC 36 (Nashville: Thomas Nelson, 1999), 61. Cf. Deut. 12:1–14; John 11:48, where English Bibles often translate *topos* as "temple"; also Acts 6:13–14 and 21:28, which include both "place" and "holy place" to designate the temple.

71. Thettayil, *In Spirit and Truth,* 68. See, e.g., Deut. 12:2–5; 2 Chron. 6:6; 7:12; Ps. 78:68; Acts 7:7, 49; John 11:48.

by contrasting two geographic *topoi* with a figurative *topos*. Jesus's answer points to a nonlocative reality, a place of sorts, but not a geographically situated one. Clearly, an apples-to-apples comparison is not in play.

To say, as Schnackenburg does, that the contrast points to a difference between a human-empowered temple and a God-empowered temple seems largely to miss the point. It is to belie, in fact, the words of Yahweh concerning tabernacle and temple worship.[72] Brown's suggestion, shared by Burge, that the shift in view is "from the place of worship (20–21) to the manner of worship" seems equally unsatisfying.[73] If the Old Testament prophetic critique is to be believed, the manner of worship played an equally important role in Israel's worship.[74] Walter Bauer's assertion that true worshipers are those who are "freed from every chain that binds men to the realm of the flesh, to sacred times and places and ceremonies," reflects a widespread but flawed conviction in Protestant circles.[75]

Over against these approaches, I suggest four ways in which the contrast might be understood. "Spirit and Truth" stand in relation to the *topoi* (1) as physical localities, (2) as singular localities, (3) as representative of the cult practiced in the respective localities, or (4) as symbolic of their singular localities, along with their respective singular cultic practices. All four possibilities presume that the primary concern is the question of space, whether literal or figurative. I suggest that option 4 is the more plausible view of the contrast. On one side of the equation stands the Jerusalem temple, whose significance lies in both its exclusive geographic place, as well as in the ceremonies that fundamentally oriented its corporate life, while on the other side stands the as-yet enigmatic space marked out by "Spirit and Truth."[76] In Jesus's reference to these *topoi*, then, he speaks of a complex symbol whose unique physical and ceremonial role had come to an end, yielding to the sphere of *pneumati kai alētheia*.[77]

---

72. Schnackenburg, *St. John*, 437. Cf. Exod. 25–40; Lev. 6–16; Num. 1:48–51; 1 Kings 6–8. See also John Witvliet's excellent essay "The Former Prophets and the Practice of Christian Worship," in *Worship Seeking Understanding*, 23–38.

73. Brown, *John*, 180; Burge, *The Anointed Community*, 164–65.

74. See, for example, Amos 5:21–26; Mic. 4:1–2; 6:6–8; Hosea 8:11–13; Jer. 7:21–26; Ezek. 16:15–21; Pss. 15; 24; 119. For a picture of the future when God would renew Israel's worship, see Isa. 19:19–21; 56:6–7; 60:7; Jer. 17:24–27; 33:10–11, 17–18; Ezek. 20:40–41.

75. Cited in Hoskyns, *The Fourth Gospel*, 244.

76. Thompson, *The God of the Gospel of John*, 194–208, proposes a helpful taxonomy of the views of worship that characterized the period of Second Temple Judaism.

77. Another possible contrast involves the idea of time rather than of space. The contrast, in this perspective, involves a tension between "old time" and "new time," with

The more acute point perhaps is the fact that John 4:23–24 remains silent on the question of materiality per se. Materiality itself obtains neither a negative nor a positive judgment in Jesus's oblique assertion. An antimaterial polemic or the dismissal of symbolic place can only be inferred. In fact, the text declares only that the symbolic and exclusive geographic *topoi* that Gerizim and Jerusalem occupied no longer serve the purposes of the Father in this eschatological hour.[78] The physical locality of worship and whatever symbolic qualities it will assume in the new age will need to be discerned, somehow, someway, in the sphere of the "Spirit and Truth."[79]

Conclusion

If worship in "Spirit and Truth" is not chiefly about an interiorized, immaterial worship, and if 4:23–24 does not represent an antimaterial polemic, then what positive relation, if any, obtains between "Spirit and Truth" and the material aspect of worship envisioned in John's Gospel? What does this "sphere" look like? Is it materially "simple," or is it otherwise? Three brief observations can be suggested in our conclusion.

First, John 4 does not answer this exact question, because the text is frankly not interested in the question. Where commentators have concluded that the text proposes a certain material shape of worship, whether minimal or maximal, whether positive or negative, it owes more to the presuppositions of the commentator than to the logic of the text. Jesus does not tell the woman where or how worship spatially must occur, because his central concern is not a locative or geographic one. His concern is theological.

Second, the idea of "simple" worship is foreign to the meaning of John 4:23–24. It is an inference that Calvin draws in light of his own theological and liturgical presuppositions, but it is also an erroneous one, a foreign import at odds with this locus classicus on worship. All that the

---

space playing a derivative or secondary role. See Thompson, *The God of the Gospel of John*, 216; Thettayil, *In Spirit and Truth*, 75–78, 106–12.

78. Cf. Richard J. Bauckham, "James and the Jerusalem Church," in *The Book of Acts in Its Palestinian Setting*, ed. Richard Bauckham (Grand Rapids: Eerdmans, 1995), 425.

79. See Thettayil, *In Spirit and Truth*, 162. He suggests that "the use of ἐν may be taken either as *local* or *metaphorical*" (emphasis original), and he believes that there is an analogous relationship to the language of ἐν Χριστῷ (in Christ).

text supposes is that space and matter have acquired a new significance in light of the work of Christ and the gift of the Spirit.

Third, the text does state that these two *topoi*, Gerizim and Jerusalem, will no longer suffice for the kind of worship that the Father seeks. A new thing is required. The narrative as such prods us to look to a kind of worship that will take place in the "sphere" of *pneumati kai alētheia*. It prods us to ask how materiality fares in this new "hour" of worship, as John discerns it.

CHAPTER 9

The Trinitarian Space of Worship

True worshippers must be empowered by the Spirit of God
in order to encounter God in worship, as they respond to the
Father in exclusive worship by recognizing his divine reality of
eschatological life found in the True Temple of God.

Stephen Um, *The Theme of Temple Christology in John's Gospel*

It is little wonder that the Reformed liturgical aesthetic that
emerged in Calvin's legacy regarded simplicity as the essence of
beauty, and proper ordering, modesty, and gravity as the essence
of decorum.

Philip Butin, "John Calvin's Humanist Image
of Popular Late-Medieval Piety"

Since the glory of God ought, in a measure, to shine in the several
parts of our bodies, it is especially fitting that the tongue has been
assigned and destined for this task, both through singing and
through speaking.

Calvin, *Institutes*

Without an explicit statement in John 4:23-24 regarding the material shape
of worship, as I have argued in the previous chapter, it is necessary to look to
patterns of thought in the Johannine narrative that might orient an answer

one way or another. Three patterns of thought lead me to believe that we might, in fact, find a positive answer: (1) the way in which the Fourth Gospel regards Jesus as the new "holy place," (2) a motif of new creation as it touches upon the Spirit's work, and (3) the intrinsic link between *sēmeia* (signs) and materiality. Largely parting ways with Calvin's reading of John, I argue here that the fundamental trajectories of the Johannine narrative invite us to infer a positive relationship between materiality and worship, not one that is merely ambivalent or even expressly negative.[1]

Jesus the Holy Place

First, Jesus as the new "holy place" in John establishes the definitive goodness of materiality. In a comment on John 1:14, Calvin remarks that, though God hid himself "under the lowliness of the flesh," yet this flesh still manifested the divine glory.[2] Christ's body is the "abode" of his divinity: "For we know that the Son of God so clothed Himself with our nature that in the flesh which He assumed the eternal majesty of God dwelt as in His Sanctuary."[3] From heaven, as it were, Christ descends to put on human flesh in order that, "by stretching out a brotherly hand to us, He might raise us to heaven along with Himself."[4] This idea of union with God is particularly evident in Calvin's commentary on John 6. Through Christ's flesh, in fact, the entire redemption of humanity is accomplished: "In it a sacrifice was offered to atone for sins, and an obedience yielded to God to reconcile Him to us; it was also filled with the sanctification of the Spirit; finally, having overcome death, it was received into the heavenly glory."[5] Christ's flesh, in fact, is Spirit-vivified and Spirit-vivifying for those who receive it in faith. Calvin puts the matter in vivid terms: "It is necessary to eat the crucified flesh for it to benefit us."[6]

Yet, as positively as Calvin is able to speak of Christ's flesh, he believes that John's use of *sarx* implies a mitigated benefit. The *sarx* that Je-

---

1. While Calvin says plenty else about the incarnation of Christ, the work of the Spirit in creation, and the purpose of material symbols in worship, for the purposes of this chapter I restrict myself to Calvin's observations on John's Gospel.

2. *Comm.* John 1:14.

3. *Comm.* John 2:19.

4. *Comm.* John 3:13.

5. *Comm.* John 6:51.

6. *Comm.* John 6:63; cf. his comments on 8:36.

sus is said to take on in 1:14 is not a euphemism for corrupt human nature but rather a description of mortal humanity: "It denotes derogatorily his frail and almost transient nature."[7] Calvin exclaims, "How great is the distance between the spiritual glory of the Word of God and the stinking filth of our flesh!"[8] When Christ shows his wounded body to the disciples, Calvin assumes an act of condescension is at work. Jesus exhibits his wounds, that is, for the sake of a weak faith. To believe that these wounds are permanently inscribed in Jesus's body, moreover, is "ridiculous."[9] In Thomas's experience of touching the wounded side and the pierced hands, Calvin accuses the doubting disciple of "binding faith (which springs from hearing and ought to be entirely fixed to the Word) to the other senses."[10]

Against this reading, with its admittedly rhetorically heightened quality, I argue that the Johannine narrative involves no explicit denigration of Christ's flesh, nor a sense that the wounded body of Jesus is a cause for embarrassment to the disciples. John 2 is decisive, for it is here that the reader discovers the proper telos of 1:14.[11] The Logos becomes *sarx* because it is Jesus's body-as-temple that shall now serve as the new "holy place." Jesus hereby replaces both tabernacle and temple and becomes the embodied place of meeting. As Craig Koester observes, Jesus assumes for John the role of the new portable presence of God.[12] This presence is touched, anointed, bathed, caressed, leaned against, poked, pulled, torn, and then offered for the life of the world. It is through this flesh that God tabernacles with humanity and exhibits his glory. Through this flesh God's glory becomes tangible, not tangential, in the revelation of the Messiah. Through this flesh the restoration of the cosmos properly begins.

It is especially noteworthy that the language of tabernacle and temple, which John uses to describe Jesus's life (1:14; 2:19, 21), appears elsewhere only once. In Revelation 21:3, the tabernacle of God is said to be with humanity, while in Revelation 15:5, the language of temple, taberna-

---

7. *Comm.* John 1:14. This understanding is in contrast to what he believes is being addressed in John 3:6.

8. *Comm.* John 1:14; cf. *Comm.* John 6:53.

9. *Comm.* John 20:20.

10. *Comm.* John 20:29.

11. Cf. Gale A. Yee, *Jewish Feasts and the Gospel of John* (Wilmington, DE: Michael Glazier, 1989).

12. Koester, *Dwelling of God*, 100–115. Cf. uses in Wisd. of Sol. 9:15; 2 Cor. 5:1, 4; and LXX for the Israelite tabernacle. Cf. also Rev. 21:3, as well as Ezek. 47:1–12, with its imagery of water flowing out from under the threshold of the temple, echoing both Gen. 2 and Ps. 1.

cle of meeting, and divine glory are employed to recount John's vision of a sign.[13] And if the author of the Fourth Gospel can be linked to the First Epistle of John,[14] then the multisensory language of 1 John 1:1–3 serves only to underscore the important relation between God's self-revelation and materiality in Johannine perspective. It is precisely this Christ, "who was revealed in the flesh" (1 Tim. 3:16), whom the church confesses. It is through this wounded flesh that Jesus offers his body. It is in this pierced body that the faithful discover not a condescension to a weak faith, regrettably in need of palpable attestation, but rather a radical vision of the Man of Sorrows, sympathetic to the somatic condition of human creatures.

Stressing the pneumatic dimension of this embodied presence, Dorothy Lee argues that "the Spirit who abides on Jesus draws believers to the Son as the heavenly yet material *topos*: the site of worship of the Father."[15] Worship in John's Gospel, then, can be said to occur through the humanity of Jesus *by way of* the Spirit.[16] As the new holy place, Jesus occupies a Spirit-empowered corporeal space through which encounter with the Father is made possible.[17] Whatever else worship "in" Christ means, it means nothing less than worship mediated through the flesh of Christ, capable of unmarred habitation by the Spirit.[18] To worship "in Truth," in a Johannine sense, points therefore to a worship that occurs not only *because* of Jesus, with its accompanying soteriological and eschatological significance, but also *in and on account of his Spirit-formed corporeality*, with implications for creation itself.[19]

In John, the Logos becomes *sarx* and redeems all *sarx*. All *sarx*, and by implication all of the material creation, is implicated in this renovative work of Jesus. If all of creation is renewed through the body of Christ, then I contend that the material shape of worship cannot be excluded

13. Cf. Rev. 7:15. I do not suggest here a common author for the Gospel and the Revelation; I simply notice an intertextual echo.

14. This is a big "if," though not by any means unwarranted. R. E. Brown, *The Epistles of John*, Anchor Bible 30 (New York: Doubleday, 1982), 20ff., lists scholars who argue one side or the other of this issue.

15. Lee, "In the Spirit of Truth," 285.

16. Cf. Trevor Hart, "Humankind in Christ and Christ in Humankind: Salvation as Participation in Our Substitute in the Theology of John Calvin," *Scottish Journal of Theology* 42 (1989): 67–84.

17. This is to argue against Davies, *Gospel and the Land*, 295.

18. Cf. Lee, *The Symbolic Narratives of the Fourth Gospel*, 82.

19. John 20:27 could be seen to play a significant role in supporting this point. Cf. Thompson, *The God of the Gospel of John*, 216–17.

from this renewing work. It too must somehow give expression to a world that has been healed and reconfigured on account of Christ's body. To speak of the reconfiguring work of Christ's flesh, moreover, is surely also to speak of the *Spirit's* reconfiguration of the place of worship.

The Spirit's Work of Re-creation

Second, the Spirit's work of re-creation in John points to the ongoing goodness of materiality for the church's worship. Calvin is sensitive to the way in which the Spirit functions, so to speak, in adjectival fashion.[20] To speak of the spiritual work of God, as often as not, is to speak of the work of the Spirit, the *interior magister*.[21] As such, the only way to receive the benefits of Christ's work is to receive them Spirit-ually.[22] With John's Gospel, Calvin attends to specific pneumatological activity. It is the Spirit who illumines darkened creatures, who places the Word in the hearts of the faithful, who establishes faith in them, while also increasing in them an appetite for grace, and who leads the faithful toward "the school of Christ," equipping and empowering the disciple for God's mission.[23] And it is the Spirit whom Jesus gives to his disciples in order to complete the work of salvation in them: "Christ was the Patron of His own so long as He lived in the world. Afterwards He committed them to the protection and guardianship of the Spirit. . . . While He dwelt in the world, He openly manifested Himself as their Patron. Now He guards us by His Spirit." While Calvin regards Christ's work in John as atonement and redemption, the work of the Spirit, he believes, "is to make us partakers not only of Christ Himself, but of all His blessings."[24]

As noted in previous chapters, Calvin is especially concerned with the soul-ish work of salvation.[25] The corporeal shape of renewed humanity receives much less emphasis. The sacramental bread, Calvin writes, is given for "the spiritual nourishment of the soul."[26] The language of "rivers" in 7:38 points to "the multiple graces of the Spirit, which are neces-

---

20. *Comm.* John 6:63.
21. *Comm.* John 14:16.
22. *Comm.* John 14:16; 20:22.
23. *Comm.* John 6:46; 7:37; 8:32; 15:26; 16:14; 20:22.
24. Pitkin, "Calvin as Commentator on the Gospel of John," 193.
25. *Comm.* John 15:26.
26. *Comm.* John 6:32.

sary for the spiritual life of the soul."[27] Because the soul is seen to take priority over the body in the redemptive work of Christ, the organs of hearing and speaking take priority over the organs of sight and sense. God "sounds in our ears by the mouth of men; and He addresses us inwardly by His Spirit."[28] Neither oracles nor visions should be sought, he adds, since the Spirit-empowered preached Word, which is "in our mouth and heart," suffices.[29]

Calvin's commentary on John 20:22 is emblematic of his construal of material symbols of worship in the Fourth Gospel. When "Popish theologasters" surmise from this text the liturgical practice of "breathing," or when they infer a sacrament of penance from 20:23, Calvin views this as a gross misunderstanding of the gospel. No sacramental practice is to be inferred from Christ's action to breathe upon his disciples.[30] What papal religion does here is to pervert the gospel. "Did the Spirit have to come down from heaven for the apostles to learn by what ceremony cups and their altars must be consecrated, church bells baptized, holy water blessed and Mass celebrated? . . . Thus, by a false claim to the Spirit, the world has been bewitched to leave the simple purity of Christ."[31]

Such a conclusion is, of course, consistent with what Calvin supposes is the purpose of John's Gospel. As he explains in his commentary preface, while the Synoptic Gospels exhibit Christ's "body," the Fourth Gospel presents his "soul." Though external aids to faith have their place in public worship, Calvin believed that singular emphasis should be placed on the work of the Spirit in the interior life of the Christian.

To take this line of thought, however, is to underestimate the importance of the Genesis subtext in John, with its implications for the material creation.[32] Beginning with John's theological reworking of Genesis 1 (in John 1:1–18), through to the end where the Beloved Disciple evokes the language of Yahweh as Gardener from Genesis 2–3 (John 20:15), the Fourth Gospel witnesses throughout to the new-creational work of Christ

27. *Comm.* John 7:38.
28. *Comm.* John 14:26; cf. *Comm.* John 15:27.
29. *Comm.* John 14:26; cf. *Comm.* John 16:8; 20:29.
30. *Comm.* John 20:22.
31. *Comm.* John 16:12, 14.
32. See John R. Levison, *Filled with the Spirit* (Grand Rapids: Eerdmans, 2009); John Painter, "Rereading Genesis in the Prologue of John?" in *Neotestamentica et Philonica* (Boston: Brill, 2003), 179–201; Elaine Pagels, "Exegesis of Genesis 1 in the Gospels of Thomas and John," *JBL* 118.3 (1999): 477–96.

and the Spirit.[33] Dunn notes that, for John, "Jesus is the author of the new creation as he was of the old."[34] And it is the Spirit who effects this work of re-creation. John 20:22 serves as an exemplar of this work.[35] The larger setting reads as follows: "Jesus said to them again, 'Peace be with you. Just as the Father has sent me, so I send you.' And having said this, he breathed on them and said to them, 'Receive the Holy Spirit.'"

As commentators have pointed out, the verb "breathe" (or "in-breathe") appears only here in the New Testament, although language very similar appears in Genesis 2:7 (LXX), Ezekiel 37:9 (LXX), and the Wisdom of Solomon 15:15. Each of these texts, in turn, describes the creation or re-creation of human beings.[36] Stephen Um deduces from this intertextual connection that "the Evangelist's use of this rare term was intended to imply that Jesus actually imparted the eschatological Spirit or new creational breath of life."[37] Just as the language of John 3:5 points to the sovereign work of the Spirit to effect new life in the disciple,[38] so too the language of 20:22 underscores the work of new creation that the Spirit accomplishes through the Son.[39] In giving the Spirit to his disciples, Jesus's action evokes the eschatological promises of God that Israel's prophets announced long ago, when "the Spirit is poured upon us from on high, and the desert becomes a fertile field" (Isa. 32:15).[40] On that day, shalom will characterize both the state of the land and relations between humans.

It is no coincidence, then, that Jesus in 20:21 speaks this peace to his disciples (cf. 14:27), his emissaries of the new age of the Spirit.[41] In three

33. Martin Hengel, "The Prologue of the Gospel of John as the Gateway to Christological Truth," in *The Gospel of John and Christian Theology*, ed. Richard Bauckham and Carl Mosser (Grand Rapids: Eerdmans, 2008), 289.

34. James D. G. Dunn, *Baptism in the Holy Spirit: A Re-examination of the New Testament Teaching on the Gift of the Spirit in Relation to Pentecostalism Today* (Philadelphia: Westminster, 1970), 180.

35. See esp. Cornelis Bennema, "The Giving of the Spirit in John 19–20: Another Round," in *The Spirit and Christ in the New Testament and Christian Theology: Essays in Honor of Max Turner*, ed. I. Howard Marshall, Volker Rabens, and Cornelis Bennema (Grand Rapids: Eerdmans, 2012), 86–105.

36. Cf. Bennema, "The Giving of the Spirit in John 19–20," 95.

37. Stephen T. Um, *The Theme of Temple Christology in John's Gospel* (London: T&T Clark, 2006), 181.

38. Linda Belleville, "'Born of Water and Spirit': John 3:5," *Trinity Journal* 1 (1980): 137.

39. Cf. 2 Cor. 5:17; Thiselton, *The Holy Spirit*, 137.

40. Cf. Ps. 104:30; Ezek. 36:33–36; 37:4–5; Isa. 44:3.

41. Cf. Jub. 1:23–25.

distinctive actions—speaking peace, breathing the Spirit, and entrusting to his disciples a priestly vocation—the reader hears echoes of Yahweh's activity in the early chapters of Genesis, which the prophets in various ways apply to Israel's vocation.[42] Where Israel fails to fulfill this calling, however, Jesus is shown in John's Gospel to be the one who perfectly fulfills God's will.[43] John's Gospel also suggests that the Spirit will continue Jesus's work in the lives of the disciples. In the so-called Upper Room Discourse, Jesus commissions his disciples to be agents of this new life, announcing the new creation that the Spirit achieves in them in fulfillment of God's promise to make a new people, called by his name (Ezek. 36).[44] As Lee summarizes, "The Spirit is central to the creative and re-creative work of God, played out in the mission and ministry of Jesus."[45]

Over against Calvin, I suggest that the eschatological work of the Spirit concerns not only a redeemed community but also a renewed creation. The material particulars of the eschatological era, including the particulars of worship, cannot be seen to stand outside of the Spirit's concerns. To do so is to ignore the comprehensive scope of Christ's redemptive work. It is also to fail to reckon with John's presentation of the Spirit as the one who, as agent of both the Father and the Son, realizes and fulfills the divine will *on earth*.[46] Though Calvin is right to stress the work of the Spirit to renew the hearts and minds of people, he largely overlooks the multiple ways in which John advances a positive relationship between the Spirit and the new creation.

The Material Signs of Christ

Third, the symbolic work of Jesus in John's Gospel, as *sēmeia* that reveal his glory, underscores the goodness of materiality in the symbols of the church's worship. When John 1:32 states that the Spirit descends "as a dove" on Jesus, Calvin understands this to be an example of metonymy:

42. Cf. Rikki E. Watts, *Isaiah's New Exodus in Mark* (Grand Rapids: Baker Books, 2000).

43. John 1:29; 5:14; 8:7–11; 16:7–11.

44. Marianne Meye Thompson, "The Breath of Life: John 20:22–23 Once More," in *The Holy Spirit and Christian Origins*, ed. Stanton, Longenecker, and Barton, 78.

45. Lee, "In the Spirit of Truth," 284.

46. Stephen Smalley, "Pneumatology in the Johannine Gospel and Apocalypse," in *Exploring the Gospel of John*, ed. Culpepper and Black, 292.

"Not that it is really the Spirit, but it shows Him in a way man can grasp," as a sign of gentleness.[47] This way of figuring things symbolically, he adds, "is usual in the Sacraments." It is also "a frequent and common way of speaking in Scripture."[48] With respect to the "visible sign" of water, God testifies and seals the new life that Christ accomplishes in the faithful through the Spirit. When Jesus says that the wind blows where it wills, Calvin believes this is a way of speaking of the incomprehensible power of God's Spirit to preserve "the estate of our bodies."[49]

Calvin reasons that all the outward symbols that Jesus employs in John's Gospel involve a positive purpose: "Christ freely and often adorned the outward symbols with His miracles, either to accustom believers to the use of signs, or to show that all things were under His will, or to testify that there is just so much power in each of His creatures as He chooses to give."[50]

And yet, as often as not, Calvin worries that these material symbols will also lead the faithful astray.[51] The six waterpots that feature in Jesus's miracle at Cana are, for Calvin, a sign of Jewish superstition. The line of thought he argues here is typical of his general anxiety over external aids to worship: "As the world is prone to excess in externals, the Jews, not satisfied with the simplicity enjoined by God, amused themselves with continual sprinklings; and since superstition is ambitious, it undoubtedly led to ostentation."[52]

Much like the Jews of Jesus's day, the papacy arranges its public worship "for pure display."[53] The weak faith of the Jews in 2:23 led them to cling "to the world and earthly things." Calvin explains: "For because we are carnal, nothing is harder than to tear from our minds this foolish attitude by which we drag down Christ from heaven to us."[54] Echoing his sentiments on music, he adds, "We know how cold and sluggish our attention is if we are not excited by something external."[55] Jesus's command

47. *Comm.* John 1:32. Calvin cites Isa. 42:3 as a backdrop for this idea.
48. *Comm.* John 3:5.
49. *Comm.* John 3:8.
50. *Comm.* John 9:7.
51. This is a worry that Calvin's contemporaries did not share to the same degree. See Barbara Pitkin, "Seeing and Believing in the Commentaries on John by Martin Bucer and John Calvin," *Church History* 68 (1999): 883–85.
52. *Comm.* John 2:6.
53. *Comm.* John 2:6. See also Pitkin, "Calvin as Commentator on the Gospel of John," 185.
54. *Comm.* John 16:7.
55. *Comm.* John 20:31. In a note on John 10:38, Calvin writes, "For rebels want to

to wash one another's feet, in John 13, is interpreted as a general principle, whereas the papists "hold a theatrical feet-washing" that results only in a shameful mockery of Christ.[56] Finally, they wrongly practice the laying on of hands as a sign of apostolic succession, when all that is needed, Calvin argues, is to witness "the gifts of the Holy Spirit" in the ordained person.

While some disciples are weak, Calvin believes others are hard-hearted, as Thomas is seen to be. Rather than viewing Thomas's experience of the resurrection of the Wounded One as positive, Calvin sees Thomas's request to feel Christ's wounds as a sign of a monstrous "stupidity and wickedness."[57] Where future disciples are commended for believing in Jesus apart from sensory confirmation, Thomas feels the need to be "drawn violently to faith by the experience of his senses."[58] As Calvin reasons, the need for such a "sensual judgment" is the opposite of faith.[59] Even more strongly, he asserts that "all our senses fade away and fail when we have to do with God."[60] In contrast to this weak faith, the kind of faith that Christ commends is that which acquiesces "in the simple Word and does not depend at all on the sense and reason of the flesh."[61]

None of these arguments should surprise us. By now we have witnessed a consistent pattern of thought in Calvin. While he commends material symbols in John, he qualifies this commendation by noting their limited benefit or by stressing the habit of humans to pervert them by placing inordinate trust in them. Although this danger is real in John's record of Jesus's ministry, it does not tell the whole story. Where Calvin qualifies the benefit of the *sēmeia* at every turn, no qualification of *sēmeia* is required according to the Johannine narrative. Though never ends in themselves, the *sēmeia* by which the Beloved Disciple frames his story are regarded as central to God's self-disclosure in Jesus Christ. And while they are not capable of automatically generating saving faith, the material property of the *sēmeia* is not seen to pose an intrinsic problem to this saving faith. Quite the opposite—an intimate link between sign and materiality is posited in the Fourth Gospel.

---

know before they believe. And yet God indulges us so far as to prepare us for faith by a knowledge of His works." See also *Comm.* John 2:11, 23; 4:53; 7:31; 11:45.

56. *Comm.* John 13:14–15.

57. *Comm.* John 20:24, 27. Cf. *Comm.* John 6:30; 3.2.5; Pitkin, "Calvin as Commentator on the Gospel of John," 194–96.

58. *Comm.* John 20:29.

59. *Comm.* John 20:25.

60. *Comm.* John 3:13.

61. *Comm.* John 20:29.

For one, "sign" in John is not to be confused with "sign" as it is popularly used. Dorothy Lee explains, "Whereas the sign stands [in the everyday, non-Johannine sense] for something absent, the symbol brings to expression that which is present." Furthermore, in John an important connection exists between symbolic form, narrative development, and theological meaning.[62] Lee writes, "Each narrative is created to unfold a central symbol and the development of the symbol, in turn, draws out the narrative. . . . In theological terms, the narratives reveal the way in which material reality becomes symbolic of the divine."[63] The material aspect of the *sēmeia*, in this light, is fundamental to the revelatory and soteriological purposes of God, not a concession to the weaknesses of human faith, as Calvin imagined.[64]

More particularly, rather than negating Jesus's life and ministry, the *sēmeia* substantiate it as evidence of God's presence and favor.[65] Thus, for example, in John 5 Jesus heals a man at the pool on a Sabbath, for this is what God does: heal human bodies. In John 6 Jesus feeds an impossibly large crowd of people, for again this is what God does: feed human bodies. In John 9 Jesus heals a man born blind on a Sabbath day, for this is what God does: mend human bodies. He does more than this, to be sure, but according to the Fourth Evangelist he does no less, for through these intensively material acts, Jesus displays the Father's glory.[66] The *sēmeia*, then, not only point to God's *doxa*; they express it. In Johannine perspective they are in some way constitutive of Christ's identity rather than accidental to it or mere accommodations to a "rude" people.

For John, to speak of the sphere in which worship is actualized in this new hour is to speak of a symbolic reality.[67] Yet this does not entail

62. Lee, *The Symbolic Narratives of the Fourth Gospel*, 16.

63. Lee, *The Symbolic Narratives of the Fourth Gospel*, 11. See also Sandra Schneiders, "History and Symbolism in the Fourth Gospel," in *Évangile de Jean* (Gembloux, Belgium: Duculot, 1977), 371–76; and "Symbolism and the Sacramental Principle in the Fourth Gospel," in *Segni e sacramenti nel vangelo di Giovanni* (Rome: Editrice Anselmiana, 1977), 223, 229.

64. Cf. Marianne Meye Thompson, *The Humanity of Jesus in the Fourth Gospel* (Philadelphia: Fortress, 1988), 53–86; Barrett, *St. John*, 76.

65. Thompson, *The Humanity of Jesus in the Fourth Gospel*, 86: the *sēmeia* "are concrete manifestations of God's glory in the human sphere, which John views as a primary—if not the primary—clue to Jesus' identity." Thomas H. Olbricht, "The Theology of the Signs in the Gospel of John," in *Johannine Studies: Essays in Honor of Frank Pack*, ed. James E. Priest (Malibu, CA: Pepperdine University Press, 1989), 174. Cf. John 1:49; 20:31.

66. Cf. Craig R. Koester, *Symbolism in the Fourth Gospel: Meaning, Mystery, Community* (Minneapolis: Fortress, 2003), 3.

67. Lee, *The Symbolic Narratives of the Fourth Gospel*, 82: the Samaritan woman "is

an antithetical or ambivalent relationship to the material sphere. In John's Gospel, there are no such things as "mere" *sēmeia*; nor are *sēmeia* to be confused for figures of speech. Quite the opposite, the symbols here entail a *particular* material shape: a Christomorphic, Spirit-empowered shape. As such, what the language of "Spirit and Truth" points to is a symbolic instantiation of worship in a new-covenantal era, with implications for not only the content and activities but also the material configuration of actual liturgies. To worship in the sphere of Christ and the Spirit, then, points to a material reality in which the glory of God is inevitably *configured* and *expressed*, much like the *sēmeia* throughout John.

The Johannine *sēmeia*, in summary, not only represent a series of significant events that mediate and reveal the power of God, they also indicate a symbolic habit of being, describing baptism and table fellowship, footwashing and healings, feastings and breathings. The *sēmeia* convey an efficacious embodied presence, with implications for the entire shape of the community's life, not just doctrinal concepts or matters of the heart. When viewed this way, it is not unreasonable to suppose that the disciples would carry on this kind of symbolic way of life, entrusted as they were with the Spirit's power to perpetuate Jesus's mission.[68]

Materially and Symbolically Mediated Worship

Fourth, whatever else worship "in Spirit and Truth" may be, whether simple or fulsome, for John it is materially and symbolically mediated worship rooted in the activity of the triune God. We can therefore state the following points with a high measure of confidence.

The Work of the Triune God

For one, the primary accent in John's Gospel rests on the work of the triune God to enable disciples to worship God rightly; it does not rest on the work of the human creature.[69] This point, I suggest, is fundamentally

---

not offered a 'spiritualized' [i.e., nonmaterial] understanding of worship which stands over against the physical, but rather a symbolic one."

68. Wright, "Worship and the Spirit in the New Testament," 24, links a Trinitarian reading to this concern about materiality.

69. Cf. R. G. Gruenler, *The Trinity in the Gospel of John: A Thematic Commentary on*

sympathetic to Calvin's liturgical theology. As he comments in book 4 of the 1559 *Institutes*: "Believers have no greater help than public worship, for by it God raises his own folk upward step by step." Hughes Oliphant Old summarizes what Calvin scholars have widely observed when he says, "What Calvin has in mind is that God is active in our worship. . . . For Calvin the worship of the church is a matter of divine activity rather than human creativity."[70] Inasmuch as this statement can be said to represent a Calvinian picture of public worship, it coheres with the basic vision of worship in John's Gospel.

Yet this is not exactly the tack that Calvin takes in his exegesis of John 4. In this instance, Calvin interprets Jesus's pronouncement on worship as a statement about the essence of God rather than about the activity of the Trinity. Calvin also believes the interior condition of the worshiper is at stake rather than the conditions under which the triune Persons enable right worship to occur. Consistent with the Trinitarian shape of the Fourth Gospel, however, I argue that a Trinitarian reading of John 4 makes better sense of the literary, narrative, and theological data.[71] Employing language similar to that which I advanced in chapter 4, Bruner wonderfully elucidates this dynamic activity:

> How do we come to God the Father? By Spirit and Truth, Jesus now teaches, that is to say, by *the Spirit's* going *down deep* into the human hearts and moving them *upward* to faith in and focus on the living Truth who is *Jesus*, who then in tandem with the Spirit brings us spiritually, or ever since his Ascension brings us through the outward means of grace—the Church, the Word, the sacraments, and the Christian people in the world, materially—*upward still more* to the heart's goal: to God the Father . . . down, down, and down; up, up, and up; and then in a moment, out, out, and out into the wide world.[72]

---

the *Fourth Gospel* (Grand Rapids: Baker Books, 1986); Hengel, "The Prologue of the Gospel of John," 292.

70. Old, "John Calvin and the Prophetic Criticism of Worship," in *John Calvin and the Church: A Prism of Reform*, ed. Timothy George (Louisville: Westminster John Knox, 1990), 234. Witvliet, "Images and Themes in John Calvin's Theology of Liturgy," 145: "At the heart of Calvin's vision is the notion that worship is charged with divine activity."

71. On this point, see Lee, "In the Spirit of Truth," 296; Wright, "Worship and the Spirit in the New Testament," 11.

72. Bruner, *The Gospel of John*, 263–64, emphasis original.

Mediated Worship

Second, worship in a Johannine perspective will be a materially and symbolically mediated worship. Calvin nowhere doubts that God himself has provided the church with suitable material symbols of worship. God has furnished his people with external helps of worship according to the need of the times ("old" or "new") and in a manner that befits the human condition in its earthly pilgrimage. The purpose of these helps is to allow the body to be "exercised" at the same time as the soul.[73] Indeed, all bodily exercises are seen to be useful insofar that they serve the "practice of godliness," which concerns the integrity of the human creature.[74] As he explains in a comment on Genesis 12:7, "The inward worship of the heart is not sufficient, unless external profession before men be added."[75] On this view, Calvin rightly perceives that John's presentation of Jesus's miracles involves a certain adornment by outward symbols, which, in turn, gives evidence of the need for both soul and body to be involved in the experience of genuine faith.[76]

Yet, inasmuch as Calvin believes that external confession is an apt fruit of the confession that arises from the heart, the dominant stress is placed on the heart and mind.[77] A certain regret is eventually attached to the human need for sensory attestation of God in worship. I contend that Calvin qualifies the value of material media, whereas the Johannine narrative requires none. While Calvin is right to issue a caution against the misunderstanding or abuse of material symbols of worship, he is wrong to regard them as marginal to the work of worship or as radically subordinate to the activities of the soul. G. K. Beale identifies in John 4 an aspect that Calvin perceived, namely, that Jesus's statement to the Samaritan woman involved the offer of greater intimacy with the Father.[78] Yet, like plenty

73. "On the Necessity of Reforming the Church," 127.

74. *Comm.* 1 Tim. 4:8. Calvin adds, in 3.19.8, that, if they have not been commanded by the Bible, such bodily exercises should be left a matter of Christian freedom; no one's conscience ought ever to be constrained to perform them.

75. *CO* 23:181.

76. *Comm.* John 9:7.

77. 3.3.16: "When we have to deal with God nothing is achieved unless we begin from the inner disposition of the heart."

78. G. K. Beale, "Jesus as the Temple of the New Creation in John" (paper presented at ETS, Baltimore, November 2013). Beale believes that temple-like worship in a New Testament era will be focused on activities of teaching, evangelism, discipleship, and making more worshipers. For Beale, this is what a "spiritual service of worship" entails.

of theologians in Calvin's wake, Beale fails to grasp the implications of Jesus's words for the material and symbolic shape of the church's worship.

This connection matters because John's Gospel involves a contest not only of disputed beliefs but also of disputed practices.[79] Practices are not regarded as irrelevant in John. Instead, they are transfigured with the advent of Christ and the gift of the Holy Spirit.[80] The need for a symbolically informed place of worship, moreover, is not replaced by the allegedly superior nonmaterial activities of heart and mind. Rather, new symbols are required by the faithful to give expression to worship in this new hour. "Living waters" do not endlessly swirl in the depths of the human soul; they spring out symbolically in the practice of baptism. The miracle of Jesus at Cana does not signal messianic replacement or, as Calvin supposed, a "carnal" need for material expressions of God's kingdom; rather, it signals messianic fullness.[81] God's abundant life, symbolized in the exorbitant production of wine, is given expression in both the body of Christ, poured out for the life of the world, and in the eucharistic body, which, "like a rich and inexhaustible fountain," pours into the faithful the life of God.[82]

To put my point otherwise, worship in the Johannine picture is not an immediate experience of God. It is a mediated experience: in the Spirit, through the Truth, while also through the church, through its people and its practices.[83] Worship that the Spirit makes possible is in this way enfleshed in the new life that God in Christ makes possible in his disciples: in their speech, their actions, their bodies, and the material media that liturgically symbolize the new life in Christ.[84] Richard Hays argues that, despite the common perception of John as otherworldly and ethereal, "this gospel's aesthetic vision is deeply grounded in the *particular*, the *palpable*, and the *embodied*."[85] Though the material creation in John

---

79. Marianne Meye Thompson argues this point persuasively in "Reflections on Worship in the Gospel of John," *Princeton Seminary Bulletin* 19 (1998): 259–78.

80. Thettayil, *In Spirit and Truth*, 122.

81. Thompson, "Reflections on Worship in the Gospel of John," 266.

82. 4.17.9.

83. Cf. Lee, *The Symbolic Narratives of the Fourth Gospel*, 82–83.

84. It is noteworthy that the Scriptures include numerous examples of material objects that—both accompanied by and apart from faith—mediate the power and presence of God: the tabernacle altar, Moses's rod, Elijah's mantle, Elisha's bones, Paul's handkerchief, and Jesus's own robe.

85. Richard B. Hays, "The Materiality of John's Symbolic World," in *Preaching John's Gospel: The World It Imagines*, ed. David Fleer and Dave Bland (St. Louis, MO: Chalice Press, 2008), 6, emphasis original.

obtains a provisional status on account of its frail and sinful character, it also obtains a fundamentally positive status because of Christ's resurrection and the Spirit, who enables the disciples to live this resurrected life.[86] John's Gospel points us therefore to a new-covenantal worship where the material creation plays an indispensable role: narratively through the story it tells (e.g., in footwashing) and dramatically through the story it enacts (e.g., by way of eucharistic gatherings).[87]

The Supposition of Simple Worship

Additionally, simple worship is not an explicit description or requirement that John 4 encourages. Simplicity, whatever may be meant by that term, is something that must be inferred from an exegesis of the broader text. While not incompatible as a general principle for worship, a simple material and ceremonial shape of worship is not a necessary conclusion from John 4:23–24. Though Calvin's language about simple worship involves the possibility of ambiguity, there is much less doubt about that which stands on the opposite side of simplicity. With respect to rhetoric in general, it would have included for Calvin all manner of prolixity, philosophical cleverness, and "fineness of style" that distorts the meaning of the gospel, along with anything that deluded "simple folk." Calvin rightly expressed repeated concern over empty showmanship, ostentatious external aids, chasing after paltry glory, liturgical ornamentation that obscured Christ or disguised rather than disclosed the gospel, and anything that intoxicated the senses or precluded a communal experience of worship.[88]

It is important to concede here that the historical circumstances in which he executed his liturgical reforms offer a plausible explanation for Calvin's prescriptions of a "moderate" adornment of churches and a "simple" exercise of liturgical ceremonies.[89] Even if public worship ought to be somehow simple, it is not self-evident that "simplicity" involves *less* use of material media.[90] No doubt, this conclusion is taken as self-evident

---

86. Cf. Brown, *John*, 131, 140–41, 296, 299ff.; also John 6:63; Isa. 40:6–8.

87. Cf. Wright, "Worship and the Spirit in the New Testament," 23.

88. Cf. 3.20.30.

89. See my comments at the end of chap. 1 for specific details on Calvin's historical context.

90. Cf. Calvin's comments on the requirement of moderation in the adornment of churches in 4.5.18.

in the Reformed tradition. Terry Johnson embraces this legacy when he states that "the worship of Reformed Protestantism is simple. We merely read, preach, pray, sing and see the Word of God. . . . True worship then must be primarily (though not absolutely) non-material, non-sensual, and non-symbolic."[91] Yet the requirement that the material media of worship be simple, Spartan, moderate, seemly, economical, or decent is an inference that must be drawn on the basis of theological presuppositions, for nowhere in the New Testament is this a normative goal for public worship. While the shape and activities of worship must be protected from idolatrous, hypocritical, and superstitious uses, there is no necessary injunction in the Gospels or Epistles that it be materially, let alone aesthetically, simple.

In fact, John's Gospel may invite just the opposite conclusion. From the outset it is clear that God's self-revelation in Christ involves "fullness" (1:14). What sort of fullness? John tells and shows the reader. At Cana Jesus turns water into an excessive amount of wine, as much as 680 liters (2:1–11). When Jesus might have spoken a mere word to the man born blind (9:1–7), he indulges in an extravagant drama of mud and water. He raises a dead body from the grave (11:1–44), he authorizes a large catch of fish (21:1–11), and he feeds an extraordinary number of people—roughly 5,000, not counting women and children (6:6–13). These are not the signs of a parsimonious regard for the material creation. Nor do they signal a bias for soul over body. These are the sign of a fullness (*plērōma*) of life that Jesus bestows on his disciples (1:16).

More succinctly, in John we discover no disparagement of material space, no "sacred space," no secularizing of space.[92] We discover instead the possibility of an opening out of space significantly imbued with "Spirit and Truth." We discover a way in which the material creation has been reconfigured by the triune God. We discover a vision in which materiality has been freed by the Spirit to extend beyond the designs of the Jerusalem temple in order to take full advantage of the "stuff" of creation to give a Christomorphic expression to worship rendered in a new-covenantal key.[93] It is therefore a sympathetic extension of John's presentation of

---

91. Johnson, *Reformed Worship*, 38. Cf. Robert M. Stevenson, *Patterns of Protestant Church Music* (Durham, NC: Duke University Press, 1953), 21.

92. Cf. H. Wayne Johnson, "John 4:19–24: Exegetical Implications for Worship and Place" (paper presented at ETS, Baltimore, November 2013).

93. Contra Urban C. von Wahlde, *The Gospel and Letters of John*, vol. 2: *Commentary on the Gospel of John* (Grand Rapids: Eerdmans, 2010), 183.

worship, rather than a contravention of it, for the church, in due time and under the right conditions, to explore a broad range of aesthetic possibilities for the material and symbolic shape of worship that occurs in the Son, by the Spirit, to the Father's glory.

Conclusion

If all of creation is renewed through Jesus's *flesh*, as John's Gospel implies and as Calvin's reading of John 6 suggests, then the material shape of worship cannot be excluded from this renewing work. The good news of Jesus also holds good news for the physical creation in a liturgical context. The Holy Spirit, as the Executor of the new creation, continues this good work by effecting a *Spirit-ual* renewal, not only of invisible matters but also of visible matters. To worship in the sphere of Christ and the Spirit, then, points to a material reality in which the glory of God is expressed, whether ornately or simply, whether "excessively" or economically. If the logic of Scripture opens up a way for the arts, as material artifacts, to feed and form the faithful in the context of public worship, and if Calvin's theology of materiality was to be seen as including potential trajectories for the flourishing of the liturgical arts, then these possibilities can be only glimpsed in this book, not fully developed. It is to this possibility for the liturgical arts that we now turn.

Conclusion

Just what is it that we expect a work of art to do *in liturgical space?*

Trevor Hart, "Unseemly Representations"

If it is the Christian God who comes to be revealed in the "re-enchanted" world, then material forms will no longer be encountered as brute or threatening presences but will instead speak to us in the accents of love.

Mark Wynn, "Re-enchanting the World"

But love will best judge what may hurt or edify; and if we let love be our guide, all will be safe.

Calvin, *Institutes*

A cursory glance at Calvin's ideas about musical instruments may lead the average reader to believe that his thinking is simple on this point. Looking at the matter more closely, as we have done in this book, is to discover a far more complicated but also far more interesting terrain of thought. While commentators have observed that Calvin excludes musical instruments because they belonged to the era of "figures and shadows," they have often overlooked critical emphases in Calvin's thinking. As Calvin reasons, not only do musical instruments belong to the era of "shadows," characteristic of an old-covenantal worship, but they also fail to meet the requirements of new-covenantal worship: that it be "spiritual," "simple," and "articulate." To be sure, there is a consistent anxiety in Calvin over the capacity of materiality to distort the public worship of God and to mislead the worship of the faithful in idolatrous or superstitious ways. But it also the case that Calvin's language of "shadow," "spiritual," "simple," and "articulate" is far from straightforward.

With the presumption that we would discover the fate of the liturgical arts only after we examined Calvin's view of materiality in public worship, this book has undertaken a concentrated investigation of Calvin's ideas about the material creation (the "shadows"), the resurrected body of Christ (the "spiritual"), and the material character of worship (the "simple"), setting aside, for now, Calvin's concern for "articulate" worship. Two basic patterns of thought can be observed in Calvin's thinking. When considered within a liturgical context, Calvin's theology of materiality is marked by a line of thought that gives preference to the essence of God, accenting the invisible, immaterial nature of God, and by an emphasis on the interior domain of the human creature, focused on the internal activities of the soul. When considered outside of a liturgical context, though, a conspicuously Trinitarian pattern of thought marks Calvin's theological frame of mind. Here we discover a distinctly christological and pneumatological reading of materiality; here also we discover a more positive regard for the material creation, for physical bodies, and for material symbols in God's economy.

While I part with Calvin where I believe that he has failed to take the logical implications of his Trinitarian theology far enough, I nonetheless discover a theology of materiality in Calvin that offers itself as a rich resource for considering the nature of Christian worship. Calvin's "creaturely pessimism," in point of fact, is unwarranted on his own terms. What the Spirit accomplishes in Christ's whole humanity, to which the faithful are made partakers by that same Spirit, on Calvin's own terms augurs a much more positive outcome, for instance, for human bodies in public worship. The material condition of public worship, then, is not to "get out of the way" but rather to be caught up in the work of the Two Hands of God. A more integral role for the physical creation and therefore also for the arts, under this light, is possible on Calvinian terms. And a Trinitarian grammar of thought opens up hereby a fruitful way for understanding the mutual relationship between the logic of public worship and the logic of the arts, where the arts can be seen to serve the purposes of worship in their own way, though not on their own terms. Even then, as Calvin perceives that God appropriates material things, such as eucharistic bread or the "sweetness" of creation, to form and feed the church, so I believe that God may also take the liturgical arts to form and feed the church and in this way enable them to flourish in the public worship of the faithful.

The Flourishing of the Liturgical Arts on Calvinian Terms

The question that our study has left outstanding is the following: How exactly may the liturgical arts be said to flourish on Calvinian terms? For some, it is presumed that there is nothing interesting to discover in Calvin's liturgical theology. So the answer to this question is moot. Others may feel that nothing more *should* be said; Calvin has already said everything that could be said about the liturgical arts in light of his biblical arguments, or his social location predetermines the sorts of things that might have been said.[1] Still others may dismiss his views as theologically problematic (dualistic, pessimistic, Platonic) and therefore inimical to a fruitful investigation of the arts in worship. In this book I contend, however, that there is in fact something interesting to discover in Calvin's theology. But before we can discover what that is, we need to define the term "flourishing." Two senses can be suggested. One sense of flourishing envisions an increase in the number, kind, and uses of the arts in public worship. A second sense of flourishing points to the right conditions in which any kind of liturgical art, whether few or many, whether "high" or "low," will effectively serve the purposes of public worship. In this conclusion, I focus on the second sense.

Hewing closely to Calvin's explicit theological and exegetical concerns, the flourishing of the liturgical arts might look something like the following: As products of human making, arising out of the stuff of creation, the arts flourish in a liturgical context *if they are inextricably linked to Word and Spirit, promote order, exhibit beauty, render pious joy, and prompt the faithful to "lift their hearts" to God together, rather than remain*

1. On this point it seems that Richard Muller, in his "Historiography in the Service of Theology and Worship: Toward Dialogue with John Frame," *Westminster Theological Journal* 59 (1997): 309, has confused a pastoral rationale for the liturgical arts with a theological rationale: "In a historical context where musical instruments do not appear as the trappings of ecclesiastical abuse, the theological reasons for excluding them no longer apply. They fall into the realm of *adiaphora* and are permitted as means to glorify God."

entrapped in self-absorbed concerns, and "return" with God to earth, rather than remain unmoved by the ethical and missional realities that await them in the world at large.

While this statement represents one way to render Calvin's liturgical ethos, I wish to propose a more synthetic view that extends beyond what Calvin himself imagined but that remains faithful to his Trinitarian theology and to his fundamental vision for ecclesial life. I propose that the liturgical arts flourish on Calvinian terms *(1) when they are regarded as creaturely media that (2) participate in the work of the triune God to establish right worship for the church and (3) fittingly serve the activities and purposes of public worship.*

1. The liturgical arts are creaturely media.

While there is no such thing as a theologically neutral understanding of creation, I place this criterion first in order to follow the basic movement of this book: from a consideration of the physical creation in general, to a consideration of materiality in the specific context of public worship. I suggest that the liturgical arts should be seen chiefly as creaturely media; as such, they possess a God-given integrity to be particularly "themselves," through which the glory of the triune God is disclosed.

From Calvin's perspective, creation represents the "hands and feet" of Christ and the abundant provision of God, which the human creature is invited to enjoy for both "useful" (practical and biological) and "nonuseful" (aesthetic) reasons. On this view, creation is a place *for* something: for goodness, for discovery, for beauty, for vitality and fruitfulness, for action, for the worship of God, and for the mediation of God's presence to humanity. Though sin vitiates humanity's capacity to enjoy God in and through creation, sin does not rob creation of its capacity to stage a spectacle of God's powers. And while it is only with the help of the law, faith in Christ, and the internal witness of the Holy Spirit that the faithful are able to enjoy creation fully, for Calvin the faithful are, in fact, capable of discerning, and indeed of becoming ravished by, the glory of God *through* creation. If the church's praise can be said to be ontologically inseparable from creation's own praise, then the purpose of the liturgical arts will not be to "get out of the way" but rather to serve the purposes of the liturgy on behalf of creation. The purpose of liturgical artists will be to offer "articulate" voice to creation's praise, while never seeking to replace creation's own praise.[2] Their work will be to welcome the familiar and strange voice of creation into the liturgical sphere in response to the familiar and strange voice of God.

Calvin rightly stresses that the triune God has distinguished an innumerable variety of things in creation and has "endowed each kind with its own nature, assigned functions, appointed places and stations."[3] This is another way of saying that God has endowed the things of creation with their own integrity, which demands careful, respectful, and loving attention. One task for liturgical artists, therefore, would be to understand the logics and powers of the material stuff of creation. It would involve asking how color, stone, wood, metal, fabric, glass, and wind "work." What do they "do" and "say" and "tell" us about the world that God so loves and about our place in it as earthlings? If, as Calvin believes, a combination of empirical and sanctified sight afford the faithful right understanding of creation, what, then, might we observe about the dynamics of creation: its patterns and spontaneity, its simplicity and extravagance, its order and nonorder, its spare and ornate quality? Liturgical artists would likewise want to pay close attention to how human bodies work—how they relate to both material and social environments, how they connect to mind and emotions, how they acquire a "feel for the game" in a liturgical context.[4] Liturgical artists would want to discern how the built environment "works."[5] How do spaces and dwellings "inform" their inhabitants over time and thereby form a *habitus*, a way of being in the world? How do they open up and close down possibilities for relational, theological, spiritual, and missional formation within the context of corporate worship?[6]

If the liturgical arts function as a vehicle of God's glory through creation, to put the point sharply, it is only because the triune God enables creation to be *fit for* such a task. The liturgical arts are *capax Dei*: enabled by God to serve the praise of God on earth as it is in heaven.[7]

2. Cf. Begbie, "Christ, Creation, and Creativity," 169–85.
3. 1.14.20.
4. Pierre Bourdieu, *The Logic of Practice*, trans. Richard Nice (Stanford, CA: Stanford University Press, 1990), 66.
5. Ellen F. Davis, "The Tabernacle Is Not a Storehouse: Building Sacred Spaces," *Sewanee Theological Review* 49 (2006): 306: "A sanctuary has a kind of creative capacity of its own."
6. Plenty of good work has been done on these questions, not least by James K. A. Smith in *Imagining the Kingdom: How Worship Works* (Grand Rapids: Baker Academic, 2013).
7. 1.15.5. Cf. Peter J. Leithart, "Embracing Ritual: Sacraments as Rites," *Calvin Theological Journal* 40 (2005): 9: "Grace is not a thing or energy but God's attitude of favor to-

2. *The liturgical arts participate in the triune activity.*

For conversations revolving around the "disenchantment" of the late modern era, decried by theologians of all stripes,[8] Calvin's Trinitarian instincts on the material creation have much to commend themselves. Over against tendencies to view the liturgical arts as a neutral or negative force, as is often the case in biblicist or Reformed circles, or as inherently charged with a divine force, as might be the case in Radical Orthodox or Catholic circles, Calvin's account of materiality offers a way to construe the material media of worship in "relational" terms. On this account, it is not that architecture or bodies or choral songs are intrinsically endowed with "spiritual power," but rather that they are caught up in the dynamic activities of the triune God. As I have argued in this book, it is not so much that the liturgical arts mediate a transcendent experience for the faithful, nor do they possess automatic capacities to mediate divine grace. Instead it is that the Holy Spirit enables these very creaturely things to serve the activities of public worship in order to conform God's people to the image of his Son. The issue at hand is the telos of the liturgical arts— as christologically oriented, pneumatologically ordered, always aiming at the glory of the Father. To argue in this manner is to argue, with Trevor Hart, against a "free-for-all in which any and every material form may be appealed to as a likely site of encounter with" God, instead emphasizing

---

ward us, manifested in his coming near to us through his Spirit to form and renew covenant friendship, to have personal communion with us, and to offer us the gifts and blessings of Word and Sacrament."

8. As representative of this discussion, see, for example, Catherine Pickstock, "Liturgy and the Senses," in *Paul's New Moment: Continental Philosophy and the Future of Christian Theology*, ed. John Milbank, Slavoj Zizek, Creston Davis, with Catherine Pickstock (Grand Rapids: Brazos Press, 2010), 125–45; *Radical Orthodoxy: A New Theology*, ed. John Milbank, Catherine Pickstock, and Graham Ward (New York: Routledge, 1999); James K. A. Smith, *Thinking in Tongues: Pentecostal Contributions to Christian Philosophy* (Grand Rapids: Eerdmans, 2010); John Milbank, Graham Ward, and Edith Wyschogrod, *Theological Perspectives on God and Beauty* (Harrisburg, PA: Trinity Press International, 2003); Hans Boersma, *Heavenly Participation: The Weaving of a Sacramental Tapestry* (Grand Rapids: Eerdmans, 2011); and Charles Taylor, *A Secular Age* (Cambridge, MA: Belknap Press of Harvard University Press, 2007); for Taylor there is a particular blame that Calvin bears for expunging the world of "good" magic, "a world shorn of the sacred" (79–80). For a possible rebuttal of this view, see Laura Smit, "'The Depth behind Things': Toward a Calvinist Sacramental Theology," in *Radical Orthodoxy and the Reformed Tradition: Creation, Covenant, and Participation*, ed. James K. A. Smith and James H. Olthuis (Grand Rapids: Baker Books, 2005), 205–27.

what God chooses to do—and indeed *wishes* to do.[9] While Calvin may not articulate this idea himself, it is not wholly unwarranted to say that it remains faithful to the logic of his own Trinitarian sensibilities.

A Christological Reading of the Liturgical Arts Because Christ stands at the center of the cosmic order, the created realm can be properly regarded as the beloved world of God. Because Christ is the mediator of "the whole world,"[10] "the lawful heir of heaven and earth, by whom the faithful recover what they had lost in Adam,"[11] and the one who cares and keeps "all of creation in its proper state,"[12] creation discovers itself in motion: from the Father who has caught up the cosmos in the beloved life of his Son by the power of his Spirit. As the incarnate temple of God, Christ also grounds, orients, and gathers up all of creation's praise in a gift of love to the Father. Christ's praise, transposed in the church's praise, under this light, becomes an actual and symbolic prelude to the restoration of creation's perfect praise. The liturgical arts function hereby as a *partner* of Christ's praise and a *poet* to creation's praise. On the one hand, they join Christ's praise for the Father's marvelous works and offer praise *of* Christ *through* the Spirit. On the other, they join the praise of the cosmos, but also translate and transpose that praise through metaphoric and material language. From our study we have frequently noted that God's self-revelation in Christ involves a "fullness." If such fullness or excess were applied to the liturgical arts, I submit that they would not need to be seen as hindrances but rather as helps to the worship that the Father seeks and that the Spirit makes possible in Jesus's disciples. I further suggest that we might discover ways that seeing and sensing, not just hearing and speaking, adequately reflect Christ's life, freedom, and mystery.[13]

A Pneumatological Reading of the Liturgical Arts For Calvin, at his best, there is never *mere* materiality. There is always materiality *headed*

9. Trevor Hart, "Unseemly Representations," in *Between the Image and the Word: Theological Engagements with Imagination, Language and Literature* (Surrey, UK: Ashgate, 2013), 178.

10. *Comm.* Col. 1:17.

11. *Comm.* Ps. 8:6.

12. *Comm.* Heb. 1:3.

13. Butin, "Constructive Iconoclasm," 138. Butin summarizes what he believes are Calvin's own views on this issue in "Calvin's Humanist Image of Popular Late-Medieval Piety," 429–30.

somewhere, following the pull of the Spirit's work to bring all things into fellowship with God in Christ. Three things may be suggested for the liturgical arts in light of this understanding. First, if the Spirit is responsible for creation's order, then it is important not to think of this order like that of a military or factory assembly line, where precision and sameness figure largely. It is instead a creative order, neither homogenous nor topsy-turvy. It is the kind of order that is capable of surprising and enthralling. The liturgical arts, on this view, may contribute to a dynamic order, yielding new configurations of life and prompting praise to a God whose goodness is revealed through such fecundity. Second, if the Spirit is the one who gifts each thing in creation with a "space to be itself," in the same way that the Spirit enables the Son to occupy a particular space in the triune life, then the church may be encouraged to welcome the particular gifts that a given art medium may offer to public worship, trusting that the Spirit will incorporate all things in Christ and enable each thing to find its place in the kind of worship that the Father seeks. Finally, if the Spirit is the one who corrects "the inordinate desires of the flesh," conforming the lives of the faithful to the ordinate life of Christ, then it is with such a confidence in the Spirit's work that the faithful are freed both *from* undue anxiety over artistic "excesses" and *for* righteous pleasure in this theater of artistic abundance. To welcome this work of the eschatological Spirit in the liturgical arts is to welcome the work of the one who offers a fore-taste of the age to come.[14]

3. The liturgical arts serve the activities and purposes of the liturgy.

To argue that the liturgical arts should be seen as servants of the activities and purposes of public worship (whatever those may be in any given ecclesial context) is to argue, on the one hand, against the presumption that the arts should be allowed to do their own thing on their own terms, and, on the other, against the presumption that the arts have nothing unique to contribute. More positively, it is to argue that the primary purpose of public worship is conformity to Christ by his Spirit—out of which arise communion with God and an intimate commitment to God's purposes for the world—and that the various activities of worship contribute to this purpose in a broad range of ways.

14. *Comm.* Acts 2:2.

At a fundamental level, the Christomorphic orientation to the liturgical arts means that they are caught up in the movement *of* Christ *by* the Spirit to enable creation to become a dynamic theater *for* God's praise. It means that the liturgical arts are caught up in the movement of Christ himself: downward to earth by symbol and the Spirit, as Calvin might put it, outward for the life of the world, and upward in glorious ascent to fellowship with the Father.[15] It means that the liturgical arts do not merely exist but are rather caught up in a network of forces: if left to themselves, disintegrating on account of sin ("the world, the flesh, and the devil"); if submitted to God in Christ, reintegrated on account of the healing powers of the Spirit. Against Calvin's worries over the power of the arts to arouse errant passions, I suggest that the liturgical arts contribute to the sanctification of the church, countering the idols of the mind, the forgetfulness of memories, a will that is bent against God, and the disorder of broken bodies and dysfunctional affections. Against Calvin again, I suggest that the liturgical arts, as sensory attestations of God's holiness, contribute to a distinctly Christian cosmology. As indispensable rather than dispensable material media that liturgically symbolize the new life in Christ, the liturgical arts form the church in a holy imagination, enabling the faithful to live "in Christ," "as Christ," in the rest of their lives, for the sake of a cosmos marked by shalom.[16]

If the liturgical arts fulfill their purpose by serving the actions of public worship, such as praise and prayer, thanksgiving and confession, then the following may hold, to paraphrase Nicholas Wolterstorff: the liturgy calls for art; any action of the liturgy can be enhanced by art; all art used should enhance one or another action of the liturgy; the character of the action must fit the liturgical action it serves; and fittingness, not style, should primarily govern our decisions about the art used. It will also be true that liturgical arts will serve public worship in their own way, giving a broad range of artistic expression to liturgical activities.[17] The aim of the liturgical arts, however, is not to take creation's own praise onto some higher plane. Their aim is rather to invite the church to delight in cre-

15. Cf. 4.17.24.

16. Leithart, "Embracing Ritual," 14–15.

17. Contra Terry Johnson, *Reformed Worship*, 60–61: "Ostentatious displays of zeal, whether by shouting, by raising hands, by leaping about, or by other physical manifestations, have been restrained in Reformed circles by a sense of what is appropriate in a public worship service, as well as the desire not to draw attention to oneself or to claim too much for oneself."

ation's "endlessly remarkable quiddity" on behalf of the fundamental purposes of public worship.[18] Anything that risks distracting the faithful from these purposes of public worship requires careful scrutiny.[19] Such would include unnecessary multiplication (aesthetic engorgement), hypocrisy (engagement of body without heart and mind), idolatry (confusing Creator and creature), superstition (confusing the Source of power), and the dissociation of Word from any given liturgical art, thereby robbing it of its upward, or Godward, inertia.

The Liturgical Arts Feeding and Forming the Church

This entire line of thought is simply another way of saying what was proposed at the outset of this project: that the liturgical arts are a means for feeding and forming the church. On Calvinian terms, I suggest that the language of feeding is interchangeable with the language of "life-giving." To be fed by the liturgical arts is to be nourished with new life. Inasmuch as Calvin believed that God gave attestations of his grace by outward aids, or that the similitude of sound and smell (by way of the bells and pomegranates of the Jerusalem temple) "naturally leads us to the honoring of grace,"[20] it remains sympathetic to Calvin's Trinitarian instincts about the physical creation to propose that the liturgical arts also contribute to a grace-filled life. While caution is needed not to move too quickly from Calvin's eucharistic theology, with its rich regard for material media, to a theology of the liturgical arts, as material artifacts, it is not unreasonable to suppose that his Trinitarian theology opens up a way to perceive the arts in worship as media capable of feeding the faithful in God's grace, precisely because the Spirit of Christ makes this function possible.

On Calvinian terms, the liturgical arts serve the purposes of Christian formation into a holy and healthy life.[21] Such a formative view of the liturgical arts would mean that it is never impossible, only perhaps difficult, for a congregation to learn a new medium of liturgical art. This step would require right training, patience, and a willingness to learn. The case of children and the psalms in Geneva might well provide a paradigm

18. Bauckham, "Joining Creation's Praise of God," 52.

19. Cf. Abraham Kuyper, "Calvinism and Art," in *Lectures on Calvinism* (Grand Rapids: Eerdmans, 1931), 143.

20. *Comm.* Exod. 28:31; cf. *Comm.* Ps. 132:7; 4.17.24.

21. *Comm.* 1 Cor. 14:40.

THE THEATER OF GOD'S GLORY

for mature experiences of growth in a new liturgical art.[22] New liturgical arts *can* be learned, in point of fact, and therefore become intelligible over time, and in this way serve to edify the church. Sympathetic to Calvin's belief that the "affluence, sweetness, variety and beauty" of creation could train men and women to choose the good and to reject the evil and thereby to honor the Creator, I contend that the liturgical arts may disclose the knowledge of God, train the church in the "school of beasts," awaken desire for God through the beauty of the cosmos, foster obedience and love, chide ingratitude and pride in humanity's failure to acknowledge God's abundant provision, and summon the faithful to the praise of God in the common life of worship.

That being said, this book raises plenty of questions that have not been adequately addressed. What were the specific historical circumstances of worship in Geneva in relation to the kinesthetic character of that worship? What could we discover by bringing Calvin's liturgical theology into conversation with both Calvin's contemporaries (fellow Reformers and humanists) and the received tradition (medieval and patristic)? How might Calvin's interest in "rational" and "irrational" worship, by way of metaphoric and analogical language, open up possibilities for the arts? In what way exactly does the Spirit summon praise from "irrational creatures," prompt edifying adoration from the disciples at Pentecost who spoke in "unknown tongues," empower the teaching of Jesus through parables, inspire the writers of Holy Scripture through poetic media? How precisely might the liturgical arts, as largely metaphoric media, promote the "articulate" and therefore edifying worship for the church? How might the idea of accommodated language cohere with ideas of language that fittingly correspond to human creaturely capacity?

Might Calvin's Trinitarian theology open up different ways to conceive of liturgical architecture or liturgical imagery? Might Calvin's pneumatology offer insight into his ideas about art in worship? Might specific figures in the Reformed tradition broaden our understanding of the Spirit's work in the material shape of worship, such as John Williamson Nevin (with respect to the Spirit's role in the material elements of the Eucharist) or J. J. von Allmen (with respect to a recovery of the Spirit's role in the material forms of public worship) or Colin Gunton (with respect to the Spirit's work in the material creation)? What sorts of theological and

22. On this point, see Bruce Gordon, *Calvin* (New Haven: Yale University Press, 2009), 135–38.

194

practical models might offer wisdom for the increased use and variety of arts in public worship, specifically on Calvinian terms? Finally, how might Calvin's Trinitarian theology illuminate our understanding of order, to-getherness, or intelligibility with respect to the liturgical arts, in a way that remains largely absent in the Reformed tradition? While remaining outside of the proper scope of this book, all of these questions deserve careful, charitable consideration by scholars and clergy alike.

Conclusion

If the liturgical arts are viewed through the work of the Spirit in the light of Christ, as I have argued throughout this book, then the church in pub-lic worship is looking not at an escape from the material creation but rather at the preservation, healing, and liberation of the physical world so that the liturgical arts, as intensively material media, can be what the Father has eternally purposed for them. Rather than being seen as accom-modations to human weakness, the liturgical arts can be seen as media that fittingly symbolize the church's worship in light of the resurrection. Instead of being regarded as concessions to corporeal life this side of the eschaton, they can be regarded as physical media that remain commen-surate with the creaturely condition and that function as foretastes of the age to come.

On this view, the liturgical arts do not diminish corporate worship. Nor do they endanger the "acceptable" worship of God. Instead, they ably serve the economy of God in the public praise of God, as a portrait of God's glory in and through the physical creation. They become norma-tive, rather than incidental, to the church's vision of the good world that the Father has remade by way of his Two Hands. They complement and enhance, rather than merely illustrate, the verbal activities of worship. And they enable us to bring our whole humanity, along with the whole people of God, in an enactment of prayer and praise before the whole Godhead, for the sake of the whole world. What is the appropriate re-sponse of the faithful to God's gift of the liturgical arts? It is gratitude in the form of stewarding and then offering them back to God in love.

Select Bibliography

Original, Edited, and Translated Works by John Calvin

Battles, Ford Lewis, trans. *Catechism or Institution of the Christian Religion.* Pittsburgh: Pittsburgh Theological Seminary, 1972. Rev. ed., 1976.

———, trans. *Institutes of the Christian Religion (1536).* Rev. ed. Grand Rapids: Eerdmans, 1986.

Baum, Guilielmus, Eduardus Cunitz, and Eduardus Reuss, eds. *Ioannis Calvini opera quae supersunt omnia.* 59 vols. Brunswick: Schwetschke, 1863–1900.

Beveridge, Henry, trans. *Institutes of the Christian Religion (1559).* 2 vols. 1845–46. Reprint, Grand Rapids: Eerdmans, 1989.

———, trans. *Tracts and Treatises of John Calvin.* 3 vols. 1844–51. Reprint, Eugene, OR: Wipf & Stock, 2002.

Beveridge, Henry, and Jules Bonnet, eds. *Selected Works of John Calvin: Tracts and Letters.* 7 vols. 1844–58. Reprint, Grand Rapids: Baker Book House, 1983.

Bingham, Charles W., trans. *Commentaries of John Calvin.* 46 vols. Edinburgh: Calvin Translation Society, 1844–55. Reprint, Grand Rapids: Baker Book House, 1979.

Bonnet, Jules, comp. and ed. *Letters of John Calvin.* Translated by D. Constable (vols. 1–2) and M. R. Gilchrist (vols. 3–4). 4 vols. 1855–58. Reprint, New York: B. Franklin, 1973.

Garside, Charles, trans. "Foreword [Preface] to the Psalter." In *John Calvin: Writings on Pastoral Piety*, edited by Elsie Anne McKee. Classics of Western Spirituality. New York: Paulist Press, 2001.

Haroutunian, Joseph, and Louise P. Smith, trans. and eds. *Calvin: Commen-*

taries. Vol. 23 of *The Library of Christian Classics*. Philadelphia: Westminster, 1958.

Kelly, Douglas, trans. *Sermons on 2 Samuel 1–13*. Carlisle, PA: Banner of Truth Trust, 1992.

McGregor, Rob Roy, trans. *Sermons on Job*. Vol. 1, *Chapters 1–14*. Edinburgh: Banner of Truth Trust, 1993.

McNeill, John T., ed., and Ford Lewis Battles, trans. *Institutes of the Christian Religion (1559)*. Vols. 20–21 of the *Library of Christian Classics*. Philadelphia: Westminster, 1960.

Parker, T. H. L., ed. *Commentarius in epistolam Pauli ad Romanos*. Ioannis Calvini Opera Exegetica 13. Geneva: Librairie Droz, 1999.

———, ed. *Calvin's New Testament Commentaries*. Edinburgh: T&T Clark, 1993.

Reid, J. K. S., trans. *Calvin: Theological Treatises*. Vol. 22 of *The Library of Christian Classics* Philadelphia: Westminster, 1954.

Selderhuis, Herman J., ed. *Calvini Opera Database* 1.0. Apeldoorn: Institute voor Reformatieonderzoek, 2005.

Torrance, David W., and Thomas F. Torrance, eds. *Calvin's New Testament Commentaries*. 12 vols. Grand Rapids: Eerdmans, 1959–72.

Calvin and Reformed Studies

Balserak, Jon. *Divinity Compromised: A Study of Divine Accommodation in the Thought of John Calvin*. Dordrecht: Springer, 2006.

Barclay, John M. G. "Πνευματικός in the Social Dialect of Pauline Christianity." In *The Holy Spirit and Christian Origins: Essays in Honor of James D. G. Dunn*, edited by Graham N. Stanton, Bruce W. Longenecker, and Stephen C. Barton, 157–67. Grand Rapids: Eerdmans, 2004.

Barth, Karl. *The Theology of John Calvin*. Grand Rapids: Eerdmans, 1995.

Battenhouse, Roy. "The Doctrine of Man in Calvin and Renaissance Platonism." *Journal of the History of Ideas* 9 (1948): 447–71.

Battles, F. L. "God Was Accommodating Himself to Human Capacities." In *Readings in Calvin's Theology*, edited by Donald K. McKim, 21–42. Grand Rapids: Baker, 1984.

Benedict, Philip. "Calvinism as a Culture? Preliminary Remarks on Calvinism and the Visual Arts." In *Seeing beyond the Word: Visual Arts and the Calvinist Tradition*, edited by Paul Corby Finney, 19–48. Grand Rapids: Eerdmans, 1999.

Billings, Todd. *Calvin, Participation, and the Gift: The Activity of Believers in Union with Christ.* New York: Oxford University Press, 2008.

———. *Union with Christ: Reframing Theology and Ministry for the Church.* Grand Rapids: Baker Academic, 2011.

Bouwsma, William J. "The Spirituality of John Calvin." In *Christian Spirituality: High Middle Ages and Reformation,* edited by Jill Raitt, 318–33. New York: Crossroad Publishing, 1987.

Butin, Philip W. "Constructive Iconoclasm: Trinitarian Concern in Reformed Worship." *Studia Liturgica* 19 (1989): 133–42.

———. *Revelation, Redemption, and Response: Calvin's Trinitarian Understanding of the Divine-Human Relationship.* New York: Oxford University Press, 1995.

Butler, Diana. "God's Visible Glory: The Beauty of Nature in the Thought of John Calvin and Jonathan Edwards." *Westminster Theological Journal* 52 (1990): 13–26.

Canlis, Julie. *Calvin's Ladder: A Spiritual Theology of Ascent and Ascension.* Grand Rapids: Eerdmans, 2010.

Casey, Edward S. *Getting Back into Place: Toward a Renewed Understanding of the Place-World.* Bloomington: Indiana University Press, 2009.

Chung, Sung Wook, ed. *John Calvin and Evangelical Theology: Legacy and Prospect.* Louisville: Westminster John Knox, 2009.

Clark, R. Scott. *Recovering the Reformed Confession: Our Theology, Piety, and Practice.* Phillipsburg, NJ: P&R Publishing, 2008.

Clive, H. P. "The Calvinist Attitude to Music and Its Literary Aspects and Sources." *Bibliothèque d'Humanisme et Renaissance* 19.1 (1957): 80–102.

Cooke, Charles L. "Calvin's Illnesses and Their Relation to Christian Vocation." In *Calvin Studies IV,* edited by John H. Leith and W. Stacy Johnson, 41–52. Davidson, NC: Colloquium on Calvin Studies, 1988.

Cottin, Jérôme. "'Ce beau chef d'œuvre du monde': L'esthétique théologique de Calvin." *Revue d'histoire et de philosophie religieuses* 89 (2009): 489–510.

Crisp, Oliver D. *Retrieving Doctrine: Essays in Reformed Theology.* Downers Grove, IL: IVP Academic, 2010.

Danner, Dan G. "Johannine Christology during the Reformation." In *Johannine Studies: Essays in Honor of Frank Pack,* edited by James E. Priest, 36–53. Malibu, CA: Pepperdine University Press, 1989.

Davis, Thomas J. "Not 'Hidden and Far Off': The Bodily Aspect of Salvation and Its Implications for Understanding the Body in Calvin's Theology." *Calvin Theological Journal* 29 (1994): 406–18.

De Klerk, Peter, ed. *Calvin and the Holy Spirit: Papers and Responses Presented at the Sixth Colloquium on Calvin and Calvin Studies.* Grand Rapids: Calvin Studies Society, 1989.

Dowey, Edward A. *The Knowledge of God in Calvin's Theology.* 1952. Expanded ed. Grand Rapids: Eerdmans, 1994.

Eire, Carlos. *War against the Idols: The Reformation of Worship from Erasmus to Calvin.* Cambridge: Cambridge University Press, 1986.

Engel, Mary Potter. *John Calvin's Perspectival Anthropology.* Eugene, OR: Wipf & Stock, 1988.

Faber, J. *Essays in Reformed Doctrine.* Neerlandia, AB: Inheritance Publications, 1990.

Finney, Paul Corby, ed. *Seeing beyond the Word: Visual Arts and the Calvinist Tradition.* Grand Rapids: Eerdmans, 1999.

Föllmi, Beati A. "Calvin und das Psalmsingen: Die Vorschichte des Genfer Psalters." *Zwingliana* 36 (2009): 59–84.

Garside, Charles. "The Origins of Calvin's Theology of Music: 1536–1543." *Transactions of the American Philosophical Society* 4 (1969): 1–36.

Gerrish, B. A. *Grace and Gratitude: The Eucharistic Theology of John Calvin.* Minneapolis: Fortress, 1993.

——. "The Mirror of God's Goodness: Man in the Theology of Calvin." *Concordia Theological Quarterly* 45 (1981): 211–22.

——. "Sign and Reality: The Lord's Supper in the Reformed Confessions." In *The Old Protestantism and the New: Essays on the Reformation Heritage,* 118–49. Chicago: University of Chicago Press, 1982.

Goodloe, James C., IV. "The Body in Calvin's Theology." In *Calvin Studies V,* edited by John H. Leith, 103–17. Davidson, NC: Colloquium on Calvin Studies, 1990.

Gordon, Bruce. *Calvin.* New Haven: Yale University Press, 2009.

Gore, R. J., Jr. *Covenantal Worship: Reconsidering the Puritan Regulative Principles.* Phillipsburg, NJ: P&R Publishing, 2002.

Greef, Wulfert de. *The Writings of John Calvin, Expanded Edition: An Introductory Guide.* Translated by Lyle D. Bierma. Louisville: Westminster John Knox, 2008.

Guicharnaud, Hélène. "An Introduction to the Architecture of Protestant Temples Constructed in France before the Revocation of the Edict of Nantes." In *Seeing beyond the Word: Visual Arts and the Calvinist Tradition,* edited by Paul Corby Finney, 133–62. Grand Rapids: Eerdmans, 1999.

Gunton, Colin E. "Aspects of Salvation: Some Unscholastic Themes from

Calvin's Institutes." *International Journal of Systematic Theology* 1.3 (1999): 253–65.

Harink, Douglas K. "Spirit in the World in the Theology of John Calvin: A Contribution to a Theology of Religion and Culture." *Didaskalia* 61 (1998): 61–81.

Hart, Trevor. "Humankind in Christ and Christ in Humankind: Salvation as Participation in Our Substitute in the Theology of John Calvin." *Scottish Journal of Theology* 42 (1989): 67–84.

Harwood, Larry D. *Denuded Devotion to Christ: The Ascetic Piety of Protestant True Religion in the Reformation*. Eugene, OR: Pickwick Publications, 2012.

Heron, Alasdair. *Table and Tradition*. Edinburgh: Handsel Press, 1983.

Hesselink, I. John. *Calvin's First Catechism: A Commentary; Featuring Ford Lewis Battles's Translation of the 1538 Catechism*. Louisville: Westminster John Knox, 1997.

Hobbs, R. Gerald. "'Quam Apposita Religioni Sit Musica': Martin Bucer and Music in the Liturgy." *Reformation and Renaissance Review* 6.2 (2004): 155–78.

Howard, Griffith. "'The First Title of the Spirit': Adoption in Calvin's Soteriology." *Evangelical Quarterly* 73.2 (2001): 135–53.

Hunsinger, George. "The Bread That We Break: Toward a Chalcedonian Resolution of the Eucharistic Controversies." *Princeton Seminary Bulletin* 24 (2003): 241–58.

Joby, Christopher Richard. *Calvinism and the Arts: A Re-assessment*. Dudley, MA: Peeters, 2007.

Johnson, Terry. *Reformed Worship: Worship That Is according to Scripture*. Greenville, SC: Reformed Academic Press, 2000.

Kim, Jae Sung. "Unio Cum Christo: The Work of the Holy Spirit in Calvin's Theology." PhD diss., Westminster Theological Seminary, 1998.

Kinder, Ernst. "The Reformers' Doctrine of Man." *South East Asia Journal of Theology* 5 (1964): 32–42.

Kingdon, Robert M. "The Genevan Revolution in Public Worship." *Princeton Seminary Bulletin* 20.3 (1999): 264–80.

Krusche, Werner. *Das Wirken des Heiligen Geistes nach Calvin*. Göttingen: Vandenhoeck & Ruprecht, 1957.

Kuyper, Abraham. *Lectures on Calvinism*. Grand Rapids: Eerdmans, 1961.

Lee, Philip J. *Against the Protestant Gnostics*. Oxford: Oxford University Press, 1993.

MacDonald, Neil B., and Carl Trueman, eds. *Calvin, Barth, and Reformed Theology*. Milton Keynes, UK: Paternoster, 2008.

McDonald, Suzanne. "Beholding the Glory of God in the Face of Jesus Christ: John Owen and the 'Reforming' of the Beatific Vision." In *The Ashgate Research Companion to John Owen*, edited by Mark Jones and Kelly Kapci, 141–58. Aldershot, UK: Ashgate, 2012.

McDonnell, Killian. *John Calvin, the Church, and the Eucharist*. Princeton: Princeton University Press, 1967.

McKee, Elsie Anne. "Context, Contours, Contents: Towards a Description of the Classical Reformed Teaching on Worship." *Princeton Theological Seminary Bulletin* 16 (1995): 172–201.

———. "Reformed Worship in the Sixteenth Century." In *Christian Worship in Reformed Churches Past and Present*, edited by Lukas Vischer, 3–31. Grand Rapids: Eerdmans, 2003.

McKim, Donald K., ed. *Calvin and the Bible*. Cambridge: Cambridge University Press, 2006.

———. *The Cambridge Companion to John Calvin*. Cambridge: Cambridge University Press, 2004.

———. *Major Themes in the Reformed Tradition*. Grand Rapids: Eerdmans, 1992.

Miles, Margaret R. "Theology, Anthropology, and the Human Body in Calvin's Institutes of the Christian Religion." *HTR* 74 (1981): 303–23.

Millet, Oliver. "Art and Literature." In *The Calvin Handbook*, edited by Herman J. Selderhuis, translated by Henry J. Baron, Judith J. Guder, Randi H. Lundell, and Gerrit W. Sheeres, 418–27. Grand Rapids: Eerdmans, 2009.

———. *Calvin et la dynamique de la parole: Étude de rhétorique réformée*. Geneva: Slatkine, 1992.

Moeller, Pamela Ann. "Worship in John Calvin's 1559 *Institutes*, with a View to Contemporary Liturgical Renewal." PhD diss., Emory University, 1988.

Muller, Richard A. "Christ in the Eschaton: Calvin and Moltmann on the Duration of the Munus Regium." *HTR* 74 (1981): 31–59.

———. "Fides and Cognitio in Relation to the Problem of Intellect and Will in the Theology of John Calvin." *Calvin Theological Journal* 25 (1990): 207–24.

———. "Historiography in the Service of Theology and Worship: Toward Dialogue with John Frame." *Westminster Theological Journal* 59 (1997): 301–10.

————. *The Unaccommodated Calvin: Studies in the Foundation of a Theological Tradition.* Oxford: Oxford University Press, 2000.

Muller, Richard A., and John L. Thompson, eds. *Biblical Interpretation in the Era of the Reformation: Essays Presented to David C. Steinmetz in Honor of His Sixtieth Birthday.* Grand Rapids: Eerdmans, 1996.

Nevin, John Williamson. *The Mystical Presence: A Vindication of the Reformed or Calvinistic Doctrine of the Holy Eucharist.* Philadelphia: J. B. Lippincott, 1846.

Nichols, James H. *Corporate Worship in the Reformed Tradition.* Philadelphia: Westminster, 1968.

————. "The Liturgical Tradition of the Reformed Churches." *Theology Today* 11 (1954): 210–24.

Oberman, Heiko. "The 'Extra' Dimension in the Theology of Calvin." *Journal of Ecclesiastical History* 21.1 (1970): 43–64.

————. "The Pursuit of Happiness: Calvin between Humanism and Reformation." In *Humanity and Divinity in Renaissance and Reformation*, edited by John O'Malley, 251–83. Leiden: Brill, 1993.

Old, Hughes Oliphant. "John Calvin and the Prophetic Criticism of Worship." In *John Calvin and the Church: A Prism of Reform*, edited by Timothy George, 230–46. Louisville: Westminster John Knox, 1990.

————. *The Patristic Roots of Reformed Worship.* Zürcher Beiträge zur Reformationsgeschichte 5. Zürich: Theologischer Verlag, 1975.

————. *Worship: Reformed according to Scripture.* Louisville: Westminster John Knox, 2002.

Parker, T. H. L. "Calvin's Commentary on Hebrews." In *Church, Word, and Spirit: Historical and Theological Essays in Honor of Geoffrey W. Bromiley*, edited by James E. Bradley and Richard A. Muller, 135–40. Grand Rapids: Eerdmans, 1987.

————. *Calvin's Doctrine of the Knowledge of God.* Edinburgh: Oliver & Boyd, 1969.

————. *Calvin's Old Testament Commentaries.* Edinburgh: T&T Clark, 1986.

Parratt, John. "Witness of the Holy Spirit: Calvin, the Puritans, and St. Paul." *Evangelical Quarterly* 41.3 (1969): 161–68.

Partee, Charles. "The Soul in Plato, Platonism, and Calvin." *Scottish Journal of Theology* 22 (1969): 278–96.

————. *The Theology of John Calvin.* Louisville: Westminster John Knox, 2008.

Pitkin, Barbara. "Calvin as Commentator on the Gospel of John." In *Calvin and the Bible*, edited by Donald K. McKim, 164–98. Cambridge: Cambridge University Press, 2006.

————. "Seeing and Believing in the Commentaries on John by Martin Bucer and John Calvin." *Church History* 68 (1999): 865–85.

————. *What Pure Eyes Could See: Calvin's Doctrine of Faith in Its Exegetical Context*. Oxford: Oxford University Press, 1999.

Prins, Richard. "The Image of God in Adam and the Restoration of Man in Jesus Christ: A Study in Calvin." *Scottish Journal of Theology* 25 (1972): 32–44.

Quistorp, Heinrich. *Calvin's Doctrine of the Last Things*. Translated by Harold Knight. London: Lutterworth Press, 1955.

Ray, Richard A. "John Calvin on Theatrical Trifles in Worship." In *Calvin Studies VI*, edited by John H. Leith, 99–109. Davidson, NC: Colloquium on Calvin Studies, 1992.

Rogers, Eugene F., Jr. "The Mystery of the Spirit in Three Traditions: Calvin, Rahner, Florkensy; or, You Keep Wondering Where the Spirit Went." *Modern Theology* 19.2 (2003): 244–60.

Rozeboom, Sue A. "The Provenance of John Calvin's Emphasis on the Role of the Holy Spirit regarding the Sacrament of the Lord's Supper." PhD diss., University of Notre Dame, 2010.

Scholes, Percy A. *The Puritans and Music in England and New England: A Contribution to the Cultural History of Two Nations*. London: Milford, 1934.

Schreiner, Susan E. *The Theater of His Glory: Nature and the Natural Order in the Thought of John Calvin*. Durham, NC: Labyrinth Press, 1991.

Schwöbel, Christoph. "The Creature of the Word: Recovering the Ecclesiology of the Reformers." In *On Being the Church*, edited by Colin Gunton and Daniel Hardy, 110–55. Edinburgh: T&T Clark, 1989.

Selderhuis, Herman J., ed. *The Calvin Handbook*. Translated by Henry J. Baron, Judith J. Guder, Randi H. Lundell, and Gerrit W. Sheeres. Grand Rapids: Eerdmans, 2009.

————. *Calvin's Theology of the Psalms*. Grand Rapids: Baker Academic, 2007.

Selinger, Suzanne. *Calvin against Himself: An Inquiry in Intellectual History*. Hamden, CT: Archon Books, 1984.

Shu-Ying, Shih. "The Doctrine of Holy Spirit in the Theology of John Calvin." *Taiwan Journal of Theology* 31 (2009): 77–96.

Steinmetz, David. *Calvin in Context*. Oxford: Oxford University Press, 1995.

————. "The Reformation and the Ten Commandments." *Interpretation* 43 (1989): 256–66.

Tanner, Kathryn. *God and Creation in Christian Theology: Tyranny or Empowerment?* Oxford: Blackwell, 1998.

Taylor, John V. *The Go-Between God: The Holy Spirit and the Christian Mission*. Philadelphia: Fortress, 1973.

Torrance, T. F. *Calvin's Doctrine of Man*. Grand Rapids: Eerdmans, 1957.

———. "Calvin's Doctrine of the Trinity." *Calvin Theological Journal* 25 (1990): 165–93.

———. "Komm, Schöpfer Geist." *Theologische Zeitschrift* 21.2 (1965): 116–36.

Tylenda, Joseph. "Christ the Mediator: Calvin versus Stancaro." *Calvin Theological Journal* 8 (1973): 5–16.

Van der Kooi, Cornelis. *As in a Mirror: John Calvin and Karl Barth on Knowing God; A Diptych*. Translated by Donald Mader. Leiden: Brill, 2005.

VanderWilt, Jeffrey T. "John Calvin's Theology of Liturgical Song." *Christian Scholar's Review* 25.1 (1995): 63–82.

Vischer, Lukas. "Reich, bevor wir geboren wurden: Zu Calvins Verständnis der Schöpfung." *Evangelische Theologie* 69 (2009): 142–60.

Walt, B. J. van der, ed. *Calvinus Reformator: His Contribution to Theology, Church, and Society*. Transvaal, South Africa: Potschefstroom University for Christian Higher Education, 1982.

Wencelius, Léon. *L'esthétique de Calvin*. Geneva: Slatkine, 1979.

Willis, David, and Michael Welker, eds. *Toward the Future of Reformed Theology: Tasks, Topics, Traditions*. Grand Rapids: Eerdmans, 1999.

Witvliet, John D., and Nathan Bierma. "Liturgy." In *The Calvin Handbook*, edited by Herman J. Selderhuis, 407–17. Grand Rapids: Eerdmans, 2009.

Zachman, Randall C. *Image and Word in the Theology of John Calvin*. Notre Dame, IN: University of Notre Dame Press, 2007.

Secondary Sources

Arnold, Bill T. "Soul-Searching Questions about 1 Samuel 28: Samuel's Appearance at Endor and Christian Anthropology." In *What about the Soul? Neuroscience and Christian Anthropology*, edited by Joel B. Green, 75–83. Nashville: Abingdon, 2004.

Aston, Margaret. *England's Iconoclasts*. Oxford: Clarendon, 1988.

Auksi, Peter. *Christian Plain Style: The Evolution of a Spiritual Ideal*. Montreal and Kingston: McGill-Queen's University Press, 1995.

———. "Simplicity and Silence: The Influence of Scripture on the Aesthetic Thought of the Major Reformers." *Journal of Religious History* 10.4 (1979): 343–64.

Averbeck, Richard E. "Breath, Wind, Spirit, and the Holy Spirit in the Old

Testament." In *Presence, Power, and Promise: The Role of the Spirit of God in the Old Testament,* edited by David G. Firth and Paul D. Wegner, 25–37. Downers Grove, IL: IVP Academic, 2011.

————. "Holy Spirit in the Hebrew Bible and Its Connections to the New Testament." In *Who's Afraid of the Holy Spirit?* edited by M. J. Sawyer and D. B. Wallace, 15–36. Dallas: Biblical Studies Press, 2005.

Badcock, Gary D. *Light of Truth and Fire of Love: A Theology of the Holy Spirit.* Grand Rapids: Eerdmans, 1997.

Barrett, C. K. *The Gospel according to St. John.* 2nd ed. Philadelphia: Westminster, 1978.

Barth, Karl. *Church Dogmatics.* Vol. II/1. Edited by G. W. Bromiley and T. F. Torrance. Edinburgh: T&T Clark, 1957. §31.3.

————. *Church Dogmatics.* Vol. III/1. Translated by J. W. Edwards, O. Bussey, and Harold Knight. Edinburgh: T&T Clark, 1958. §§40–41.

————. *Church Dogmatics.* Vol. III/2. Translated by Harold Knight, G. W. Bromiley, J. K. S. Reid, and R. H. Fuller. Edinburgh: T&T Clark, 1960. §§43–44.

Bartholomew, Craig G. *Where Mortals Dwell: A Christian View of Place for Today.* Grand Rapids: Baker Academic, 2011.

Bauckham, Richard J. "James and the Jerusalem Church." In *The Book of Acts in Its Palestinian Setting,* edited by Richard Bauckham, 415–80. Grand Rapids: Eerdmans, 1995.

————. "Joining Creation's Praise of God." *Ecotheology* 7 (2002): 45–59.

————. *The Theology of the Book of Revelation.* Cambridge: Cambridge University Press, 2003.

Bauckham, Richard J., and Trevor Hart. *Hope against Hope: Christian Eschatology at the Turn of the Millennium.* Grand Rapids: Eerdmans, 1999.

Beale, G. K. "The Descent of the Eschatological Temple in the Form of the Spirit at Pentecost." *Tyndale Bulletin* 56 (2005): 73–102.

————. "Jesus as the Temple of the New Creation in John." Unpublished paper, presented at the Evangelical Theological Society, Baltimore, MD, November 2013.

————. *The Temple and the Church's Mission: A Biblical Theology of the Dwelling Place of God.* Downers Grove, IL: IVP, 2004.

Begbie, Jeremy S. "The Future of Theology amid the Arts: Some Reformed Reflections." In *Christ across the Disciplines: Past, Present, Future,* edited by Roger Lundin, 152–82. Grand Rapids: Eerdmans, 2013.

————. "Looking to the Future: A Hopeful Subversion." In *For the Beauty of the Church: Casting a Vision for the Arts*, edited by W. David O. Taylor, 165–86. Grand Rapids: Baker Books, 2010.

———. *Music, Modernity, and God*. Oxford: Oxford University Press, 2013.

———. "Music, Word, and Theology Today: Learning from John Calvin." In *Theology in Dialogue: The Impact of the Arts, Humanities, and Science on Contemporary Religious Thought; Essays in Honor of John W. de Gruchy*, edited by Lyn Holness and Ralf Wustenberg, 3–27. Grand Rapids: Eerdmans, 2002.

———. *Voicing Creation's Praise: Towards a Theology of the Arts*. Edinburgh: T&T Clark, 2000.

Belleville, Linda. "'Born of Water and Spirit': John 3:5." *Trinity Journal* 1 (1980): 125–41.

Benedict XVI. "Meeting with Artists." Address at the Sistine Chapel, November 21, 2009. www.vatican.va/holy_father/benedict_xvi/speeches/2009 /november/documents/hf_ben-xvi_spe_20091121_artisti_en.html.

Bennema, Cornelis. "The Giving of the Spirit in John 19–20: Another Round." In *The Spirit and Christ in the New Testament and Christian Theology: Essays in Honor of Max Turner*, edited by I. Howard Marshall, Volker Rabens, and Cornelis Bennema, 86–105. Grand Rapids: Eerdmans, 2012.

Bennetch, J. H. "John 4:24a: A Greek Study." *Biblioteca Sacra* 107 (1950): 71–83.

Bernard, J. H. *Gospel according to St. John*. Vol. 1. ICC. Edinburgh: T&T Clark, 1928.

Berry, Wendell. "The Body and the Earth." In *The Art of the Commonplace: The Agrarian Essays of Wendell Berry*. Berkeley, CA: Counterpoint Press, 2002.

Block, Daniel I. *The Book of Ezekiel: Chapters 25–48*. Grand Rapids: Eerdmans, 1998.

Blume, Friedrich. *Protestant Church Music: A History*. New York: Norton, 1974.

Brown, Christopher Boyd. *Singing the Gospel: Lutheran Hymns and the Success of the Reformation*. Cambridge, MA: Harvard University Press, 2005.

Brown, Raymond E. *The Gospel according to John*. Vol. 1. Anchor Bible. Garden City, NY: Doubleday, 1966.

Bruner, Frederick Dale. *The Gospel of John: A Commentary*. Grand Rapids: Eerdmans, 2012.

Burge, Gary M. *The Anointed Community: The Holy Spirit in the Johannine Tradition*. Grand Rapids: Eerdmans, 1997.

Carson, D. A. *The Gospel according to John*. Grand Rapids: Eerdmans, 1991.

Chan, Simon. "The Liturgy as the Work of the Spirit: A Theological Perspective." In *The Spirit in Worship—Worship in the Spirit*, edited by Teresa Berger and Bryan D. Spinks, 41–58. Collegeville, MN: Liturgical Press, 2009.

Chaplin, Adrienne D. "The Invisible and the Sublime: From Participation to Reconciliation." In *Radical Orthodoxy and the Reformed Tradition: Creation, Covenant, and Participation*, edited by James K. A. Smith and James H. Olthuis, 89–106. Grand Rapids: Baker Books, 2005.

Chua, Daniel K. L. *Absolute Music and the Construction of Meaning*. Cambridge: Cambridge University Press, 1999.

Clines, David J. A. "The Image of God in Man." *Tyndale Bulletin* 19 (1968): 53–103.

Cortez, Marc. *Theological Anthropology: A Guide for the Perplexed*. London: T&T Clark, 2010.

Davies, Horton. *Worship and Theology in England*. Vol. 1, *From Andrewes to Baxter and Fox, 1603–1690*. Princeton: Princeton University Press, 1975.

Davies, W. D. *Gospel and the Land: Early Christianity and Jewish Territorial Doctrine*. Berkeley: University of California Press, 1974.

Davis, Ellen F. "The Tabernacle Is Not a Storehouse: Building Sacred Spaces." *Sewanee Theological Review* 49 (2006): 305–19.

Dean, Jeffrey. "Listening to Sacred Polyphony c. 1500." *Early Music* 25.4 (1997): 611–36.

Destro, Adriana, and Mauro Pesce. "Self, Identity, and Body in Paul and John." In *Self, Soul, and Body in Religious Experience*, edited by Albert I. Baumgarten, J. Assmann, and G. G. Stroumsa, 184–97. SHR 78. Leiden: Brill, 1998.

Di Vito, Robert A. "Here One Need Not Be Oneself: The Concept of 'Self' in the Hebrew Scriptures." In *The Whole and Divided Self*, edited by David E. Aune and John McCarthy, 49–88. New York: Crossroad Publishing, 1997.

Dodd, C. H. *The Interpretation of the Fourth Gospel*. Cambridge: Cambridge University Press, 1958.

Dumbrell, William J. *The End of the Beginning: Revelation 21–22 and the Old Testament*. Grand Rapids: Baker Books, 1985.

Dunn, James D. G. *Baptism in the Holy Spirit: A Re-examination of the New*

Testament Teaching on the Gift of the Spirit in Relation to Pentecostalism Today. Philadelphia: Westminster, 1970.

———. "1 Corinthians 15:45—Last Adam, Life-Giving Spirit." In *Christ and the Spirit in the New Testament: Studies in Honor of C. F. D. Moule*, edited by Barnabas Lindars and Stephen S. Smalley, 127–42. Cambridge: Cambridge University Press, 1973.

———. *Jesus and the Spirit: A Study of the Religious and Charismatic Experience of Jesus and the First Christians as Reflected in the New Testament.* London: SCM Press, 1975.

———. *The Partings of the Ways: Between Christianity and Judaism and Their Significance for the Character of Christianity.* London: SCM Press, 1991.

Dyrness, William A. *Poetic Theology: God and the Poetics of Everyday Life.* Grand Rapids: Eerdmans, 2011.

———. *Reformed Theology and Visual Culture: The Protestant Imagination from Calvin to Edwards.* Cambridge: Cambridge University Press, 2004.

Edgar, William. "The Arts and the Reformed Tradition." In *Calvin and Culture: Exploring a Worldview*, edited by David W. Hall and Marvin Padgett, 40–68. Phillipsburg, NJ: P&R Publishing, 2010.

Enns, Peter. *The Evolution of Adam: What the Bible Does and Doesn't Say about Human Origins.* Grand Rapids: Brazos Press, 2012.

Farley, Michael A. "What Is 'Biblical' Worship? Biblical Hermeneutics and Evangelical Theologies of Worship." *Journal of the Evangelical Theological Society* 51 (2008): 591–613.

Fee, Gordon D. *God's Empowering Presence: The Holy Spirit in the Letters of Paul.* Peabody, MA: Hendrickson, 1994.

Ferguson, Everett. "Toward a Patristic Theology of Music." *Studia Patristica* 24 (1993): 266–83.

Filson, Floyd V. "The Significance of the Temple in the Ancient Near East IV: Temple, Synagogue, and Church." *Biblical Archaeologist* 7 (1944): 77–88.

Frame, John. *Worship in Spirit and Truth: A Refreshing Study of the Principles and Practice of Biblical Worship.* Phillipsburg, NJ: P&R Publishing, 1996.

George, Victoria Ann. *Whitewash and the New Aesthetic of the Protestant Reformation.* London: Pindar Press, 2012.

Gorman, F. H., Jr. *The Ideology of Ritual: Space, Time, and Status in the Priestly Theology.* Sheffield, UK: JSOT Press, 1990.

Green, Joel B. *Body, Soul, and Human Life: The Nature of Humanity in the Bible.* Grand Rapids: Baker Academic, 2008.

————. "Eschatology and the Nature of Humans: A Reconsideration of Pertinent Biblical Evidence." *Science and Christian Belief* 14 (2002): 33–50.

————. *The Gospel of Luke.* NICNT. Grand Rapids: Eerdmans, 1997.

Gundry, Robert H. *Sōma in Biblical Theology, with Emphasis on Pauline Anthropology.* Cambridge: Cambridge University Press, 1976.

Gunton, Colin. *Christ and Creation.* Grand Rapids: Eerdmans, 1992.

————. "The Church on Earth: The Roots of Community." In *On Being the Church: Essays in the Christian Community,* edited by Colin E. Gunton and Daniel W. Hardy, 48–80. Edinburgh: T&T Clark, 1989.

————, ed. *The Doctrine of Creation: Essays in Dogmatics, History, and Philosophy.* London: T&T Clark, 2004.

————. *Father, Son, and Holy Spirit: Essays toward a Fully Trinitarian Theology.* London: T&T Clark, 2003.

————. *The One, the Three, and the Many: God, Creation, and the Culture of Modernity.* Cambridge: Cambridge University Press, 1993.

————. *The Triune Creator: A Historical and Systematic Study.* Grand Rapids: Eerdmans, 1998.

Guthrie, Steven R. *Creator Spirit: The Holy Spirit and the Art of Becoming Human.* Grand Rapids: Baker Academic, 2011.

————. "Temples of the Spirit: Worship as Embodied Performance." In *Faithful Performances: Enacting Christian Tradition,* ed. Trevor A. Hart and Steven R. Guthrie, 91–108. Aldershot, UK: Ashgate, 2007.

Hardy, Daniel W. "Calvinism and the Visual Arts: A Theological Introduction." In *Seeing beyond the Word: Visual Arts and the Calvinist Tradition,* edited by Paul Corby Finney, 1–18. Grand Rapids: Eerdmans, 1999.

Hart, Trevor. *Between the Image and the Word: Theological Engagements with Imagination, Language, and Literature.* Surrey, UK: Ashgate, 2013.

Hauerwas, Stanley. "On Keeping Theological Ethics Imaginative." In *Against the Nations: War and Survival in a Liberal Society.* San Francisco: Harper & Row, 1985.

————. "The Significance of Vision: Toward an Aesthetic Ethic." In *Vision and Virtue: Essays in Christian Ethical Reflection.* Notre Dame, IN: Fides Publishers, 1974.

Hays, Richard B. "The Materiality of John's Symbolic World." In *Preaching John's Gospel: The World It Imagines,* edited by David Fleer and Dave Bland, 5–12. St. Louis, MO: Chalice Press, 2008.

Helm, Paul. "John Calvin, the 'Sensus Divinitatis,' and the Noetic Effects of Sin." *International Journal for Philosophy of Religion* 43 (1998): 87–107.

Hengel, Martin. "The Prologue of the Gospel of John as the Gateway to

Christological Truth." In *The Gospel of John and Christian Theology*, edited by Richard Bauckham and Carl Mosser, 265–94. Grand Rapids: Eerdmans, 2008.

Henry, Matthew. *Matthew Henry's Commentary on the Whole Bible*. Vol. 5, *Matthew to John*. Old Tappan, NJ: Fleming H. Revell, 1986.

Herl, Joseph. *Worship Wars in Early Lutheranism: Choir, Congregation, and Three Centuries of Conflict*. Oxford: Oxford University Press, 2004.

Higman, Francis. "Music." In *The Reformation World*, edited by Andrew Pettegree, 491–504. London: Routledge, 2000.

Horton, Michael. "Image and Office: Human Personhood and the Covenant." In *Personal Identity in Theological Perspective*, edited by Richard Lints, Michael S. Horton, and Mark R. Talbot, 178–203. Grand Rapids: Eerdmans, 2006.

Humbert, Paul. *Études sur le récit du paradis et de la chute dans la Genèse*. Neuchâtel: Secretariat de l'Université Neuchâtel, 1940.

Jacobs, Alan. *The Book of Common Prayer: A Biography*. Princeton: Princeton University Press, 2013.

Jenson, Robert W. *Systematic Theology*. Vol. 2, *The Works of God*. Oxford: Oxford University Press, 1999.

Jewett, Robert. *Paul's Anthropological Terms: A Study of Their Use in Conflict Settings*. AGJU 10. Leiden: Brill, 1971.

John Paul II. "Letter of His Holiness Pope John Paul II to Artists." April 4, 1999. http://w2.vatican.va/content/john-paul-ii/en/letters/1999/documents/hf_jp-ii_let_23041999_artists.html.

Johnson, H. Wayne. "John 4:19–24: Exegetical Implications for Worship and Place." Unpublished paper presented at the Evangelical Theological Society, Baltimore, MD, November 2013.

Johnston, George. *The Spirit-Paraclete in the Gospel of John*. SNTSMS 12. Cambridge: Cambridge University Press, 1970.

Jones, Beth Felker. *Marks of His Wounds: Gender, Politics, and Bodily Resurrection*. Oxford: Oxford University Press, 2007.

Jones, Paul S. "Calvin and Music." In *Calvin and Culture: Exploring a Worldview*, edited by David W. Hall and Marvin Padgett, 217–53. Phillipsburg, NJ: P&R Publishing, 2010.

Kearney, P. J. "Creation and Liturgy: The P Redaction of Ex 25–40." *Zeitschrift für die alttestamentliche Wissenschaft* 89 (1977): 375–78.

Koester, Craig R. *Dwelling of God: The Tabernacle in the Old Testament, Intertestamental Jewish Literature, and the New Testament*. Washington, DC: Catholic Biblical Association of America, 1989.

————. *Symbolism in the Fourth Gospel: Meaning, Mystery, Community.* Minneapolis: Fortress, 2003.

Korrick, Leslie. "Instrumental Music in the Early Sixteenth-Century Mass: New Evidence." *Early Music* 18.3 (1990): 359–65, 367–70.

Köstenberger, Andreas J. *John.* BECNT. Grand Rapids: Baker Academic, 2004.

————. "John." In *Commentary on the New Testament Use of the Old Testament,* edited by G. K. Beale and D. A. Carson, 415–512. Grand Rapids: Baker Academic, 2007.

Lathrop, Gordon W. *Holy Ground: A Liturgical Cosmology.* Minneapolis: Fortress, 2004.

Lee, Dorothy A. "In the Spirit of Truth: Worship and Prayer in the Gospel of John and the Early Fathers." *Vigiliae Christianae* 58 (2004): 277–97.

————. *The Symbolic Narratives of the Fourth Gospel: The Interplay of Form and Meaning.* JSNTSup 95. Sheffield: JSOT Press, 1994.

Lee, Philip J. *Against the Protestant Gnostics.* Oxford: Oxford University Press, 1993.

Leith, John. H. *An Introduction to the Reformed Tradition: A Way of Being the Christian Community.* Atlanta: John Knox Press, 1977.

Leithart, Peter J. "Embracing Ritual: Sacraments as Rites." *Calvin Theological Journal* 40 (2005): 6–20.

————. "Synagogue or Temple? Models for the Christian Worship." *Westminster Theological Journal* 63 (2002): 119–33.

Levenson, Jon D. *Resurrection and the Restoration of Israel: The Ultimate Victory of the God of Life.* New Haven: Yale University Press, 2006.

————. "The Temple and the World." *Journal of Religion* 64 (1984): 297.

Levison, Jon R. *Filled with the Spirit.* Grand Rapids: Eerdmans, 2009.

Lockwood, Lewis. "Music and Religion in the High Renaissance and the Reformation." In *The Pursuit of Holiness in Late Medieval and Renaissance Religion,* edited by Charles Trinkaus, with Heiko A. Oberman, 496–502. Leiden: Brill, 1974.

Loewe, Andreas. "'Musica est Optimum': Martin Luther's Theory of Music." http://mcd.academia.edu/loewe/Papers/1074845/Musica_est_opti mum_Martin_Luthers_Theory_of_Music, 33–38.

Luter, A. Boyd., Jr. "'Worship' as Service: The New Testament Usage of *latreuō.*" *Criswell Theological Review* 2 (1988): 335–44.

McHugh, J. F. *A Critical and Exegetical Commentary of John 1–4.* ICC. Edinburgh: T&T Clark, 2009.

Michaels, J. Ramsey. *The Gospel of John*. NICNT. Grand Rapids: Eerdmans, 2010.

Michalski, Sergiusz. *The Reformation and the Visual Arts: The Protestant Image Question in Western and Eastern Europe*. London: Routledge, 1993.

Moffitt, David. *Atonement and the Logic of Resurrection in the Epistle to the Hebrews*. Leiden: Brill, 2011.

Moloney, F. J. *Experiencing God in the Gospel of John*. New York: Paulist Press, 2003.

Moltmann, Jürgen. *God in Creation: A New Theology of Creation and the Spirit of God*. Minneapolis: Fortress, 1993.

―――. *The Source of Life: The Holy Spirit and the Theology of Life*. London: SCM, 1997.

―――. *The Spirit of Life: A Universal Affirmation*. Minneapolis: Fortress, 1992.

Morris, Leon. *The Gospel according to John*. Grand Rapids: Eerdmans, 1995.

Music, David W. *Instruments in Church: A Collection of Source Documents*. Lanham, MA: Scarecrow Press, 1998.

Newbigin, Lesslie. *The Light Has Come: An Exposition of the Fourth Gospel*. Grand Rapids: Eerdmans, 1982.

Niditch, Susan. "Ezekiel 40–48 in a Visionary Context." *Catholic Bible Quarterly* 48.2 (1986): 208–24.

Perrin, Nicholas. *Jesus the Temple*. Grand Rapids: Baker Academic, 2010.

Pickstock, Catherine. "Liturgy and the Senses." In *Paul's New Moment: Continental Philosophy and the Future of Christian Theology*, edited by John Milbank, Slavoj Zizek, Creston Davis, with Catherine Pickstock, 125–45. Grand Rapids: Brazos Press, 2010.

Piper, John. "Worship God!" Sermon given on November 9, 1997. www.desiringgod.org/ResourceLibrary/TopicIndex/60/1016_Worship_God.

Porsch, Felix. *Pneuma und Wort: Ein exegetischer Beitrag zur Pneumatologie des Johannesevangeliums*. Frankfurt: Josef Knecht, 1974.

Reese, Gustave. *Music in the Renaissance*. New York: Norton, 1959.

Riches, J. K. *Conflicting Mythologies: Identity Formation in the Gospels of Mark and Matthew*. Edinburgh: T&T Clark, 2000.

Rogers, Eugene F., Jr. *After the Spirit: A Constructive Pneumatology from Resources outside the Modern West*. Grand Rapids: Eerdmans, 2005.

―――, ed. *The Holy Spirit: Classical and Contemporary Readings*. Chichester, UK: Wiley-Blackwell, 2009.

Ross, Allen P. *Recalling the Hope of Glory: Biblical Worship from the Garden to the New Creation*. Grand Rapids: Kregel, 2006.

Routledge, Robin. "The Spirit and the Future in the Old Testament: Restoration and Renewal." In *Presence, Power, and Promise: The Role of the Spirit of God in the Old Testament*, edited by David G. Firth and Paul D. Wegner, 362–66. Downers Grove, IL: IVP Academic, 2011.

Saliers, Don. "Liturgy and Ethics: Some New Beginnings." In *Liturgy and the Moral Self: Humanity at Full Stretch before God*, edited by E. Byron Anderson and Bruce T. Morrill, 15–35. Collegeville, MN: Liturgical Press, 1998.

Sayers, Dorothy. *Further Papers on Dante.* Vol. 2: *His Heirs and His Ancestors.* Eugene, OR: Wipf & Stock, 2006.

Schmidt, Werner H. *Die Schöpfungsgeschichte der Priesterschrift.* Neukirchen-Vluyn: Neukirchener Verlag, 1964.

Schnackenburg, Rudolf. *The Gospel according to St. John.* Vol. 1. New York: Seabury, 1968.

Schneiders, Sandra. "History and Symbolism in the Fourth Gospel." In *Évangile de Jean*, edited by Marinus de Jonge, 371–76. Gembloux, Belgium: Duculot, 1977.

———. "Symbolism and the Sacramental Principle in the Fourth Gospel." In *Segni e sacramenti nel vangelo di Giovanni*, edited by Pius-Ramon Tragan, 221–35. Rome: Editrice Anselmiana, 1977.

Schnelle, Udo. *The Human Condition: Anthropology in the Teachings of Jesus, Paul, and John.* Minneapolis: Fortress, 1996.

Seerveld, Calvin. *Rainbows for a Fallen World: Aesthetic Life and Artistic Task.* Toronto: Toronto Tuppence Press, 1980.

Senn, Frank. *New Creation: A Liturgical World View.* Minneapolis: Fortress, 2000.

Smith, D. Moody. "John." In *The Harper Collins Bible Commentary*, edited by James L. Mays, 956–86. San Francisco: HarperSanFrancisco, 1988.

Smith, James K. A. *Desiring the Kingdom: Worship, Worldview, and Cultural Formation.* Grand Rapids: Baker Academic, 2009.

———. *Thinking in Tongues: Pentecostal Contributions to Christian Philosophy.* Grand Rapids: Eerdmans, 2010.

Stevenson, Robert M. *Patterns of Protestant Church Music.* Durham, NC: Duke University Press, 1953.

Stone, Lawson G. "The Soul: Possession, Part, or Person? The Genesis of Human Nature in Genesis 2:7." In *What about the Soul? Neuroscience and Christian Anthropology*, edited by Joel B. Green, 47–61. Nashville: Abingdon, 2004.

Thettayil, Benny. *In Spirit and Truth: An Exegetical Study of John 4:19–26 and* a *Theological Investigation of the Replacement Theme in the Fourth Gospel.* Leuven: Peeters, 2007.

Thiselton, Anthony C. *The First Epistle to the Corinthians: A Commentary on the Greek Text.* NIGTC. Grand Rapids: Eerdmans, 2000.

———. *The Holy Spirit—in Biblical Teaching, through the Centuries, and Today.* Grand Rapids: Eerdmans, 2013.

Thomas, Günter. "Resurrection to New Life: Pneumatological Implications of the Eschatological Transition." In *Resurrection: Theological and Scientific Assessments,* edited by Ted Peters, Robert John Russell, and Michael Welker, 255–76. Grand Rapids: Eerdmans, 2002.

Thompson, Marianne Meye. *The God of the Gospel of John.* Grand Rapids: Eerdmans, 2001.

———. "The Historical Jesus and the Johannine Christ." In *Exploring the Gospel of John: In Honor of D. Moody Smith,* edited by R. Alan Culpepper and C. Clifton Black, 21–42. Louisville: Westminster John Knox, 1996.

———. *The Humanity of Jesus in the Fourth Gospel.* Philadelphia: Fortress, 1988.

Torrance, James B. *Worship, Community, and the Triune God of Grace.* Downers Grove, IL: IVP Academic, 1996.

Um, Stephen T. *The Theme of Temple Christology in John's Gospel.* London: T&T Clark, 2006.

Underhill, Evelyn. *Worship.* Eugene, OR: Wipf & Stock, 2002.

Von Allmen, Jean-Jacques. "Short Theology of the Place of Worship." *Studia Liturgica* 3.3 (1964): 155–71.

———. "Theological Frame of a Liturgical Renewal." *Church Quarterly* 2.1 (1969): 8–23.

———. "Worship and the Holy Spirit." *Studia Liturgica* 2.2 (1963): 124–35.

———. *Worship: Its Theology and Practice.* Translated by Harold Knight and W. Fletcher Fleet. London: Lutterworth Press, 1965.

Von Rad, Gerhard. *Old Testament Theology.* Translated by D. M. G. Stalker. Vol. 1. New York: Harper & Row, 1962.

Wainwright, Geoffrey. *Doxology: The Praise of God in Worship, Doctrine, and Life; A Systematic Theology.* New York: Oxford University Press, 1980.

Walton, John H. "Creation in Genesis 1:1–2:3 and the Ancient Near East: Order out of Disorder after *Chaoskampf.*" *Calvin Theological Journal* 43 (2008): 48–63.

Webster, John. *Holy Scripture: A Dogmatic Sketch.* Cambridge: Cambridge University Press, 2003.

Weder, Hans. "*Deus Incarnatus*: On the Hermeneutics of Christology in the Johannine Writings." In *Exploring the Gospel of John: In Honor of D. Moody Smith*, edited by R. Alan Culpepper and C. Clifton Black, translated by Douglas W. Stott, 327–45. Louisville: Westminster John Knox, 1996.

Wells, Samuel. *God's Companions: Reimagining Christian Ethics*. Oxford: Blackwell, 2006.

Wenham, Gordon J. "Sanctuary Symbolism in the Garden of Eden Story." In *"I Studied Inscriptions from before the Flood": Ancient Near Eastern, Literary, and Linguistic Approaches to Genesis 1–11*, edited by Richard S. Hess and David T. Tsumura, 399–404. Winona Lake, IN: Eisenbrauns, 1994.

Westcott, B. F. *The Gospel according to John*. Grand Rapids: Eerdmans, 1958.

Westermann, Claus. *Genesis 1–11: A Commentary*. Translated by John J. Scullion. Minneapolis: Augsburg, 1984.

Witvliet, John D. *The Biblical Psalms in Christian Worship: A Brief Introduction and Guide to Resources*. Grand Rapids: Eerdmans, 2007.

———. "Toward a Liturgical Aesthetic: An Interdisciplinary Review of Aesthetic Theory." *Liturgy Digest* 3 (1996): 4–86.

———. *Worship Seeking Understanding: Windows into Christian Practice*. Grand Rapids: Baker Academic, 2003.

Wolterstorff, Nicholas J. *Art in Action: Toward a Christian Aesthetic*. Grand Rapids: Eerdmans, 1980.

———. "Beyond Beauty and the Aesthetic in the Engagement of Religion and Art." In *Theological Aesthetics after Von Balthasar*, edited by Oleg V. Bychkov and James Fodor, 119–33. Aldershot, UK: Ashgate, 2008.

———. *Hearing the Call: Liturgy, Justice, Church, and World*, edited by Mark R. Gornik and Gregory Thompson. Grand Rapids: Eerdmans, 2011.

Wood, Donald. "Maker of Heaven and Earth." *International Journal of Systematic Theology* 14 (2012): 381–95.

Wright, N. T. "Freedom and Framework, Spirit and Truth: Recovering Biblical Worship." *Studia Liturgica* 32.2 (2002): 176–95.

———. *Jesus and the Victory of God*. Minneapolis: Fortress, 1996.

———. "Mind, Spirit, Soul, and Body: All for One and One for All; Reflections on Paul's Anthropology in His Complex Contexts." Paper presented at the Society of Christian Philosophers: Regional Meeting. Fordham University, March 18, 2011.

———. "Worship and the Spirit in the New Testament." In *The Spirit in*

Worship—Worship in the Spirit, edited by Teresa Berger and Bryan D. Spinks, 3–24. Collegeville, MN: Liturgical Press, 2009.

Wynn, Mark. "Re-enchanting the World: The Possibility of Materially Mediated Religious Experience." In *Theology, Aesthetics, and Culture: Responses to the Work of David Brown*, edited by Robert McSwain and Taylor Worley, 115–27. Oxford: Oxford University Press, 2013.

Yates, John. "Role of the Holy Spirit in the Lord's Supper." *Churchman* 105 (1991): 350–59.

Yong, Amos. "Ruach, the Primordial Chaos, and the Breath of Life: Emergence Theory and the Creation Narratives in Pneumatological Perspective." In *The Work of the Spirit: Pneumatology and Pentecostalism*, edited by M. Welker, 183–204. Grand Rapids: Eerdmans, 2006.

Index

INDEX